Organization and Administration of Adult Education Programs

A volume in
Adult Education Special Topics:
Theory, Research, and Practice in Lifelong Learning
Kathleen P. King, *Series Editor*

Organization and Administration of Adult Education Programs

A Guide for Practitioners

Steven W. Schmidt
East Carolina University

Susan M. Yelich Biniecki
Kansas State University

INFORMATION AGE PUBLISHING, INC.
Charlotte, NC • www.infoagepub.com

Library of Congress Cataloging-in-Publication Data

A CIP record for this book is available from the Library of Congress
http://www.loc.gov

ISBN: 978-1-68123-635-3 (Paperback)
        978-1-68123-636-0 (Hardcover)
        978-1-68123-637-7 (ebook)

Contents

1

Introduction

The Business Side of Adult Education

What is educational program management, and why do we, as adult educators, study the topic? Hopefully, by the time you finish reading this book, you will have a good understanding of the answers to both of these questions. To begin with, educational program management is a specific and distinct aspect of adult education. There is research on the topic; there are systems, models, and best practices in place. There are jobs in program management, and many adult education and human resource development (HRD) practitioners have positions that involve aspects of program management. (Some have entire careers in the field.) There are also books written on the topic (including this one).

The management of programs is often a topic that adult educators study in formal learning environments. Most adult education and HRD programs feature at least one course on the management of educational programs. These courses are run under a variety of names: the organization and administration of adult educational programs, educational program management, educational program administration, and others. Yet,

Organization and Administration of Adult Education Programs, pages 1–11
Copyright © 2016 by Information Age Publishing
All rights of reproduction in any form reserved.

as instructors in graduate-level educational program management courses, the authors regularly find that students coming into these courses don't see the importance or applicability of the topic in the field of adult education. Even in graduate programs, educational program organization and administration is often limited to a single course, and often it is viewed by students as simply a requirement that must be taken in order to graduate.

The Difference in Organization and Administration

The topics associated with educational program management (the term *management* will be used as a blanket term, covering administration and organization) are different from many other adult education and HRD-related topics for a few reasons. First, program administration is typically done on a level that can be far removed from instructors and learners. Much of the focus of adult education and HRD programs is on instruction, individual learners, classroom methods, and related topics. The management of educational programs takes place at a level above the instructor or learner level (Figure 1.1). Organization and administration focuses on the management of a series of courses or educational programs. The overall management of a series of educational programs is quite different from the work educators do in teaching adult learners. This type of work involves things like budgeting, marketing, recruiting and hiring instructors, strategic planning, and a variety of other topics. As a result, a variety of knowledge and skills is required, assorted issues are faced, and multiple and diverse topics of study become important Many of those topics will be addressed in this book.

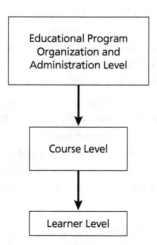

Figure 1.1   The levels on which we can study adult education.

The second reason why educational program administration and organization is different from other adult education or HRD topics is because it combines two disciplines—those of business and education. In order to successfully manage adult education and HRD programs, one has to have an understanding of business or management principles as well as an understanding of adult education. The multidisciplinary nature of the topic means that it does not necessarily fit nicely into either education or business fields. It also means that the topic of educational program administration can be more difficult to understand (and more difficult to relate to) by those who are focused on adult education at the learner or course level. After developing our concept for this book, the authors submitted a proposal to a publisher for review. The reviewer questioned the need for such a book and noted that it seemed too business-like for the field of adult education. The reviewer also inquired as to why students interested in this topic couldn't simply read a business book or take a business course. Our topic does straddle two disciplines, and that makes it difficult for people in either individual discipline to completely understand. Yet there is a need for this type of text and these types of courses in adult education and HRD. Textbooks and courses in business are typically not focused enough on adult education, and there are unique aspects of adult education that affect how programs are managed. Conversely, textbooks and courses in adult education are typically focused on the learner or classroom level rather than on the organization and administration of educational programs.

Why Educational Program Management Is Important to You

In reading this book, or at least reading this introductory chapter to this point, you might now be starting to understand how the topics of organization and administration are different from other adult education and HRD-related topics. Some of you may already be in program management–type positions, and you may already understand the importance of the topic and the program manager position. For those of you who are already involved in educational program management, this book may serve as reinforcement for what you are already doing. It may also provide you with a variety of perspectives and a number of methods you can use to perform the tasks associated with your positions. If you are not involved in program management, however, you may still be wondering if, or why, you should learn more about it. If you fall into this category of reader, the next sections of this book are for you.

Those working in the fields of adult education or HRD should consider the issue of longer-term career planning in those fields. Many adult educators are very happy teaching courses and working with adult learners, and many do not desire additional responsibilities at work beyond teaching. There is certainly nothing wrong with that. However, it may be that after a few years of classroom experience, some of you may find yourselves interested in being promoted to higher levels in your organization. Organizations often promote the best employee in a group to a leadership position within that group, without understanding that additional sets of skills are required in that higher-level position. As noted earlier, skills required for educators and program managers, though related in some senses, are vastly different. An understanding of management-related issues within adult education can be beneficial if you find yourself in that situation and if you are interested in furthering your career by moving into a management position.

You may not be interested in organization and administration as a career. However, changes in personnel or department or organizational restructuring may still result in your being assigned to some organizational or administrative duties, regardless of your interest. For example, an existing program manager may leave their organization for another opportunity, and those left in the organization may be asked to step in and temporarily handle those duties.

Even volunteers are asked to help with some management-related tasks. You may be involved in adult education from a volunteer standpoint. You may simply be interested in contributing to an organization that provides education to adults in need. Nonprofit and community-based organizations rely on volunteers to help fulfill their missions, and your knowledge of educational program organization and administration may make you a more valuable and well-rounded volunteer. Knowledge of program organization and administration may mean you are able to help the organization on a different level than most volunteers.

The above points are all similar in that they all involve the changing nature of work and the ever-present issue of resource acquisition, allocation, and management. It is safe to say that these days, all of us in every aspect of adult education and HRD are being asked to do more with fewer resources. That means that those who specialize in one aspect of adult education, such as teaching or curriculum development, are now being asked to broaden their knowledge and skills so they can take on more responsibilities within their organizations. Those additional responsibilities may be related to topics discussed in this textbook, so knowledge of program management–related issues may prove beneficial to you by making you a more well-rounded employee or volunteer.

As experienced practitioners in the organization and administration of adult education programs, the authors have seen all of the above scenarios happen many times. Sometimes these situations are handled smoothly, and sometimes they result in exactly what all involved hope for. Other times they are handled poorly, and those in the organization find themselves "thrown in" to situations they were neither expecting nor prepared to handle. The key is being prepared to handle many types of situations that might occur in adult education organizations regardless of the circumstances around you. That preparedness can start with an understanding of topics discussed in this book.

You may have noticed that the writing style in the above section of this textbook changed in the above few paragraphs. In many textbooks, and at the start of this book, the third-person point of view is used (the adult educator, the program administrator). In the above section, pronouns were changed from third to first and second person (we, you). The remainder of this book is written using the first-person point of view, as we (the authors) believe that it is important for you (the reader) to put yourself in the position of program manager as you read through the book. We believe this will help you to envision yourself as a program administrator (should you actually find yourself in that position) and to examine the topics discussed as if you were that administrator. This will also be helpful as you consider the questions, case studies, and issues that are presented throughout this text.

Functions of Educational Program Management

Noted earlier in this chapter is the idea that organization and administration are managerial-type functions. As such, they are different than the topics that we typically study in adult education. A discussion of managerial-type functions in general is necessary in order to put the rest of this textbook in proper context.

Henri Fayol was a French industrialist and management theorist in the early 20th century. Fayol identified several primary functions of management that must be performed by those in the organization if that organization is to operate more effectively and efficiently than the individual (alone) might operate (Stroh, Northcraft, & Neale, 2002). These functions are still considered relevant today, and, as one researcher noted, "Fayol's elements of management are not refuted but rather reinforced by more recent findings (on management theory)" (Fells, 2000). Fayol's management functions (Figure 1.2) are as follows: planning, organizing, commanding,

Figure 1.2   Five functions of management. Adapted from Stroh et al., 2002.

coordinating, and controlling (Fells, 2000). These functions were used as a basis for determining the contents of this text.

Fayol's five functions of management are each described in more detail in Table 1.1. In the left column of the table, each function is discussed in the context of the overall concept of management. In the right column of the table, we look at those five functions of management from the context of educational program management. Like many managerial functions, the concept of program management is broader than may be believed at first glance. Effective program management encompasses all five functions of management noted on the left. However, the way in which those functions

TABLE 1.1   Functions of Management in the Context of Adult Education Program Management

Five Functions of Management	Five Functions of Management in the Context of Adult Education Program Management
Planning: Managers have to plan for future conditions. They must consider how the organization will proceed or move forward. Key in the planning stage are the identification of strategies and tactics that will help the organization to achieve goals. Planning is done on both short and longer term bases.	**Planning:** Managers have to plan educational programs in response to what they believe will be the future needs of their learners, while keeping in mind the needs of other stakeholders (who may not be learners). They must consider how their organizations will proceed or move forward and how education they provide will address learners' needs. They must identify strategies and tactics for program management that are in line with organizational goals.
Organizing: Organizing is done based on planning efforts above. Organization is the process associated with arranging people, materials, tasks, and products so that goals can be met. Managers are involved in the actual organizing of all of the above entities.	**Organizing:** Once plans have been completed, organization must occur. The organizer of learning programs must consider the process associated with arranging people, materials, tasks, and products so that the organization can operate smoothly and efficiently and programs can be run. Organizational resources and constraints, learner needs, and unique learner situations must also be considered.

(continued)

TABLE 1.1   Functions of Management in the Context of Adult Education Program Management (continued)

Five Functions of Management	Five Functions of Management in the Context of Adult Education Program Management
Commanding: Managers must supervise the work being done by those in the organization to make sure it is being done to the desired level. This task also involves communication of company expectations, goals, policies, and related messages to the employee. Treatment of employees or those in the organization is important to note, as well. Managers must treat employees in line with standards set forth by the organization.	**Commanding:** In some cases, the management of educational programs may include supervision of the work being done by those who manage and instruct in the course or program. Supervision of employees or volunteers responsible for teaching may also be part of the program manager's job duties. Even if direct supervision is not involved, the program manager may be tasked with communication of organizational expectations, goals, policies, and related messages to the employee. They must operate ethically and must treat employees or volunteers in line with standards set for by the organization.
Coordinating: Managers must ensure that the proper structure is in place for employees to perform their jobs. Coordinating includes such things as identifying job duties for each employee and determining the structure of the organization and relationships between employees.	**Coordinating:** Program managers may be charged with ensuring that the proper structure is in place for employees to perform their jobs and ensuring that the organization structure is appropriate for supporting the educational program. Coordinating includes such things as identifying job duties for each employee, managing processes and workflow, and determining the structure of the organization and relationship between positions. Coordinating involves ensuring those in the organization are all on the same page with regard to organizational and program goals.
Controlling: Controlling involves management oversight with regard to company goals. Managers must be continually mindful of the progress the organization is making toward those goals, and taking action when those goals are not being met. Important in controlling is the evaluation of performance at the individual and overall product levels (Fells, 2000).	**Controlling:** Program managers must always keep track of the degree to which their educational programs are meeting overall organizational goals and objectives. They must also monitor the degree to which programs are staying within the financial and organizational constraints. Progress must be continually monitored, and action must be taken when issues arise that may cause goals to not be met. Ongoing evaluation of the entire process associated with the organization of programs (in the context of all the above variables) must be monitored. This may include the evaluation of performance at the individual and overall product levels.

relate to educational program management may be a bit different from the traditional ways of management.

You can see by this list of functions that educational program management includes many types of duties and responsibilities. On any given day, the program manager may be involved in any or all of these five functions. They must have the knowledge, skills, and abilities necessary to do all of these things.

As an example of this complexity, consider the tasks of an educational program manager at a large hospital in a midsized city. In one day, that manager may attend a planning team meeting, at which ideas for new educational programs are discussed. The manager may then have to address an issue with a long-running educational program on nutrition, as attendance for the program has been decreasing over the last several years. This may involve brainstorming ideas for the marketing of this program. The manager may reserve time to review attendance figures for courses offered by his/her department in the last month, and he or she may do some analyzing of attendance and revenue figures in general. The manager may then have to make copies of materials for a course being run that day because the person who usually manages this function is out sick. It is easy to see where the job of program organizer may be overwhelming at times.

Educational program managers need to know about a lot of different topics in order to be successful in their work. Those topics are the focus of this book. This book was written and organized to provide educational program managers with the tools they need to be successful in all of the five functions of management noted above. Chapter topics included are as follows:

- **Methods of Program Organization:** This chapter covers the many different ways that both organizations and educational programs can be organized. It also addresses issues to consider when making organizational decisions and includes a process for making those decisions.
- **Leadership and Administration:** The concept of leadership in organizations is examined here, along with the duties and responsibilities of those in educational program administration. The relationship between leadership and administration is also examined.
- **Budgeting:** Program managers must have a thorough understanding of the budgeting process and how budgeting systems work. Content on budgets is the focus of this chapter, which includes a model for developing a budget.
- **Funding and Support:** Directly related to budgets (but different in focus), funding and support programs deal with the ways in which organizations can procure financial resources to support their missions.
- **Marketing:** Every organization must have a plan for marketing and promoting their services. This chapter covers the basics of

marketing and the development of marketing plans. Steps in the development of a marketing plan are also presented.

■ **Human Resources:** Most organizations rely on people to fulfill their missions. Sometimes those people are employees and sometimes they are volunteers. Regardless of position, a basic understanding of human resource issues, including recruitment, hiring, training, and recordkeeping, is a necessity for educational program managers.

■ **Strategic Planning:** All organizations should be involved in ongoing strategic planning efforts. This chapter covers processes associated with strategic planning. Prerequisites for successful strategic planning are presented, along with a model that can be used to work through the process of strategic planning.

■ **Program Evaluation:** Providing educational programs is the primary mission of those in educational program management. The evaluation of those programs can be done many different ways and for many different reasons. This chapter details the ways in which different aspects of educational programs can be evaluated.

■ **Legal Issues and Ethical Considerations:** Ethics and legal issues must be considered in all decisions program managers make. This chapter looks at both ethical and legal issues from an educational program management standpoint.

■ **Scenarios, Role Plays, and Activities:** The very last chapter in the book includes scenarios, case studies, group activities, and questions that pull together many different aspects of educational program management.

Throughout this book, you will see connections among topics presented. None of the topics covered in any single chapter happens, or is dealt with, strictly by itself. Educational program management is multifaceted work that typically involves the interplay of many of these topics at the same time. Marketing is affected by strategic planning, and strategic planning depends on an organization's budget and funding and support programs, for example. Human resource–related tasks must be done with budgetary, organizational, and legal issues in mind. Ethical issues flow through every topic in this book, and leadership and administration can influence all other aspects of program management. Nothing related to program management happens in a vacuum, and the scenarios included in the last chapter of this book illustrate that point. They also help you to consider real-world situations and practice your program management skills.

Similarly, topics presented in this book are done so on a general level. There are volumes of books written specifically on each of the individual topics discussed in each chapter. Each chapter in this book presents you with an overview of, and basic information on, the topic discussed. Additionally, each successive chapter is designed to introduce you to a certain topic and prepare you with a working knowledge of that topic in a broad sense. Hopefully you will find areas of interest in this book that you can then study more in-depth using other resources.

Book Organization

Each chapter in this book is organized similarly. Each one starts with an opening question or scenario. For example, the chapter on marketing starts with a discussion of the concepts of "learner" and "customer" and discusses whether or not learners should be considered customers when viewed from a marketing perspective. Other questions and scenarios provide historical context on the topics included in the chapter or questions for you to ponder as you read through the text. Opening case studies or questions are also provided to help you consider actual situations involving chapter topics. Following this opening content, each topic is defined, and the topic is then discussed in the context of educational program management. Throughout each chapter, questions for discussion are provided, and at the end of each chapter, you will find a more comprehensive list of questions, scenarios, and case studies that can be considered. As noted above, the final chapter contains more broad-level case studies, activities, and questions that can be used to pull together content from multiple chapters.

The End of the Beginning

Now that you have come to the conclusion of this first chapter, you should have a better idea about what educational program management entails as well as why it is important to learn about the topic. Whether you are reading this book as part of a course assignment or whether you are reading it to further your own knowledge on topics associated with educational program management, we hope you find it useful and informative.

QUESTIONS FOR DISCUSSION

1. Consider your own abilities. Which of Fayol's five functions of management are strengths for you? Which ones do you need to work on? Now consider your supervisor or a leader in your organization.

Which of the five functions are strengths for that person? Which are weaknesses?

2. Pick one of Fayol's five functions of management and consider, in more detail, how that function is different in the context of adult education or HRD. What aspects of adult learning or HRD make that function different (when considered in the context of adult education or HRD).

3. Consider your future in adult education or HRD. How does knowledge of educational program management fit with your future plans (if at all)?

4. Consider your knowledge of educational program management before you read this chapter and after you finished the chapter. What did you learn about the topic?

5. Consider your organization (or an organization you are familiar with). Knowing what you know about program management so far (by reading this chapter), what are your organization's strengths with regard to educational program management? What are its weaknesses?

References

Fells, M. J. (2000). Fayol stands the test of time. *Journal of Management History, 6*(8), 345–360. doi: http://dx.doi.org/10.1108/13552520010359379

Stroh, L. K., Northcraft, G. B., & Neale, M. A. (2002). *Organizational behavior: A management challenge.* Mahwah, NJ: Erlbaum.

2

Methods of Program Organization

Who Has Time to Organize?

Why is educational program organization important? Often, educational programs are organized in a haphazard fashion, if they are even organized at all. Practitioners who work in training and development typically manage an array of educational programs, but they are often at a loss to explain the method and procedures used to organize those programs. In fact, methodical ways of organizing programs are not often used. Rather than using formal methods of organization, we often just add programs here and there, and give program-related responsibilities to employees who volunteer to take them on (or to those who are asked to take them on). Given the fast-paced environments in which adult educators work, one could argue that there is not any need to formally organize and, even if there were a need, there is no time to formally organize. Is program organization necessary, given the environment in which the adult educator works?

As you read through this chapter, consider these questions. Also consider what factors influence your thoughts regarding the importance of program organization. Did your opinions about program organization change

Organization and Administration of Adult Education Programs, pages 13–32
Copyright © 2016 by Information Age Publishing
13

by the time you reached the end of the chapter? Or were they reinforced? Consider the following scenarios.

Anita manages educational programs at a literacy center that has started offering a new series of courses on technology and computer-related literacy. The courses have become more popular than originally anticipated, and now she is struggling with how to manage them successfully while continuing to provide positive experiences for the learners.

Joe is the manager in an HRD department. He observes that several of his employees who conduct employee training sessions are overwhelmed with work lately. He also notices that two employees in charge of program-related administration seem to have more free time than they should.

Two hospitals in the same geographic area each offer courses to the public on pregnancy and prenatal issues. Those hospitals have recently merged, as have the departments in each hospital that offered these courses. They are now one large department.

Organization Defined

The thing that the above scenarios all have in common is that they involve organizational issues of one type or another. Before looking at these issues, it is first important to define the concept of organization. Organization (or organizing) is the assembling of resources necessary to attain objectives and the arranging of those resources into a purposeful order and structure (Business Dictionary, n.d.a, n.d.b). It is the grouping of activities to attain goals and it provides the framework for things like accountability, authority, and responsibility (Bhattacharyya, 2009). In the context of educational programs, organizing involves the making of preparations and the coordination of activities associated with developing, managing, and facilitating those programs for adult learners.

Why is organization important? Organization allows for both effectiveness and efficiency in program planning and management. Each of those concepts is defined below.

- *Effectiveness:* The ability of an organization to accomplish an important goal, purpose, or mission. Purposeful and thoughtful program organization allows program planners (and organizations, overall) to be more effective in meeting their goals. (Daft, 2013)
- *Efficiency:* The maximization of productivity of organizational resources, such as labor and capital. Well-organized programs enable organizations offering educational programs to run more

efficiently. Well-organized programs also allow potential learners to easily find, enroll (in), and participate in those educational opportunities. (Stroh, Northcraft, & Neale, 2002, p. 7)

Typically, an organization (as a structure) should match (or be related to) the way that its programs are organized. The phrase "form follows function" is a principle used in architecture to mean that the design of something (like a building, in the case of architecture) should be based on the intended purpose or use for that thing. In a similar vein, there should be commonalities or relationships between how an organization is structured and in how its educational programs are organized. In the following section, we will discuss ways in which educational programs can be organized. These are also ways in which the organization that manages these programs can be organized or structured.

As you read through the next section, consider how the programs at your organization are organized. Also, consider your organization from a structural standpoint. How is your organization structured? Is that structure related to how its programs are organized? What is the relationship between the way those programs are organized and the effectiveness and efficiency of the overall organization?

Methods of Educational Program Organization

There are many ways in which educational programs can be organized (Figure 2.1). Remember the main reasons why we organize programs at all were discussed earlier in this chapter. Programs are organized, in one way or another, to provide increased efficiency for those involved in the program,

Ways of Organizing Educational Programs

Division or Product
Customer or Learner Segment
Geography or Territory
Demand
Method
Function
Hybrid
Matrix

Figure 2.1   Ways of organizing educational programs.

and to result in increased effectiveness of the program and the overall organization (Daft, 2013).

Programs can be organized in several different ways (The Different Ways, 2013). Seven ways will be discussed in this chapter. As you read thorough this section, consider the educational programs with which you are familiar. How are they organized? Using one of these methods or another way? Each of the ways of program organization listed in Figure 2.1 are discussed in the pages that follow.

Organization by Division or Product

Educational programs can be organized by product or product line (Figure 2.2). Organizing by product line means that all products of a similar nature are organized together. For example, a community center may offer a variety of courses for local residents. They may offer courses on fitness, nutrition, music, sports, hobbies, and a variety of other topics. All of the fitness courses, such as yoga, Pilates, and aerobics would be organized together. Nutrition courses such as weight loss and cooking courses would be organized together and so on. When new program ideas are considered, they would then fall into one of the existing categories (or maybe, if there is no appropriate existing category, a new category or product line could be developed) (Business Dictionary, n.d.c). Universities and colleges are examples of entities that organize educational programs by product. Courses on writing skills and English literature are housed in the Department of English, courses on early U.S. history are housed in the department of history, and so on. This type of organization may also be seen in entities such

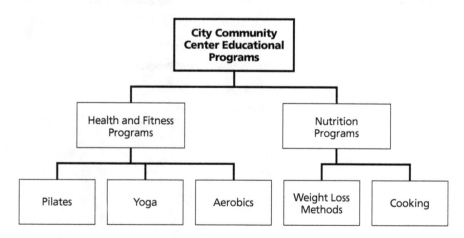

Figure 2.2 Organization by division or product.

as hospitals, where courses for the general public on nutrition and diet are handled by the Department of Family Medicine, and courses on topics related to death and dying may be handled by the hospice unit.

A main benefit of organizing by product is that all activities associated with a particular program can be managed by those with specialized knowledge of that program subject (Bhattacharyya, 2009). As a result, educational programs can be much stronger in terms of content, as they are developed and taught by experts. This expertise also adds credibility to the educational program. Learner satisfaction may be higher in programs organized by product due to the fact that all aspects of the product are managed in one area.

A disadvantage of organizing by product is the fact that it may be difficult to coordinate efforts that involve multiple products. Those who work in organizations that are organized by product may have a lot of skills in a variety of areas related to that product, but they may not be able to develop specific skills in a single aspect of that product (Daft, 2010). In this type of organization, efficiencies may be sacrificed as well. If each separate function or category of program is managed by a different program organizer, whenever a new program idea is proposed, the organizer has to go through the entire program development process. At the same time, the organizer of another function or category of programs may also be working on a new program idea and going through the exact same steps. In organizing educational programs by division or product, sometimes economies of scale are missed because of the autonomy associated with grouping programs by category (Gillikin, n.d.).

This is not always the case, however, as the above scenario assumes there are different organizers for each category of educational program. That is not always the situation, especially in smaller organizations.

There are many potential divisions that can be used to organize educational programs. Organization by customer or learner segment, organization by geography or territory, organization by demand, and organization by method are all variations on organization by division or product. Each is similar in that each involves organization using some method of categorizing programs.

Organization by Customer or Learner Segment

Educational programs can be organized by the customers who take advantage of those programs (or to whom programs are targeted) (Figure 2.3). This type of structure is increasing in popularity for several reasons. Educational consumers have many more choices than they ever had before,

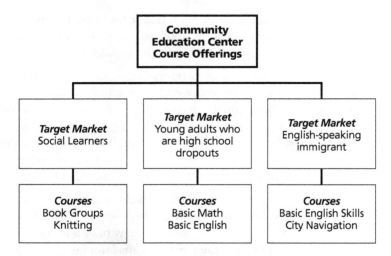

Figure 2.3 Organization by customer or learner segment.

and educational opportunities are now marketed specifically to targeted potential learners. Organization by customer or learner segment allows the program organizer to focus specifically on the needs of a particular market.

One of the biggest advantages to organizing programs this way is the knowledge of the target market. Organizers get to know the characteristics of the people in their market. This makes it easier to be proactive in the development of new programs to meet the needs of these learners (Bhattacharyya, 2009). It also can be a more responsive approach in that changes to existing programs can be made fairly quickly, again, based on the needs of the learners.

A disadvantage of this organizational approach is similar to a disadvantage of the product approach. In larger organizations, if different people are responsible for organizing programs for different markets, each of those people may end up developing a similar education program for their own market. In doing so, efficiency is lost, as each organizer may have to go through the same steps as the other organizer. However, each program may be developed specifically for the needs of that market, which is a positive thing (Gillikin, n.d.).

As an example of this approach, consider a nonprofit organization that provides basic skills education to learners in a large urban area. Educational programs offered by that center may be organized by customer or learner segment. All educational programs focused on recent immigrants who do not speak English as a primary language may be organized together. Programs in this area may focus on language skills, practical math skills, and skills associated with living and interacting in the city. All programs focused on young adults who have dropped out of high school and are interested in attaining GEDs may also be organized together. Courses in this area may include math skills and basic writing skills.

The HRD department of an organization may be organized this way as well. Courses for employees within 10 years of retiring may focus on retirement planning, health, and wellness issues. Courses for younger employees may focus on career management and financial literacy. Or courses for all employees in a particular job could be grouped together; courses for those in sales, courses for those in accounting, and so on.

Organization by Geography or Territory

Sometimes it makes sense for all educational products offered to a group of learners in the same geographic area or territory to be organized together (Figure 2.4). This approach is somewhat similar to the organization by customer or market segment noted above, but it is different in that all programs for all customers in a particular geographic area are organized together (rather than segmented by specific market or group of learners). Organizations that are spread out geographically may consider this method of educational program organization. An organization like the Salvation Army, which has locations around the country, may organize their educational programs in this way. Each office or regional territory may have its own set of educational program offerings. There may be one person in charge of overall program organization for the entity as a whole, and also organizers in each geographic region or territory.

A benefit of organization by territory is that those educational planners who work in that territory have more in-depth knowledge of the needs of the learners in that territory. They can be more responsive to those learner

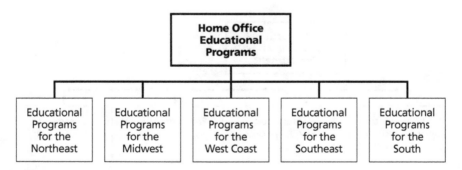

Figure 2.4 Organization by geography or territory.

needs. Different territories may teach the same topics, but may do so in different ways based on territory needs.

A negative aspect of organization by territory goes back to economies of scale. Program organizers in two different territories could be facing the same problems but resolve them in different ways. One might be a successful resolution and the other may not be successful (Daft, 2010).

Organization by Demand

Sometimes programs are organized based on the needs of stakeholders (Figure 2.5). This type of organization is similar in form to organization by customer segment. Remember that stakeholders can be customers, employees, clients, or anyone else who may participate in the educational programs to be offered. Using this method of organization, educational programs that are run often, or on regular bases would be organized together, regardless of subject matter. Programs that are run less often are also grouped together and programs that are run very infrequently organized together as well. This method of organization may be appropriate for large groups, like the HRD department in a large business, for example. Programs that the HRD department runs every month or more frequently, such as new employee orientation training, are organized together, and programs that are only run once or twice per year are organized together.

A benefit of this method of organization is that it allows the program organizer to devote appropriate amounts of time for each category of program. Programs that are run often are focused on more often than programs that are run more infrequently.

A negative aspect of this method is that it does not consider program topic. Also, care has to be taken to ensure that programs move from one category to another as stakeholder needs shift.

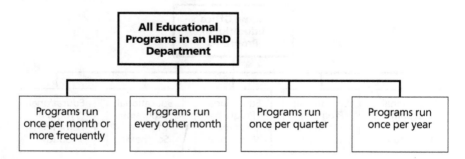

Figure 2.5 Organization by demand.

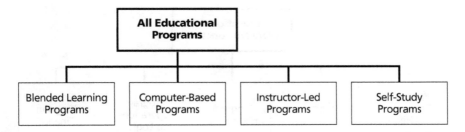

Figure 2.6 Organization by method.

Organization by Method

Educational programs can be organized by the method used to teach those programs (Figure 2.6). For example, if an organization used a wide variety of teaching methods in its educational program offerings, it could organize all Internet-based programs together, all instructor-led face-to-face programs together, all self-study programs together, and so on. Advantages to this method are similar to the advantages of organizing programs by product, subject, and demand, except this method provides for expertise in method rather than in subject.

Organization by Function

Organizing educational programs by function involves breaking down the individual components of those programs and grouping them by functional area (Figure 2.7). For example, needs analysis is considered one function, as are program design, program marketing, and program logistics. That means that all marketing efforts for all programs are grouped together in one function. All program development activities are grouped together by one function. This is a good example of a situation where the structure of the organization mimics the way their educational programs are organized. Experts in program marketing would work in the marketing of all programs, and experts in program finance would work on the financing of all programs, for example.

One of the benefits of organizing by function is that it is often more efficient to manage one aspect of all programs all together. Furthermore, the focus on one particular aspect of an educational program can help program organizers determine best practices as well as things to avoid in the future. A particular way of marketing one program that was successful, for example, might be used to market other programs. A way of structuring fees and charges for one educational program may be used on another

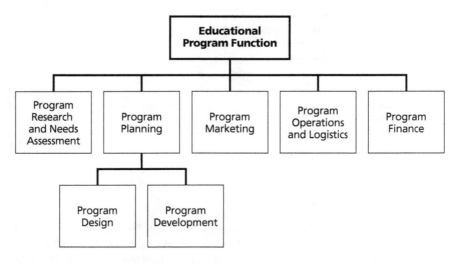

Figure 2.7   Organization by function.

program. Organization by function allows program administrators to more efficiently find what has worked in some cases and what has failed in others. It is also easier to manage activities for one function than it is to coordinate activities across multiple, different functions (Bhattacharyya, 2009).

There are disadvantages to this type of organization as well. Daft (2010) notes that this type of structure works best with a limited variety of programs. An organization with the sole focus of providing training on the use of medical records systems to various groups, for example, might find this the best way to organize. However, organizations that offer many different educational programs may not find this the best way to organize. The downside of focus and specialization on a particular function may mean that the larger-level goals of the entire educational program (and the organization) might get lost. It also can be more difficult to make decisions about an educational program that involve multiple functions (Daft, 2010).

Hybrid Organization

Hybrid methods of organizing programs pull aspects of different ways of organizing together in a way that is uniquely suited for the situation (Figure 2.8). Hybrid methods can involve the use of two or more ways of organizing. For example, a programmer may organize the educational programs for an organization by region or geographic territory. At the region or territory level, programs may be suborganized based on target market or customer. Or programs may be organized by product or division and also by customer

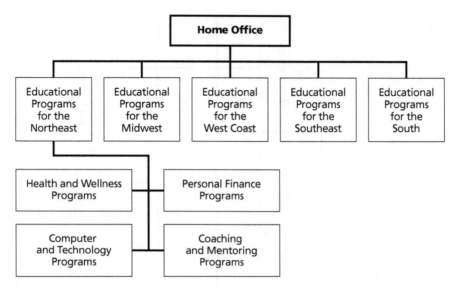

Figure 2.8 Hybrid organization.

or learner segment. Program organization is not always a case of "one size fits all." Aspects of all methods of organization can be pulled together to create individual ways of program organization (The Different Ways, 2013).

In the example below, programs are organized by geographic region or territory. Within each territory, programs are organized by product line or topical area.

Organization by Matrix Structure

Organizing programs using a matrix structure involves overlaying one method of organization on top of another. In the example in Figure 2.9, the functional approach to organization is augmented by a product approach to form a matrix or grid. Programs organized this way have the benefits of both the functional and product approaches. However, Bhattacharyya (2009) notes that "this structure requires high administrative costs, creates confusion over authority and responsibility, enhances interpersonal conflicts and overemphasizes group decision making" (p. 110).

Making Organizational Choices

Tully, Goddard, Hale, and Parsons (2014) note that "most companies do not design their organization, but they traditionally evolve over time,

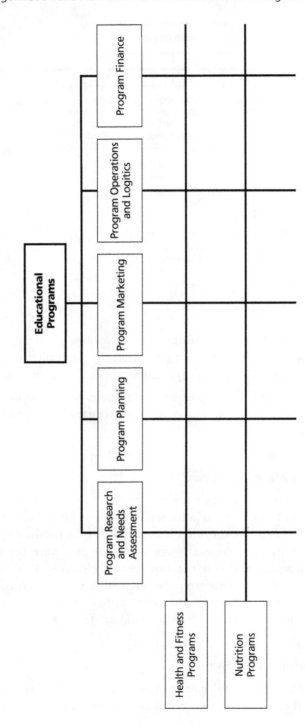

Figure 2.9 Matrix organization.

shaped more by politics than by a systematic and methodological planning process" (p. 3). However, they caution that lack of such processes can lead to inefficiencies and failure in the organization (Tully et al., 2014). Several ways of organizing educational programs have been presented in this chapter. Given these choices, how are systematic and methodological decisions on organization made? Here are some factors to consider when making those types of decisions.

Organizational Mission

As noted earlier, the overall structure of an educational organization should be based on the way that organization structures its programs. That structure should support the mission and goals of the organization (Johnson, n.d.).

For example, consider a business that operates on a national level, with one home office and six branch offices around the country. This organization's mission includes an emphasis on being very responsive to individual customer needs. It cultivates a close-to-the-customer philosophy, and its offices around the country are in place to meet the specific needs of customers in different geographic regions. The HRD department of that organization might also organize its employee training programs in a similar way—by geography or region. In doing so, they are in a better position to meet the needs of employees in each branch office. They are also consistent with the organization's overall close-to-the-customer philosophy.

Organizational Priorities

Priorities should be considered when making decisions about program organization as well. Different from an organization's mission, which is typically fairly consistent, priorities may change over time. When priorities do change, an organization's structure and way of organizing should be considered. An organization that has become very customer focused may decide to organize all educational programs using a customer or learner-segment approach to organization. They may group all educational programs for one customer all together and do the same with programs for other customers.

Sometimes more indirect factors may influence the way educational programs are organized. The HRD department in an organization that is going through a great deal of change, such as a corporate restructuring, may want to organize programs based on what is occurring within the organization. They may adjust their educational program and organizational structures to allow them to focus on topics such as change management and dealing with workplace stress.

Organizational Size, Culture, and Resources

An organization's size, structure, and resources may dictate how educational programs are organized (and therefore how the organization itself is organized) (Johnson, n.d.). For example, if an organization is very small, and there is one person in charge of program organization, educational programs may be organized all together. In larger organizations with more people, there may be more elaborate ways of organizing programs.

An organization's culture may affect how its educational programs are organized. For example, some organizations are more centralized, and others are more decentralized. In more centralized organizations, where decisions are made from the top down, educational programs may be organized differently than in flatter organizations, where employees are empowered to make decisions. Other cultural factors may influence how programs are organized. Company hierarchy, employee roles and responsibilities, and the degree to which employees are given the freedom to make decisions are factors that affect how programs are organized.

Resources can be in the form of training budgets as well as staff or human resources; and in most organizations, budgets are developed based on organizational priorities. The more resources an organization devotes to training, the more programs it can offer, and the more complex program organization may be.

Program Diversity

The variety of educational programs should be considered when determining how those programs should be organized. Some organizations may focus on one single type of educational program (such as consulting services that offer courses in one particular subject), whereas others may offer a wide variety of programs. A narrow range of program offerings could be organized using a more simple structure than would be appropriate for the organization of a wide variety of programs. The degree of diversity in an organization's educational program offerings should be a factor in determining how those programs are organized.

Competitive Environment

The environment in which the organization operates may also affect how educational programs offered by that organization are organized. An organization operating in an environment that is highly competitive, with many different organizations that offer similar products, may find different ways of organizing their educational programs than one that is the only player in the market.

For example, a consulting firm specializing in computer training for employees of local businesses may organize its programs based on market needs as well as what competing firms are doing with regard to their educational program offerings. The firm may change the way in which it organizes programs based on what competitors are doing and what its customers are demanding.

Summary: Factors to Consider

There are many ways educational programs can be organized, and there are many factors that influence how programs are organized. Many of the factors that affect decisions about program organization are continually changing as well. There is no one correct combination of factors to consider when making decisions about how to organize programs. Those who make these types of decisions should have a good understanding of all of these factors.

Making Organizational Decisions

So far in this chapter we have discussed the different ways educational programs can be organized. We have also presented factors that influence the way programs may be organized. Now we will look at the process that can be used to best determine how an organization's educational programs can be organized.

The process associated with making decisions about program organization is similar to the processes associated with making organizational-type decisions in general. Galbraith (1995) documented that process, and a modified version of his process, to focus on educational program organization, is presented in Figure 2.10.

The first thing to consider in making decisions about the way educational programs are organized is the overall mission and strategic objectives of the organization. Different stakeholders may have different criteria and different needs with regard to the way programs are organized, and these factors should be considered as well. Based on stakeholder needs and organizational mission and goals, alternatives for program organization should be developed.

Once those organizational models are developed, they should be tested, or discussed with organizational stakeholders. Feedback on the positive and negative aspects of each model should be gathered for evaluation. At this point, additional data may be collected as well. For example, benchmarking

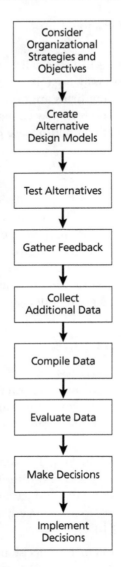

Figure 2.10 The decision-making process.

to learn about the ways in which other, similar organizations organize their programs is a good way of gathering additional information that may be valuable in the decision-making process.

Once all data has been gathered, it should be organized for use in the evaluation stage. It should be grouped together so that all involved are able to make decisions, which is the next step in the process. Once decisions are made, they can be implemented in the organization.

Signs of Success

All the variables to consider when making decisions about organization may make the task of organization seem overwhelming. How do we know when good decisions are being made? How do we know when our organization is appropriate for us? What does success look like with regard to organization? Here are some things to consider when determining the success of organizational efforts.

Appropriate organization of adult education programs (and conversely, of the organizations that offer those programs) results in efficient and effective program management. Appropriate organization is one in which learner needs are satisfied, employee or volunteer needs are satisfied, and the economic needs of the organization are satisfied (Lovey, Nadkarni, & Erdelyi, 2007). "When satisfying any one or two of these basic objectives is overemphasized at the expense of the other(s), the actualization of the other(s) will suffer and this over time will start propelling the organization in a downward spiral" (Lovey et al., 2007, p. 29–30). Effective organization results in satisfied learners who perceive value in the learning activities in which they participate. It means that those in the organization believe in the importance of their contributions and feel they are valued by the organization. It means that organizational resources are used efficiently and effectively and that the overall organization has a necessary and valued place in its environment.

Organization and Change

Keep in mind that decisions regarding organization are not set in stone. In fact, organizational decisions, whether they are related to the structure of the organization or the way in which programs are organized, should be continually examined and assessed. The ways in which programs are organized can be changed based on many variables, including the factors that influence program organization noted earlier in this chapter. Consider those variables again: Organizational mission; organizational priorities; organizational size, structure, and resources; program diversity; and the organization's competitive environment. These variables are continually evolving, which means that structures must continually evolve as well. If the organization's overall mission and strategic objectives change, for example, a change in the way programs are organized may be merited. Organizational downsizing or upsizing may require a change in structure and program organization. External factors can also influence internal change. For example, changes in immigration have resulted in greater need for courses in English-speaking and writing skills.

The Change Tightrope

Content in the above section is not meant to imply that there are daily changes to organization. That is the tightrope that those in charge of organization-related issues walk. Change is a necessary part of the continued health of an organization, but stability is important as well. People in organizations typically prefer stability to change, so change processes can be difficult. External forces, such as learner needs, societal issues, competition, technological changes, and legislative changes, may necessitate faster change with regard to organization (Salmon & de Linares, 1999). The key is in knowing when each (change and stability) is a priority for the organization. Organizations must be flexible and allow for both change and stability when necessary (Lovey et al., 2007). When change is necessary, a review of the decision-making process noted earlier in this chapter is a good start.

Also important to remember is that changes to organizations can differ with regard to size and scope, and these variables may affect the way change is done. Small changes can sometimes be made fairly easily and quickly with minimal employee or volunteer involvement. Larger changes typically require more of all of the aforementioned variables. The amount of time and other resources spent on a change related to organization should be proportionate to the size of the change and the people affected by that change.

Summary

Educational program organization is a dynamic and continually changing endeavor. It is not something that is done once and then forgotten about. Often the way programs are organized mirrors the way an organization is structured. Methods of program organization were presented in this chapter. Also included were variables to consider when making decisions related to organization along with a process that can be used to evaluated organization-related decisions. Program organization should be a thoughtful and deliberate process. These tools should be helpful to you as you work through that process.

QUESTIONS FOR DISCUSSION

1. How are the educational programs in your organization organized? Why are they organized this way? In your opinion, are they

organized in the most appropriate way, or is there a better way to organize them? Now consider other organizations with which you are familiar and address the same questions.

2. What is your organization's mission? What are its priorities? How mission and priorities reflected in the way educational programs are organized?

3. In your organization (or an organization with which you are familiar), consider how educational programs are organized. Then consider the structure of the organization. To what degree is program organization aligned with organizational structure?

4. Revisit the three scenarios at the start of this chapter. From an organization standpoint, how would you address these issues? What would you advise those in the scenarios to do?

References

Bhattacharyya, D. K. (2009). *Organizational systems, design, structure and management.* Mumbai, India: Himalaya.

Business Dictionary. (n.d.a). *Organization.* Retrieved from http://www.businessdictionary.com/definition/organization.html

Business Dictionary. (n.d.b). *Organizing.* Retrieved from http://www.businessdictionary.com/definition/organizing.html

Business Dictionary. (n.d.c). *Product organization.* Retrieved from http://www.businessdictionary.com/definition/product-organization.html

Daft, R. L. (2010). *Organizational theory & design* (10th ed.). Mason, OH: South-Western.

Daft, R. L. (2013). *Organization theory & design* (11th ed.). Mason, OH: South-Western.

Galbraith, J. R. (1995). *Designing organizations.* San Francisco, CA: Jossey-Bass.

Gillikin, J. (n.d.). Advantages & disadvantages of divisional organizational structure. *Chron.* Retrieved from http://smallbusiness.chron.com/advantages-disadvantages-divisional-organizational-structure-611.html

Johnson, S. (n.d.). How to determine the best organizational structure. *azcentral.* Retrieved from http://yourbusiness.azcentral.com/determine-organizational-structure-11025.html

Lovey, I, Nadkarni, M., S., & Erdelyi, E. (2007). *How healthy is your organization?* Westport, CT: Praeger.

Salmon, R., & de Linares, Y. (1999). *Competitive intelligence: Scanning the global environment.* London, England: Economica.

Stroh, L. K., Northcraft, G. B., & Neale, M. A. (2002). *Organizational behavior: A management challenge.* Mahwah, NJ: Erlbaum.

The different ways organizations can be structured and operated. (2013, January 10). *123HelpMe.com.* Retrieved from www.123HelpMe.com/view.asp?id=150297

Tully, P., Goddard, E., Hale, A., & Parsons, E. (2014, March 31–April 3). Engineering the organization: Providing new insights into organizational design using systems principles. In *8th Annual IEEE Systems Conference (SysCon* (pp. 439–445). doi:10.1109/SysCon.2014.6819294

3

Leadership and Administration

Leaders and Administrators: The Symbiotic Relationship

The concepts of leadership and administration have a symbiotic relationship when considered in the context of adult education and HRD. They intersect, and this intersection is demonstrated in the titles of many articles, books, academic courses, and educational programs on these topics. Titles such as "Educational Administration Leadership," "Administrative Leadership in Adult and Continuing Education," or "Leadership in Higher Education Administration" show that the two terms are often used together. However, they are not necessarily the same, and there can be differences between a leader and an administrator. A leader is not always an administrator. In fact, anyone in an organization can be a leader to some degree. An administrator is a type of a formal leader, or one in a formal position of power (Raven, 1965). That level of formality is important to the differences between the two concepts. An administrator is formally responsible for leading an organization or a unit of that organization as well as managing people and resources. Ideally, administrators are effective leaders, but unfortunately, some administrators are not. The two concepts have a symbiotic relationship, as seen in

Organization and Administration of Adult Education Programs, pages 33–60
Copyright © 2016 by Information Age Publishing
All rights of reproduction in any form reserved.

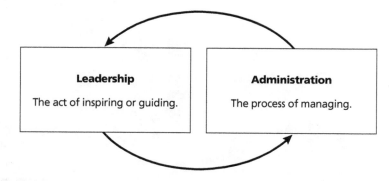

Figure 3.1 Symbiotic relationship between leadership and administration: Administrative leadership.

Figure 3.1. This relationship is the basis for articles, books, courses, and programs such as those previously mentioned.

Each concept informs the other and an understanding of both informs one's practice as an administrative leader. Consider the following scenarios.

Mark was a successful instructor in the HRD department of a mid-sized manufacturing company. He was well respected as a leader among the instructors with whom he worked and among the employees he taught. He was recently promoted to a managerial position and is struggling with his new formal leadership and administration responsibilities.

Marijo accepted a position as an educator at a community center, and was looking forward to working with her new supervisor, who talked about concepts like participatory leadership, employee empowerment, and open communication. However, Marijo has since come to learn that her new supervisor is a micromanager, who wants to be in control of everything Marijo does on the job.

Audrey is a new instructor at a wellness center. She is interested in becoming a leader and in taking on more leadership responsibility in the center at some point. She has several ideas she thinks will be popular with those she teaches.

Why Are Leadership and Administration Important in Adult Education?

Why are these two concepts important in adult education? To address that question, consider a world in which we have no adult education leaders or administrators. We need leaders and administrators to help adult education organizations operate, plan, and move forward with their objectives. Adult educators and learners don't simply show up in the same place at the same time for learning events. Leaders and administrators plan these events well in advance. They handle logistics, put systems in place, communicate with various stakeholders, make decisions, build teams, and engage in many other preparatory endeavors that will be discussed in this chapter. Leaders and administrators help create the circumstances and environments in which adult education can occur.

Chapter Overview

As stated above, leadership and administration have a symbiotic relationship. In order to fully understand that relationship, each concept will be examined separately, and then both concepts will be examined together. This chapter is organized as follows: First, leadership will be addressed. Following that, administration will be explored, specifically focusing on the topic as it relates to administration of people, resources, and processes. Last, questions and case studies will be presented to encourage dialogue. These concluding activities can be used to foster reflection regarding how ideas discussed in this chapter apply to real-world situations in the leadership and administration of adult education programs.

What Is a Leader?

Before modern organizations and administrators existed, leaders existed. Every field needs to draw on leadership approaches, and adult education and HRD are no exceptions. Leaders inspire and guide others toward a common vision or goal (Bolman & Deal, 2013). Leadership can be seen as "a process whereby an individual influences a group of individuals to achieve a common goal" (Northouse, 2015, p. 6). In order to influence others, a leader must hold some type of power. Leaders may have formal or informal power. Leaders do not necessarily have to serve in managerial or administrative roles, although some leaders do. Many effective leaders are not in official managerial or administrative positions within organizations.

Some views of leadership consider the leader an individual who affects a process and other people (Barnard, 1938). Or he/she can be considered a person who encourages organizations or groups of people to have faith in the leader's vision (Dess, Lumpkin, & Eisner, 2010). Still others see leaders more so as facilitators of learning who serve others within complex systems (Senge, 1990). Approaches to leadership are multifaceted and diverse, often with overlapping emphases, and your specific philosophical views of leadership may influence how you view effective leaders.

What Makes an Effective Leader?

Leaders may or may not have formal power. For example, leaders may not have formal, authoritative titles within organizations, but they are able to influence and motivate others. As such, leaders, by nature, have followers. Think about those people to whom everyone turns to gauge decision-making at family gatherings, outings with friends, or within meetings. Throughout history leaders have influenced and motivated others. You may think of world politicians, activists within your community, and unsung heroes who have held no formal position(s) of power, but they were able to communicate a vision and inspire people to achieve a common goal. These individuals were able to achieve goals by building a team of followers who commit to a shared purpose.

Although some think leadership traits are inherent (Stodgill, 1974), most suggest leadership can be learned (Blake & Mouton, 1964; Northouse, 2015; & Senge, 1990). Leaders possess certain traits and skills such as adaptability, decisiveness, diplomacy, intelligence, and creativity, among others (Stodgill, 1974). Since we can define specific characteristics important for leaders to have, we can also teach individuals those leadership skills. Doing so strengthens our own roles as leaders (Blake & Mouton, 1964).

In order to be successful, leaders must have an acute ability to navigate context, which means that they are able to navigate change, power, and systems without naïveté, in order to get things accomplished. Effective leaders must understand and empathize with followers. Although each of us can identify leaders who have influenced and motivated people for less than reputable purposes, ethics is an important aspect of leadership in the context of adult education and HRD (and in all other contexts as well). We define ethical leaders as those who are able to empathize with followers and act with integrity (Avolio & Gardner, 2005). These are the leaders who make fair and transparent decisions according to an ethical or moral code, for the social good.

Each of these aspects of effective leadership (Figure 3.2) will be examined in the section that follows.

An Effective Leader:

- Influences and motivates others toward a shared vision
- Navigates context
- Focuses on the social good

Figure 3.2 Effective leaders.

An Effective Leader Influences and Motivates Others Toward a Shared Vision

A vision represents the kind of world, place, or condition a person or an organization would like to see established (Levin, 2000). Visions can be individual or shared (by those in an organization, for example). They can be focused on different time frames in the future as well. You may have an individual vision focusing on personal and professional aims for your work, family, financial situation, hobbies, and other areas. A shared vision is one that a group of people is working toward. Organizations have visions, and vision statements, to ensure that everyone has a shared objective regarding the work that the organization does. A vision should provide guidance for the organization as it moves forward (Levin, 2000). Visions are different from missions. A mission (usually expressed in the form of a mission statement) deals with goals and objectives, and an organization's goals and objectives should specify ways in which the vision can be achieved (Heyes & Martin, 2015). A leader's role is to make sure that all individuals in the organization subscribe to, and work toward fulfilling, the organization's vision. Good leaders can do this, while at the same time helping individuals achieve their own goals (thereby working to achieve their individual visions).

An organization's vision is often presented in the form of a vision statement. Many organizations have vision statements that summarize their missions and desired outcomes. Examples of vision statements from several organizations follow:

- The vision statement for the American Association for Adult and Continuing Education (AAACE) is as follows: "The American Association for Adult and Continuing Education is dedicated to the belief that lifelong learning contributes to human fulfillment and positive social change. We envision a more humane world made possible by the diverse practice of our members in helping adults acquire the knowledge, skills, and values needed to lead productive and satisfying lives." (AAACE, 2015)
- The Academy of Human Resource Development vision is: "Leading human resource development through research" (AHRD, 2015). This vision also is part of the organizational tag line.
- The U.S. Army Corps of Engineers states the vision is to develop "engineering solutions for our Nation's toughest challenges." (USACE, 2015)

A leader is able to communicate to followers their vision (or their organization's vision) and the importance of that vision. Effective leaders also have the ability to communicate their visions to multiple audiences in many different situations, crafting communication to meet the needs of each audience. Consider how leaders effectively communicate their visions (or do not) in times of crisis, such as war, as well as in times of hope. Consider how visions are communicated in your organization. Who communicates them and how are they communicated?

Communication regarding vision is often followed by calls to action. A leader must be able to inspire people to work toward a vision, and they should lead by example (Kohles, Bligh, & Carsten, 2011). A positive attitude and belief in the vision are of utmost importance. If leaders don't believe their organizations can achieve their visions, how can they expect those around them (volunteers, employees, or other stakeholders) to believe they can? Leading by example is also necessary in order to inspire others. If a leader is telling others to foster a positive work culture, how is that leader fostering positive work culture him or herself? If fiscal restraint is necessary in order to make progress toward organizational goals, how is the leader modeling that restraint?

Effective leaders understand that sometimes visions and missions change or are adjusted. In these cases, leaders are able to serve as a change agents. They identify and relate to the motivations and needs of colleagues and subordinates, working to connect them to new or revised visions and goals. A leader, through symbolism, ceremony, and a variety of other methods (including plain hard work), generates energy, enthusiasm, and support for initiatives (Bolman & Deal, 2013). For example, the ceremony in which each person is rewarded for dedicated service within an organization is genuinely appreciated if the leader's actions reflect support for such an honor. If not, the ceremony is considered a disingenuous exercise to be checked off a to-do list.

Finally, effective leaders are able to build teams or followers. People follow if they understand and believe in the vision the leader has communicated. Senge (1990) states, "In learning organizations, leaders are designers, stewards, and teachers. They are responsible for building organizations where people continually expand their capabilities to understand complexity, clarify vision, and improve shared mental models—that is, they are responsible for learning" (p. 340). Leaders are directly responsible for moving their organizations forward, and that involves building the teams that help the organization work toward its vision.

An Effective Leader Navigates Context

An effective leader is a master at navigating context, which includes change, power, and systems internal and external to the organization (Bolman & Deal, 2013) (Figure 3.3). Think about what navigating means. You may envision a forest, a road, or an ocean. If you can successfully navigate

Elements of Context
• Change
• Power
• Systems

Figure 3.3 Elements of context.

through these areas, you are able to direct yourself and others to a destination. Once you are finished, you may have a clear way of charting your course that you can use for the next time. This metaphor depicts that navigating context takes practice and effective leaders have the ability to navigate the unknown to make it familiar and chart it so that they recognize signs and guideposts from past navigations and use them to move forward.

An effective leader is able to navigate change, both the small changes that happen and the astronomical changes that may occur. Leaders understand that certain approaches may be situational (Hersey & Blanchard, 1969; Tannenbaum & Schmidt, 1958) and that context is crucial to examining the right leadership approach (Fielder, 1967). Therefore, the way leaders lead might be different from one context to the next. You might recall situations in which you or another leader were very successful in one context, but using similar approaches within another context did not work as well. Contextualization emphasizes the need to clearly understand the situation, the followers, the leader's own values and beliefs, and those of others involved (Tannenbaum & Schmidt, 1958). In addition, leaders should fully understand specific forces within the environment and navigate accordingly. What is the current environmental situation, and how might that situation impact the leader, followers, and the vision moving forward? How is the environment different from the last time the leader dealt with a similar situation? The financial well-being of the organization, potential layoffs, an individual's new family responsibilities, or governmental political changes might be examples of things that may impact the environment.

Navigating context also means a leader is able to navigate power. Effective leaders recognize how power and authority are derived within the environment as well as how they derive power and authority within each specific cultural and political landscape. Being able to recognize forms of power as well as the power you possess can help facilitate ethical and effective means of working toward a vision.

Consider that there are many ways in which people derive power. Below are examples of six bases of power (French & Raven, 1959; Raven, 1965).

What kind of power do you hold in your organization? What kind of power is held by others with whom you interact? How can these bases of power be used constructively and destructively?

1. *Reward:* Power based on the ability to reward others.
2. *Coercive:* Power based on the ability to punish others.
3. *Legitimate:* Power based on formal position. As a leader you may have legitimate power in your role within the organization, such as a title, and others may hold legitimate power in relation to your position.
4. *Expert:* Power based on the knowledge and competence a person is perceived to possess. Someone in your organization may be the "go to" person about online training and this person may hold expert power in that area.
5. *Referent:* Power based on how well a person is liked and respected. For example, a person in your organization may not hold much legitimate power, but the person may hold a good deal of referent power, and others will look to this person for input or guidance before making a decision.
6. *Informational:* Power based on the ability to use information to persuade and make an argument for a position.

These bases of power help us understand how to navigate relationships and influence change. Consider that power is a fluid concept. One may have a wide range of power in one situation and a limited amount of power in the next. Understanding bases of power provides a navigation tool for leaders.

Lastly, a leader needs to have a keen ability to navigate systems. Systems are interlinked and interdependent people, places, and organizations within our lives (Bánáthy, 1992). This means that a leader is able to understand the interconnectedness of these systems and how their actions can impact them. You may think, "With all of this navigation, does a leader make any progress?" While it may seem a difficult task (and sometimes it is), an effective leader is able to skillfully navigate these systems and not become bogged down or stuck in a situation that prevents them from moving forward.

An Effective Leader Focuses on the Social Good

The foundations of adult education are grounded in the social good and so is effective leadership (Aviolo & Gardner, 2006) (Figure 3.4). Focusing on the social good means striving to understand the feelings of followers. It means acting with integrity, honesty, and moral courage in commonplace interactions and in the face of adversity. And focusing on the social good means

> **Focusing on the Social Good means:**
> - Empathizing with followers
> - Acting with integrity
> - Engaging in fair and transparent decision making

Figure 3.4 Focusing on social good.

that leaders engage in fair and transparent decision making without nepotistic actions and corrupt, imbalanced, or less-than-ethical self-interest (Crossman, 2011). Working for the social good is a basic tenet for many adult education organizations, so leaders must keep in mind its importance in all that they do.

An effective leader who focuses on social good is able to empathize with followers. Leaders who are empathetic are able to genuinely share in the feelings of others, and they possess a level of self-awareness that allows them to understand how their actions may affect the feelings of others (Mashud, Yukl, & Prussia, 2010). Leaders focusing on the social good act with integrity; they understand themselves and their moral principles. This knowledge of self and of followers should inform, and subsequently dictate, fair and transparent decision making.

An effective leader focusing on the social good engages in fair and transparent decision making. Usually this kind of decision making involves participation from followers in a democratic type of decision-making process (Lewin, Lippit, & White, 1939). Rather than a top down approach, a leader using a participative approach aims to involve followers in the decision-making process with a goal for fostering commitment to the organization, its vision and goals, and its leaders.

Qualifications for an Effective Leader

Given what we know about effective leadership, we can identify qualifications for effective leaders. These qualifications, summarized from a variety of sources, are divided into three areas: knowledge, skills, and attributes. An effective leader needs to have in-depth knowledge of the people, the power, and the environment he or she works in. That knowledge is supported by certain attributes such as empathy, resiliency, and creativity that influence the leader's actions. Knowledge and attributes help the leader to effectively use his or her skills to work toward fulfilling a vision.

It is important to note that the list in Table 3.1 is an ideal model of qualities an effective leader should have. These are qualities leaders must

TABLE 3.1	Qualities of Effective Leaders	
Knowledge	**Skills**	**Attributes**
Power	Ability to influence others	Ethical
People	Ability to motivate	Culturally competent
Environment	Decision making	Committed
	Problem solving skills	Empathetic
	Team building skills	Diplomatic
	Cultural competency skills	Resilient
	Communication skills	Creative

continually hone and improve. Each leader has strengths and weaknesses with regard to the items in Table 3.1, and not all leaders possess all of these characteristics. Good leaders are aware enough to understand their own strengths and weaknesses, so they can work on their weaknesses and use their strengths to their advantage and that of the organization.

We can all think of examples of leadership that has gone wrong, or think of leaders who fell short in the necessary knowledge, skills, or attributes at key moments in the leadership process. Consider some of those situations. In what ways did the leader fall short? What was the result? For certain, leaders begin to fail when they lose the ability to gauge the needs of followers. These leaders become removed from the real needs and motivations of their followers. Leaders can also err when their vision is not shared by enough people (or when they are not able to communicate their vision appropriately). Lastly and most destructively, a leader may become intoxicated by power and subsequently disregard or ignore the social good. If leaders only take action to keep their own power, then all other aspects of leadership erode.

Leadership Summary

The previous section discussed the concept of leadership. Approaches, definitions, and characteristics of effective leaders were also presented. Understanding leadership can help inform one's knowledge of administration, which is presented in the next section of this chapter.

What Is an Administrator?

An administrator is a person who manages processes within an organization (Kotter, 1996). An administrator is also someone who makes, and executes, decisions with regard to people, resources, and processes, focusing on short-term and long-term strategy and plans for the organization

(Dess, Lumpkin, & Eisner, 2010). The people, resources, and processes an administrator oversees are related to a variety of areas or topics, including those discussed in this book. They include

- Organizing;
- Leading;
- Managing resources, people, and processes;
- Decision making;
- Analyzing individual, team, and organizational needs;
- Budgeting;
- Securing organizational support;
- Marketing;
- Staffing;
- Stakeholder management;
- Strategic planning;
- Evaluating programs;
- Overseeing legal compliance; and
- Fostering an ethical work environment.

Administration is different from teaching, and administrators of adult education programs have very different jobs from those who teach in adult education programs. As such, additional skills are required, and those skills are not necessarily gained through time spent teaching adults (which is why many educational programs in adult education and HRD feature specific courses in program administration). Administration is the business (or operational side) of education. As noted above, administration refers to the management, organization, and operations of an organization or educational program.

In primary and secondary education, there are clear divisions between those who teach and those who work in administration. That is not always the case in adult education. Administrators working in adult education may serve at various levels of an organization, and they may wear multiple hats. If you currently serve as an administrator, you also may serve as an instructor, an accountant, or a public relations specialist. If you work in a small organization, you may be responsible for all of the subjects or areas noted above, or if you work in a larger organization with many administrators, you may be in charge of a few of them. The administrator ultimately has responsibility and oversight for what happens within the unit, department, or organization as a whole, even if work is delegated to others within the organization. Effective administration can mean the difference between a successful organization and an organization that does not last long, as administration deals with the securing of resources and the use of resources. An organization's educational programs, people's jobs, course offerings, and opportunities for learning are all dependent on the effectiveness of the administrator.

What Makes an Effective Administrator?

Think about how your organization is structured (or think about an adult education organization with which you are familiar). Some organizations are large and others are small. Some organizations have structures that are relatively simple, and others have complex structures. Regardless, some level of hierarchy exists within all organizations, and administrators are an integral part of that hierarchy. As such, they need to be able to effectively work within the structure of the organization (Figure 3.5).

An administrator's role involves managing people "up," "down," and "across." Even if you are an administrator near the top of the organizational chart, you probably have someone or some group to whom you are accountable. This could be a board of directors, a board of regents, or another overseeing body. An administrator manages up when working with that person or group. If people report to you, you typically have a management system in place for those individuals, and this is called "managing down." Working with peers on committees and in other groups, administrators manage "across" to be able to accomplish tasks and move the organization forward. Managing across may involve managing people in outside organizations or teams of people from other divisions or areas of the organization.

Administrators also are involved in managing resources, such as money, time, and educational offerings including online and face-to-face courses, workshops, and training sessions. In order to manage these things effectively, administrators must have processes in place that deal with the management of resources and the running of the organization. In smaller organizations, the administrator may manage these processes and carry them out as well. Larger organizations may be staffed by employees who perform

---

An effective administrator

- Manages people skillfully
- Manages resources effectively
- Manages processes diligently

Figure 3.5   Effective administrators.

specific duties within the organization. In these cases, the administrator may manage the employees who perform those duties.

To be an effective administrator, you need to be able manage people skillfully and manage resources and processes diligently. Administration is a delicate and diplomatic job. It is also one that is different for each organization and one that involves a wide variety of duties and responsibilities. In any given day, an administrator may ask these questions: Who is managing the budgets? How is the electric bill getting paid? Who is arranging for speaker logistics or for training program logistics? Who is evaluating programs? Who is teaching this course? Who is securing funding? All of these questions represent issues that administrators must address (and there are many more questions that could be posed here). A summary of knowledge, skills, and abilities necessary for successful administrators is discussed in the section that follows.

An Effective Administrator Manages People Skillfully

Managing people skillfully means managing interpersonal relations effectively (Figure 3.6). Managing people within the role of an adult education administrator involves three main areas: supervising, navigating systems of people, and leading. Consider a supervisor or manager you have (or have had in the past). What was most and least effective about that supervisor? What did you learn to do (and learn to not do) from that supervisor?

Administrators are responsible for supervising or managing people. Remember that the people in an adult education organization may be employees or they may be volunteers (or they may possibly exist as a combination of the two), so supervising may look different for different categories of people within an organization. An organizational chart identifies the formal relationships of individuals within an organization. However, informal structures are also key to understanding how organizations work. Navigating systems of people involves working successfully within formal structures (given formal and informal relationships among people in the organization

---

Managing people involves

- Supervising
- Navigating systems of people
- Leading

Figure 3.6 Managing people.

and outside of the organization) to get things done. As noted earlier in this chapter, leading involves moving the organization effectively and efficiently toward organizational goals. These three concepts will be discussed in the sections that follow.

Supervising

There is a reason why many job descriptions for educational program administrators require experiences supervising others; it is very sensitive and careful work. If you supervise people, you are in a formal position of power over others. Supervisors must be conscious of that power differential and understand their roles in helping individuals flourish within their productivity in addition to making sure their contributions foster a productive organization or unit. These are not easy tasks. The administrator/co-worker/worker relationships need to be absolutely central within the consideration of what you do as an administrator (Follett, 1949/1987).

Supervisors connect the individuals they supervise with the rest of the organization. A supervisor needs to make sure the goals and objectives of the organization are being met through the efforts of individual employees. This may involve implementing a process like the one described in the steps below:

1. Identify the goals and objectives of the organization;
2. Identify what is needed to accomplish these goals and objectives;
3. Determine the types of tasks that need to be addressed;
4. Discern whether long-term or short-term employees are needed to accomplish those tasks;
5. Describe the parameters of employee roles related to these tasks;
6. Establish or clarify the structure of supervision of the employees for those tasks;
7. Explore the talent the organization has, or needs, to accomplish the tasks (and secure this talent, if necessary); and
8. Cleary articulate how employees are evaluated regarding their performance of jobs and duties. (Gautam & Upadhyay, 2011)

These steps can help the administrator link the work of the individual to the goals and objectives of the organization. Because organizational goals and objectives continually evolve, this is an ongoing process, so an administrator is continually assessing these eight steps, and making modifications and improvements based on internal and external situations that affect the organization. More details on supervising are provided in the chapter on human resources (Chapter 7) as well as in Chapter 10 on legal issues.

Navigating Systems of People

Navigating systems of people means administrators understand their own positions and the positions of others, both internal and external to the organization, and that they are able to work effectively within those systems to get things accomplished. Elements of position include a person's power, job scope, influence, interests, motivations, priorities, politics, and relationships (among others) (Gardenswartz & Rowe, 2003). Navigating systems of people is sometimes like navigating the front end and back end network on a computer: although everything seems to work well on the front end, it is important to understand how systems work behind the scenes and how networks interrelate and fit with each other in order to accomplish goals. Computer network systems involve many different connections and relationships, and systems of people are no different.

Consider all the groups of people that an administrator in an adult education program may work with. Those groups may include learners, employees, volunteers, co-workers, members of the general public, associations, boards of directors, community groups, licensing and accreditation agencies, governmental bodies, and many more. Some groups may be internal to the organization and others may be external. Partnerships, working groups, and committees bring these groups of people together and are settings in which administrators should have a keen understanding of relationships in order to accomplish objectives.

An effective administrator knows how relationships work formally, such as within the organizational chart or on community boards, as well as informally, such as within friendships between people. You may know from experience that the outward appearance of relationships may not tell the complete story of a relationship. Effective administrators, especially when they are new to an organization, spend much more time investigating than making decisions and much more time listening than talking. That is because they are learning about people and relationships, so they are in better positions to navigate systems of people going forward. Before choosing allies within the organization, administrators work to understand multiple viewpoints and perspectives, and they study formal and informal hierarchies, positions relationships, and organizational structures. This type of work provides them the information they need to begin to navigate systems in an effective manner.

Navigating systems of people is ongoing work, which means that administrators are continually engaged in it. All of the elements of position noted above are continually evolving and changing, so what is true one day may not be true the next. Effective administrators understand that effective navigation of people involves continuous efforts to understand those people.

In summary, an administrator needs to understand how each part of an organization or each segment of a community works and how those parts or segments interact in a systems approach (Senge, 1990). An adult education program administrator might be considered analogous to a general practitioner rather than a specialist in the medical field. A general practitioner needs to consider how the body functions as a whole in order to be able to understand its workings, symptoms, and needs (Ricigliano, 2012). Such is the case with the administrator. If you, as an administrator, focus on only one aspect of an adult and continuing education organization, how healthy would the organization be, and how accurate would your decision making be as a result?

Leading

Leadership was addressed in the previous section, but it is important to mention it here as well. It is not possible to be even an adequate manager of people without having some leadership skills. Administrators who are effective leaders are able to supervise and navigate relationships to move the organization forward. They bring out the best of those in the organization, and they are able to help those within the organization learn and grow while contributing to the organization's success. All of the knowledge, skills, and abilities associated with leadership will enhance the effectiveness of the administrator.

An Effective Administrator Manages Resources Effectively

In addition to managing people, administrators manage a variety of other resources, and this management must be carried out effectively. Resources are defined as "money, materials, staff and other assets that can be drawn on by a person or organization in order to function effectively" (Oxford Dictionaries, 2015). Resources include certain things like an organization's physical structure, tools, equipment, course materials and supplies (human resources, which include the people who work or volunteer for the organization, are discussed in detail in the preceding section and in Chapter 7). Financial resources include the money an organization has on hand, income the organization generates and expenses it incurs, investments, and trust funds or endowments. Resources also include intangible things like an organization's goodwill and reputation. Adult education administrators need to have a keen understanding of the resources available and the resources needed in order for their organization to function well. Often the resources that an organization needs (in an ideal situation) are different from those it actually has, so issues of balance and prioritization often come into play. If one resource is impacted, such as revenue from workshop enrollment, other categories may be impacted as well (such as the organization's ability to offer new programs or provide salary increases for staff). Staff members who do not receive salary increases may find positions elsewhere, which will affect the organization's human resources. Management of resources is an ongoing task for program administrators, as both sources for, and uses of, resources are continually changing. The program administrator must have an ongoing awareness of those sources and uses in order to manage organizational resources effectively.

The concept of overseeing production sounds a bit odd because it is often discussed in the context of product manufacturing. Although education has a different focus, production, in the form of the courses or other services we offer potential consumers, is still something adult education administrators need to manage, simply because the products and services we offer potential customers are typically the largest sources and uses of resources. Managing production means that an administrator is able to maintain the fiscal soundness of a unit or organization through budget management and securing support. This is done by ensuring that incoming resources (such as tuition dollars, course fees, donations, grant money, and other sources of support for the organization) are used effectively and efficiently so the organization can offer services that meet the needs of learners and other stakeholders and also remain solvent. Products such as workshops, conferences, courses, and training sessions are related to resources in that they require resources to produce, but they also can bring in resources in the form of tuitions and fees. Products also may include consulting fees or tangible items for sale, such as DVDs, textbooks, or manuals. Administrators make ongoing decisions about which sources and uses of resources take priority over others.

Equipment and supplies are resources related to the development of instructional products as well as the day-to-day functioning of an office. Decisions about these types of things involve resource management as well. Some organizations have adopted a purely electronic (or virtual) presence, and they have eliminated phone costs or moved to using online textbooks to reduce the costs for students. However, this may affect the organization's income (which it uses to fund educational programming), so reduced costs may ultimately result in decreased income for the organization. What may seem like a good idea for cost reduction can have unintended consequences for another resource. Looking at resources as an interconnected system is critical, as administrators should be able to map potential effects of reductions (or increases) in one resource on all other organizational resources.

Administrators need to gauge use of resources in the context of each educational program offered as well as in the context of the mission of the organization or unit. The administrator should have both detailed and big-picture views and understandings of programs in order to evaluate use of resources. Administrators must consider these questions: What does success mean for my unit? What does success mean for my organization? These two answers should be very clearly tied together to determine and gauge use of resources. For example, put yourself in the position of an administrator in a division of continuing education who manages a unit responsible for cultural community programs. Some of these programs make money, some break even, and some lose money. However, the ones that lose money are important community service programs, which have been flagship initiatives in the organization for years. You are able to manage resources by taking a bit from the programs that make a lot of money to supplement the programs that lose money. Recently, a new leader in the organization has decided that all programs need to make money in order for the organization to continue to offer them. Resolving this issue would involve multiple skills as an administrator, including an understanding of the organization's tangible and intangible resources. As an administrator, how you evaluate the effective use of resources must be something you can clearly communicate to stakeholders. That means administrators must have clear standards and processes for resource management. This leads directly to the third characteristic of an effective administrator: The ability to manage processes diligently.

Managing Processes Diligently as an Administrator

All organizations have processes; however, some processes are formal and documented and others are informal. Consider all the processes in use within your organization. You probably could name quite a few. Consider processes associated with some of the resources noted in the previous two sections. From a human resource standpoint, organizations have processes for hiring, termination, performance reviews, workplace guidelines, and many others. Fiscal processes include those related to course registrations, handling cash, and accounting. Intangible processes, or those relating to goodwill, may involve guidelines for working with the media, policies for charitable contributions or donations, and, if the organization is community based, policies for working with different groups of stakeholders in the community to which the organization belongs.

Processes are directly related to the organization's structure, as the structure of an organization can affect how processes are carried out (Galbraith, Downey, & Kates, 2001). For that reason, when we discuss processes, we do so in the context of structure.

Establishing Organizational Structure

Establishing organizational structure and processes are important to managing resources. Historically much organization and promotion within systems was done very subjectively. Family and friends were hired and promoted based on relationships rather than their specific qualifications for a position (Weber, 1947). As people began to examine the downfalls of such systems, rationality and logic began to be emphasized in establishing organization. Today, rationality and logic are important in establishing a hierarchy within the organization, in how duties are assigned, and in how people are integrated and promoted within the organization. Some 100 years ago, the closest available family member, regardless of qualification(s), was asked to step in and help with the family business. Today, job descriptions listing specific qualifications are developed for each position, rubrics are used in the hiring process, and organizations search far and wide to find exactly the right candidate for positions that are available. Most organizations today have organizational charts that are graphic representations of the structure of that organization. Structures are in place so each position in the organization is listed, and job qualifications for each position are clearly documented.

There is not a single right or wrong way for an organization to be structured. As previously explained, with regard to processes, some organizational structures are formal and firm, and others are informal and flexible. The best structures are those that meet the needs of the most stakeholders and those that provide for effective and efficient operations (Galbraith al., 2001).

Processes and Structures

Organizational structures and processes need to serve each other to maximize efficiency of both (Fayol, 1949; Gilbreth, 1912/1973; Taylor, 1911; Weber, 1947). For example, an organization may process registration for training programs in a specific and standardized way, because it has found that there is one most efficient process for accomplishing this task. All employees may be instructed to follow this specific process. In another example, some institutions have a very standardized format for instruction, because evaluators have found that one approach accomplishes instructional objectives best. The instructors may have very little input into how the instruction is implemented. The approach and materials may be decided upon at a higher level, and the instructor must deliver content in a standardized way. Some higher education organizations approach instruction in this way as well. Administrators decide upon the content and format whereas teachers deliver the instruction. In other cases, an instructor may have much more control over formats and structures, and they may be able to make changes based on the needs of a particular group of learners. There may be multiple ways for learners to register for training programs. In these situations, the administrator allows for flexibility of structure, so processes associated with teaching may change at the discretion of the instructor. In both cases, however, the administrator's role is to develop processes and create a structure.

The Tension

Consider the three main things that effective administrators do: They skillfully and successfully manage people, resources, and processes. It is rare that any given administrative decision involves benefits to all three of these entities. Most often, a benefit to one entity means taking from another or making another less of a priority. There is a tension involved in managing people, resources, and processes, and in how to make decisions that take into account the needs of all stakeholders and the fair and equitable use or treatment of people, resources, and processes. One of the challenges of administrators is in trying to find a balance between their concern for people and their concern for production or the management of resources (Blake & Mouton, 1964). For example, if an administrator is only concerned about preserving his or her own power, all areas of administration will suffer—management of people, resources, and processes. In another case, an administrator might be so concerned about a particular education program that they may lose sight of the resources involved in running that program. Or an administrator becomes so concerned with getting the work of the organization done that their ability to manage people and relations suffers, and good employees start leaving their positions to work in other organizations. Alternatively, administrators may want to be everyone's friend, but their credibility and reputation may suffer because they are not adequately supervising the management of resources. Effective administrators continually try to establish a balance concerning people (staff) and resources. Although there is no one prescription for finding balance, there are avenues we can seek out to improve administrative skills.

Qualifications of an Effective Administrator

Now that we've discussed the characteristics of effective administrators, you may think that there is a substantial list of qualifications for those interested in positions as administrators (Figure 3.7). You are correct! In order to manage people, resources, and processes, an effective administrator needs specific qualifications. A certain set of knowledge, skills, and attributes is imperative for both the daily and long-term success of the organization. A

Qualifications of an Effective Administrator

Knowledge of:
- Adult education program area
- Resource management
- Process design

Skills in:
- Leadership
- Supervising
- Decision making
- Problem solving
- Team building
- Cultural competence
- Communication

Attributes:
- Self directed
- Goal oriented
- Flexible
- Organized

Figure 3.7 Qualifications of effective administrators.

list of each of these is presented below. Each directly relates to the administrator's ability to perform his or her job. Many of the knowledge, skills, and attributes on this list are discussed in detail in this book.

The Ineffective Administrator

There are many effective program administrators working in adult education and in other fields. There are also many administrators that are not very effective at all. Finding an administrator with all the required knowledge, skills, and attributes is not easy. Administrators who lack required knowledge, skills, and attributes may not be effective, and ineffective administrators can have dire consequences for organizations. Figure 3.8 enumerates some primary reasons administrators are ineffective:

The inability to prioritize is a downfall for many administrators. All administrators have overflowing email inboxes with issues that need to be addressed. The inability to prioritize how and when issues need to be addressed can make for an ineffective administrator. If an administrator fails to prioritize, time management is also likely to be an issue for the administrator.

Traits of Ineffective Administrators

- Inability to prioritize
- Favoritism
- Lack of open communication
- Inability to balance performance, reward, and improvement actions
- Conflict avoidance

Figure 3.8 Ineffective administrators.

While there are multiple areas of potential "do overs" for administrators who err, the inability to maintain fairness is a downfall from which many cannot recover. People might be able to forgive many things, but trust is broken when issues of favoritism cloud an administrator's decision-making processes. Most people have worked in organizations in which it seemed there was nepotism and favoritism. Administrators must be able to distance themselves from certain relationships and make fair decisions based on specific information and situations that arise, regardless of the relationships they hold with certain individuals. They must treat people fairly and professionally in order to be successful within their administrative positions.

Ineffective administrators also lack the ability to communicate openly. Administrators communicate with many different stakeholders at many different levels of organizations. The communication must be fair, appropriate, and clear. It should be tailored to meet the needs of each stakeholder, and thought should be put into how communication is crafted and delivered. This is especially true in the digital age, where we have many different options for communicating information. Consider when holding a face-to-face meeting might be a better option than communicating information through a text or email message, for example. Opportunities for open communication should be incorporated into regular events or meetings at check-ins throughout the year. Quickly responding to employee emails regarding their concerns and questions should be standard procedure. Ineffective administrators have difficulty crafting appropriate messages, choosing appropriate delivery methods for the communication, and communicating effectively to meet stakeholder needs.

Ineffective administrators also have difficulty balancing the recognition of successful performance and the coaching and guidance needed for performance improvement. The ways administrators manage employee performance issues will impact employee motivation and morale. We have all worked for individuals for whom it seemed we could do nothing right.

Every issue and minor detail involved severe correction or reprimand. At some point, employees may stop caring. The opposite extreme is also true. If everything is great all the time, without a critical and constructive examination of how teams and individuals may improve, it could seem as if employees don't have clear goals to work toward. Ineffective supervisors are sometimes unable to address performance in appropriate and contextual ways to benefit the individual and the organization.

Last, ineffective supervisors may avoid conflict. Conflict is a part of life, and it must be managed proactively if it is to be resolved. Understanding how power and systems work is only a part of the equation. Taking action is much more difficult. Ineffective administrators avoid conflict instead of considering conflict a way of helping individuals, teams, and organizations grow and increase their effectiveness. Conflict rarely goes away of its own accord; rather, it builds and becomes increasingly problematic if it is not addressed.

Improving Leadership and Administration Skills

The good news is that both leadership and administrative knowledge and skills can be learned (and improved upon). Even leaders and administrators who are effective in their positions should have plans for continuously improving themselves. As mentioned several times in this chapter, the environment in which leaders and administrators work is continually changing, so the skills necessary for success one day may not be adequate for success the next. There are several ways for administrators to learn and grow. A few of those are explained in this section.

If you work as an administrator, you might consider keeping a practitioner journal for a few weeks. Keeping a journal entails recording reflections about times and situations in which they felt good about their work and times and situations in which they did not. At the end of the week, the journal can be reviewed and the administrator can reflect on the challenges they faced that week and how they might better address them in the future. Successes are also reflected upon for practices and methods that should be continued in the future. The journal may identify areas in which the administrator has strong skillsets as well as areas in which they can improve, but the reflective process is not intended to place blame. Upon reflection, an administrator may find that they are more reactive than proactive, and they may consider how they can become more proactive with regard to certain situations. They may also find they managed a situation with an employee particularly well, and they may make note of what they did well in that circumstance that can be used with other employees in the future. They may find that they need to be more clear about communicating important messages in staff meetings. Whatever they find while reviewing their practitioner journal, these reflections will help them better understand their practice.

Gathering feedback from other stakeholders can also be helpful. This can be difficult when administrators are in formal roles of power, but there are ways to gather anonymous feedback from those above you, those who report to you, and others at your own level. This is sometimes called 360-degree feedback or multirater feedback. An administrator can learn a lot about how he or she is viewed by others in the organization this way. This information can also be used to continually improve practice.

Those who identify specific areas in which they would like to increase their knowledge might consider enrolling in formal or informal educational programs. Self-directed learning, in the form of reading books and articles can be helpful, as can job shadowing, working with a mentor, or enlisting a coach with whom to work on difficult issues. Degree programs, courses, seminars, workshops, and webinars abound, so it is best to do some homework and learn as much as possible about each potential learning opportunity before selecting one.

All of these methods can help administrators learn more about themselves and continually improve their performance within their positions. When administrators improve their own practice, it can also be beneficial to co-workers, employees, and other stakeholders in the organization.

Summary

After reading this chapter, what are your thoughts about the concepts of leadership and administration? How would you address the questions posed at the start of this chapter now? After exploring both sections of this chapter on leadership and administration, hopefully, you understand the symbiotic relationship between the two concepts. You should also be able to see how each of the two are multifaceted, layered, and continually changing. This means that the job of the leader and administrator is extremely complex, involving prioritization, weighing options, and making decisions, and taking actions that are not always met with favorable response from all stakeholders. That is a challenge for those in leadership and administrative roles. With the proper combination of knowledge, skills, and attributes, leaders and administrators, as well as their organizations, can thrive. People can learn to be an effective leaders and administrators. Reflection, feedback, and education can help leaders and administrators to be successful.

DISCUSSION QUESTIONS

1. Who are the leaders in your organization? Who are the administrators? Are there any names that are in one category but not in the other? If so, why?
2. Identify a situation in which you need to motivate and influence others. Which power bases are relevant? What might be the implications for accessing those power bases?
3. How do you ethically use the power you possess as an administrator?
4. What is your definition of leadership?
5. How do you view your role as a leader in an adult and continuing education organization or field?
6. What does it mean to provide leadership in adult and continuing education?
7. Locate the organizational chart for your current place of work or volunteer effort, and find where you "fit." As you consider your place on the organizational chart, how do you manage up? How do you manage down? How do you manage across? How are you managed?
8. What do you like most about how you are managed? What do you like least about how you are managed?
9. What do the answers to questions 1 and 2 (above) tell you about:
   – Your leadership and administrative approach?
   – The leadership and administrative approaches of those around you?
10. How does your leadership approach impact your approach to administration?
11. Reflect on a moment of the day in which you served as a formal leader in the role of administrator. What did you do? How do you think others perceived your interaction?
12. Reflect on a moment of the day in which you responded to a formal leader as an administrator. How did you perceive that interaction? Why is that so?
13. Create a metaphor for, or visual representation of, how you view the connection of leadership and administration in your context? What does it look like?
14. Revisit the three scenarios at the start of this chapter. From a leadership and administrative standpoint, how would you address these issues? What would you advise those in the scenarios to do?

Scenarios for Discussion

1. Scenario: It is just too much

Jane is a diversity training program manager and instructor for a community college. She has a 50% appointment to the adult education department and a 50% appointment to the Human Resource Development Administrator (you). You ask Jane to meet with you to discuss a new project. A local company has asked if you might be able to conduct diversity training for the workforce. This is a great opportunity for your community college, and Jane is a fantastic educator and program developer. This is just the kind of project that would excite her! Jane sits down in your office, and when you bring up the project, she bursts into tears. She says that she has been working 60-hour weeks just to get the basic work for the two reporting units completed, and she just can't take on one more thing. How would the leadership and administration approaches inform your analysis and your approach in this situation?

2. Scenario: Low morale

Budget cuts have just been enacted, and you have had to eliminate two instructor positions in your Basic Adult Education program. Both had the least amount of seniority, but they had a great deal of knowledge regarding technology. Morale is low among your current team of 10 (two support staff, one assistant administrator, and seven instructors). You are about to start a program with a new cohort of students. You need to plan a staff meeting. How would the concepts from this chapter influence your approach as an administrator?

References

Academy of Human Resource Development (AHRD). (2015). *About AHRD*. Retrieved from http://www.ahrd.org/?about_ahrd_2

American Association for Adult and Continuing Education (AAACE). (2015). *Who we are*. Retrieved from http://www.aaace.org/?page=WhoWeAre

Avolio, B., & Gardner, W. (2005). Authentic leadership development: Getting to the root of positive forms of leadership. *The Leadership Quarterly, 16*, 315–338.

Barnard, C. (1939). *The functions of the executive*. Cambridge, MA: Harvard University Press.

Bánáthy, B. H. (1992). *A systems view of education: Concepts and principles for effective practice*. Englewood Cliffs, NJ: Educational Technology.

Blake, R., & Mouton, J. (1964). *The managerial grid: The key to leadership excellence*. Houston, TX: Gulf.

Bolman, L., & Deal, T. (2013). *Reframing organizations: Artistry, choice and leadership.* San Francisco, CA: Jossey-Bass.

Crossman, J. (2011). Environmental and spiritual leadership: Tracing the synergies from an organizational perspective. *Journal of Business Ethics, 103*(4), 553–565.

Dess, G., Lumpkin, G. T., & Eisner, A. (2010). *Strategic management: Text & cases* (5th ed.). New York, NY: McGraw-Hill.

Fayol, H. (1949). *General and industrial management.* London, England: Pitman.

Fiedler, F. E. (1967). *A theory of leadership effectiveness.* New York, NY: McGraw-Hill.

Follett, M. P. (1949/1987) The essentials of leadership. In L. Urwick (Ed.), *Freedom and co-ordination: Lectures in business organization* (pp. 47–60). New York, NY: Garland.

French, J., & Raven, B. H. (1959). The bases of social power. In D. Cartwright (Ed.), *Studies of social power* (pp. 150–167). Ann Arbor, MI: Institute for Social Research.

Galbraith, J., Downey, D., & Kates, A. (2001). *Designing dynamic organizations: A hands-on guide for leaders at all levels.* Saranac Lake, NY: AMACOM Books.

Gardenswartz, L., & Rowe, A. (2003). *Diverse teams at work: Capitalizing on the power of diversity.* Alexandria, VA: Society of Human Resource Management.

Gautam, V., & Upadhyay, J. P. (2011, April–June). Enhancing effectiveness of employee performance management system: Strategy, organisational culture fit model (Report). *Abhigyan, 29*(1), 28.

Gilbreth, F. B. (1912/1973). *Primer of scientific management.* Hive Pub. Co.

Hersey, P., & Blanchard, K. H. (1969). An introduction to situational leadership. *Training and Development Journal, 23,* 26–34.

Heyes, A., & Martin, S. (2015). NGO mission design. *Journal of Economic Behavior & Organization, 119,* 197–210.

Kohles, J., Bligh, M., & Carsten, M. (2011). A follower-centric approach to the vision integration process. *The Leadership Quarterly, 23*(3) 476–487.

Kotter, J. P. (1996). *Leading change.* Boston, MA: Harvard Business School Press.

Levin, I. M. (2000). Vision revisited: Telling the story of the future. *The Journal of Applied Behavioral Science, 36*(1), 91–107.

Lewin, K., Lippit, R., & White, R. (1939). Patterns of aggressive behavior in experimentally created social climates. *Journal of Social Psychology, 10,* 271–301.

Mashud, R., Yukl, G., & Prussia, G. (2010). Leader empathy, ethical leadership, and relations-oriented behavior as antecedents of leader-member exchange quality. *Journal of Managerial Psychology, 25*(6), 561–577.

Northouse, P. (2015). *Leadership theory and practice* (7th ed.). Thousand Oaks, CA: Sage.

Oxford Dictionaries. (2015). *Resources.* Retrieved from http://www.oxforddictionaries.com/us/definition/american_english/resource

Raven, B. (1965). Social influence and power. In I .D. Steiner & M. Fishbein (Eds.), *Current studies in social psychology* (pp. 371–382). New York, NY: Holt, Rinehart & Winston.

Ricigliano, R. (2012). *Making peace last: A tool for sustainable peacebuilding*. Boulder, CO: Paradigm.

Senge, P. (1990). *The fifth discipline: The art & practice of the learning organization*. New York, NY: Currency Doubleday.

Stogdill, R. M. (1974). *Handbook of leadership: A survey of theory and research*. New York, NY: Free Press.

Tannenbaum, A. S., & Schmidt, W. H. (1958, March/April). How to choose a leadership pattern. *Harvard Business Review, 36,* 95–101.

Taylor, F. W. (1911). *The principles of scientific management*. New York, NY: Harper.

U.S. Army Corps of Engineers. (2015). *About*. Retrieved from http://www.us-ace.army.mil/About/MissionandVision.aspx

Weber, M. (1947). *The theory of social and economic organization*. New York, NY: Free Press.

4

Budgeting

Budgets: The Organization's Purse

Consider your first thoughts when you hear the word *budget*. Often, people's reactions are not positive. Budgets are often associated with complex calculations, with losing resources, or with having to make difficult decisions. The word *budget* is derived from the French word *bougette*, which means a purse, wallet, or little bag. "The connection between bougette and budget is made presumably because one's entire wealth could be contained within a purse—just as the organization's worth is contained within the boundaries of a budget" (Hartnett, 2009, p. 3). To many in adult education, the work surrounding the development and maintenance of a budget is uninteresting at best and painful at worst. Those who teach adults seldom go into the profession because of their interest in figures and accounting. Still, budgets are an important part of the organization and administration of adult education programs.

Some chapters in this book note that the topics discussed in those chapters can be implemented formally or informally, depending on the size and nature of the organization; the same cannot be said about budgets.

Organization and Administration of Adult Education Programs, pages 61–82
Copyright © 2016 by Information Age Publishing
61

All organizations are advised to have formal processes in place for the management of budgets, and all organizations should ensure that the ongoing maintenance of budgets, the evaluation of current budget numbers, and the preparation of future budgets are done on regular bases. An organization's budget should be up-to-date, and it should be an accurate reflection, on any given day, of the financial health of the organization. Budgeting, and budget maintenance and assessment, must be ongoing in order to ensure that this can happen. The organization's "purse" is too important to ignore, even for a very short amount of time. The good news, however, is that budgets need not be complicated, and an understanding of budgets and the budgeting process can be extremely helpful in your planning efforts. Budgets can provide you with a wealth (no pun intended) of information. Consider the following scenarios.

Guili was hired by a small nonprofit organization to formalize the budgeting process for that organization. To this point, budgeting had been done informally, with a focus on the short term. Educational programs were not planned far in advance, as the organization relied on money coming in each month to fund programs offered during the next month.

Bill is in charge of the budgets for a community center. Bill's boss just informed him that the center will have to undergo major renovations in the upcoming year, which will affect the budgets for that year and several subsequent years. To this point, the budgeting process for the center has been pretty straightforward, but these renovations will mean drastic changes to the center's budget.

Kate works in the HRD department of a midsized consumer goods organization. She has been doing some analysis and realizes that the cost of several educational programs for the organization's employees have drastically increased over the past few years. Kate knows that if the programs are to survive, she will have to find ways to cut costs associated with these programs.

Why Are Budgets Important in Adult Education?

This may be a better question: To what degree is budgeting important in adult education? The answer may depend on your position or role in the field. Educational program organization and administration are often directly involved with budgets and the budgeting process. Budgets are important to program organizers and administrators because they are the main tools that can be used to examine the financial health of an organization and to guide the organization forward. "Planning for the future enhances our understanding of the present. Budgets reduce the chance of repetition of past errors . . . and effective budgeting can lead to the preparedness necessary to deal with adversity and opportunity when either is at your doorstep" (Lalli, 2012, p. xvi).

Those with other roles may be less involved with budgets. Instructors, for example, may be more focused on teaching and curriculum-related things than on budgets (although an organization's budgets have direct effects on everyone in the organization, including instructors). Everyone in an organization should have an understanding of the organization's budget, however, so all are on the same page with regard to the organization's priorities and goals. "An emphasis on budget may help (an organization) to achieve budgetary objectives by aligning the behavior of employees with organizational goals; thereby strengthening company performance" (Kung, Huang, & Cheng, 2013, p. 136). Budgets are important in adult education because they can provide an immediate snapshot of the health of an organization and because they can be useful tools that provide guidance, aid in decision-making processes, and help organizations prepare for the future.

Chapter Overview

This chapter begins by looking at terms and definitions associated with budgets and the budgeting process. A look at roles and responsibilities of key stakeholders involved in the development and maintenance of an organization's budget is then presented. There are many different processes that can be used to develop a budget. One of those processes is presented in this chapter, and each step in the process is discussed. The chapter concludes with a section on taking action based on information gathered during the budgeting process.

Budgets Defined

A budget is defined as "The formal expression of plans, goals and objectives of management that covers all aspects of operations for a designated time period" (Shim, Siegel, & Shim, 2011, p. 1). An organization's budget is an estimate of costs or expenses, revenues, and resources over a specific period, reflecting a reading of future financial conditions and goals (Business Dictionary, n.d.a).

Important in these definitions are the following components: First, a budget is an estimate or projection of what is to happen in the future. Budgets use past and current data to help those in the organization plan for the future (Lalli, 2012). Secondly, budgets take into consideration revenues, or

> **Revenue:** The amount of money an organization takes in during a specific period
>
> **Expenses:** The costs that an organization incurs while doing business
>
> **Income:** An organization's revenues less expenses

Figure 4.1 Budget-related definitions.

the money coming into the organization, costs, or the money that is flowing out of the organization, and other resources, which may include labor, the organization's capital, expertise within the organization, and management, among others (Business Dictionary n.d.c). Third, budgets are plans and as such are subject to change. There are always unplanned things that come into play—unanticipated expenses, for example, that may not be included in the budget. In these cases, adjustments to the budget have to be made. Sometimes, budgets allow for contingencies to compensate for unanticipated expenses that arise during the course of the budget period. Unanticipated budgetary factors can also be positive; additional revenues, an unexpected donation, or the receipt of a grant, for example. Those positive factors affecting the budget can be accounted for, and dealt with, much more easily than can unexpected expenses, which may have negative effects on other parts of the budget. Fourth, budgets are time bound. They may be for a year (which is typical), a quarter, or a month (or some other time period), but some budgets span multiple years. In many cases, the budget for a longer period of time is developed by combining budgets from shorter periods of time. A monthly budget may roll into a quarterly budget, and four quarterly budgets may be combined to develop a budget for an entire year. Just as budgets are time bound, they can also be prepared for different levels of the organization. In large organizations, the budgets for separate departments may roll up into the overall budget for a division. Further, budgets for all divisions of the organization may roll into the overall organizational budget. In adult education organizations, budgets may be developed on the course level, or the program level, in addition to the overall organizational level. In some organizations, only one budget, for the overall organization, is needed. The number and type of budgets created in any one organization depends on the size and structure of that organization (Shim et al., 2011). Typically, the most detail is found in budgets designated for use during shorter time periods and for those prepared at lower or more specific levels of an organization (Shim et al., 2011). Budgets become more general at higher levels of the organization and when they cover greater (multiyear) time frames.

The definition of budget noted in the Business Dictionary (n.d.a) continues as follows: "One of the most important administrative tools, a budget serves also as a (1) plan of action for achieving quantified objectives, (2) standard for measuring performance, and (3) device for coping with foreseeable adverse situations." Indeed, the organization's budget serves many important functions. Those whose job it is to develop budgets continually monitor them to see how actual figures compare with budgeted figures. The comparison of actual figures with budgeted figures helps the organization to adjust plans and make changes going forward. These comparisons can also tell the organization where its strengths and weaknesses lie (Lalli, 2012).

An organization's budget is developed and used by many different entities in the organization. Some organizations have accountants or bookkeepers who are in charge of budget development and maintenance. In some organizations, the executive director or leader is in charge of developing and maintaining a budget. Other stakeholders within an organization play different roles with regard to the budget. Those who are in leadership positions in an organization who may be involved in budgeting for a particular division or area may be most interested in their specific parts of the overall budget. In nonprofit organizations, boards of directors or entities that provide oversight to the organization may be interested in the overall organizational budget as a tool in making decisions about the organization's future. Like most of the functions noted in this book, budget development and maintenance is not done in a vacuum. Rather, it takes the input of many different stakeholders in order to ensure accuracy (Shim et al., 2011).

To conclude this discussion on the definition of a budget, consider the following quote, which illustrates how budgets are connected to all that the organization does:

> A budget is much more than a column of numbers. It is, actually, a representation of an agreed-upon strategy, a blueprint and a map for the coming year(s). On one hand it is comprised [sic] of a series of educated guesses regarding funds that are expected to be received. On the other hand it also involves the cataloguing of probable expenses. By melding the two components, the organization is able to use good judgment to comfortably forecast its activities for the short and long term. (Hartnett, 2009, p. 3)

To conclude this section, we go back to a question posed earlier: Why are budgets important in adult education? In very basic terms, organizations cannot survive for the long term if their expenses are greater than their revenues (if they spend more than they bring in). All the good work an adult education organization may be doing for its learners may come to an end if that organization is not on solid financial ground. The topic of budgeting may not be of interest to some in adult education; however, it is a topic that must be mastered by those adult educators who are in charge of the organization and administration of programs. Some program administrators even come to enjoy the budgeting process; or at least, come to find it interesting. An understanding of budgets and the budgeting process can make the difference between a successful organization and a failed organization.

The Budget Process

"In terms of planning, coordination, control, or performance evaluation, budgeting systems are central to any management control system" (Kung et al., 2013, pp. 135–136). Every process has to start somewhere, and as is the case with many aspects of educational program administration, the first time an organization uses a new process is much more difficult than subsequent times. The budgeting process can be difficult the first time it is worked through. However, once everyone involved has become familiar with the steps in the process, it is easier, as previous work can be used as a blueprint for future work. Most organizations do have processes and procedures in place for budgeting (or if they do not, they should), so often, people new to the organization familiarize themselves with the steps in the process and start participating. People starting a new organization, however, must start from the very beginning when developing a budget process. Also, in certain situations in existing organizations, it may be decided that a change to the budget process is in order. Regardless of the situation, there should be a formal process in place, and that process should be followed consistently. Figure 4.2 is an example of a step-by-step guide to developing a basic budget.

Step 1: Determine the People Who Should Be Involved

The first step in the process of developing a budget is to determine the people who should be involved in the budgeting process. As noted earlier, many different stakeholders have interest in an organization's budget. Some may be directly involved in the budget development process, while others may be involved in the completed budget and/or the ongoing monitoring of results in comparison with the budget. The size and scope of the adult education organization is another factor that determines who is involved

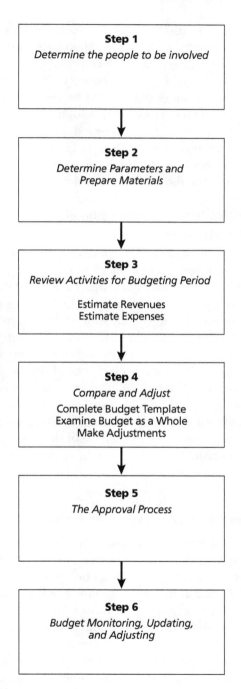

Figure 4.2 The budgeting process.

in developing the organization's budget. In some small organizations, budgeting may be done solely by the organization's administrator or director (although often when budgeting is the responsibility of one person, that person obtains input from other stakeholders in the organization). In larger organizations, a team of people may be responsible for the budget (Shim et al., 2011). A human resource development department in a large organization may be responsible for its own department budget, which is a piece of the overall organization's budget. In general, those responsible for budget development might include the organization's leader(s), program or department managers, those involved in development for the organization (in nonprofits, this includes people responsible for fundraising, grant writing, and soliciting funds for the organization), and the organization's accounting or finance employees.

It is a good idea to have budget development created by a team of people, or at least by more than one person. Input from a variety of stakeholders can result in more information upon which to build a budget, and ultimately, that can result in a more accurate budget. It is especially important to have people who work directly with budgets involved in the planning of those budgets. Organizations err when they omit these stakeholders from the budget development process. Stakeholders who manage the organization's budget, who make budget-related decisions, and who have an effect on how the organization allocates funds should be involved in the budgeting process. As a general rule, people are more invested in parts of the organization, like budgets, that they are directly involved in developing. The people in an organization must believe in the structure of the budget if they are to be successful in carrying out the organization's mission within the guidelines and scope of the budget.

―――――
Step 2: Determine Parameters and Prepare Materials

Once a group of people responsible for budgeting has been determined, plan on making decisions regarding the parameters and scope of the budget. There are also materials to gather and document templates to prepare. One of the first things to determine is a timeline for the budget. As noted earlier, budgets can be created for various time frames: monthly, quarterly, yearly, and multiyear, for example. Often budgets are developed for one year, but that year may start and end at different times of the year. A calendar-year budget runs January 1 through December 31. Fiscal year budgets also last for one year, but they may start and end at different times of the year. For example, the budget for the American Association for Adult and Continuing Education (AAACE) runs for one fiscal year. Their fiscal year begins July 1 and ends June 30. Organizations may elect to use a fiscal, rather than calendar year budget, if a majority of their revenue is earned late in the calendar year, and a majority of expenses are paid during the next calendar year. The adult education association referenced above holds its annual conference in November of each year, but many conference-related expenses are paid in January. The use of a calendar-year budget would show substantial income in November, but it would not show the corresponding expenses associated with that conference, since many of them are not paid until January. The result would be an inaccurate portrayal of year-end income if a calendar-year budget were to be used. This is the reason why a July 1–June 30 fiscal year budget makes better sense for the AAACE. Another factor to consider is that many organizations run on a calendar year basis. The time at the end of the calendar year and the start of the next year, when previous year-end accounting is done, is a very busy one for accountants and tax preparers. Using a fiscal year budget may allow an organization more immediate access to tax preparation professionals and may provide an opportunity for it to pay lower fees than would be charged during peak times (Beesley, 2013). When making these decisions, the organization's strategic plan should be used for guidance. Those who work on an organization's budget should be aware of this plan in order to make appropriate budgeting and timeline decisions.

Also important to consider at this point are formal budget review periods. As mentioned earlier, an organization's budget should be kept up-to-date on a daily basis. While doing this may be the job of a specific person within the organization, not everyone on the budget committee may be able to monitor budgets on a daily basis. In order to keep stakeholders informed, a schedule of budget updates or review periods should be developed (GFOA, 1998, p. 37). Some organizations develop monthly budgetary updates to share with members of the budget committee as well as other stakeholders. Others use a quarterly system, and they provide budget updates every 3 months. During these monthly or quarterly time periods, updates can be shared, and adjustments to the budget can be made, as become appropriate. The budget committee should decide on how updates and reviews are communicated to organizational stakeholders. It should also determine how adjustments to the budget should be made and at what points during the fiscal year.

Determining timelines for budgets typically occurs when the organization is new. Established organizations already have these timelines in place, so discussion of these types of timelines and procedures is not necessary unless the members of the budget committee feel there is good reason to change the existing timeline (GFOA, 1998, p. 38).

This step of the budget process is also the time when materials are gathered and document templates are prepared. Two types of materials are gathered and reviewed at this time. They are materials related to the organization's overall mission, goals, objectives and future plans, and materials related to the actual preparation of the budget.

In order to put the budgeting process in proper context, it is a good idea to review the plans and goals of the organization up front. Most organizations connect their budgeting processes to their strategic or long-term planning efforts. These plans typically contain information about actions and programs that are required to help the organization attain its goals (Lalli, 2012). They also include analyses of the external environment and other factors that may be important in the budgeting process. Budgets prepared in the past, current budgets, and other financial statements should also be collected at this point.

Those in the organization may have requests for new equipment, supplies, and other resources that could affect future budgets. The gathering and prioritizing of requests that may require the commitment of resources above and beyond those associated with regular operating expenses should be considered and prioritized at this point also (Costello, 2011).

Materials related to the preparation of the budget include forms and templates into which data can be entered. A budget template or a document for managing the budget should be developed at this time. That budget template may be developed so that smaller departmental budgets can become part of a larger, master budget or that so monthly and quarterly budgets can become part of yearly budgets. A calendar that includes times for budget reviews and meetings for those on the budget committee can also be developed at this time (FMA, 2012).

Step 3: Review Activities for the Budgeting Period

This step in the budget process involves examining details about the organization's past (and current, or period-to-date) revenues and expenses (Figure 4.3). If the organization has a budgeting process already in place, the examination of previous and current budgets should be straightforward. Some models of budget development note that the examination of revenues should be done before the examination of expenses, and others recommend expenses be analyzed before revenues. It is important to consider the two topics separately, however, as it makes the budget development process more orderly. In this chapter, we will address revenues first, followed by expenses.

**Reviewing Activities for the
Budget Period includes:**

Estimate Revenues

Estimate Expenses

Figure 4.3   Estimating revenues and expenses.

As stated earlier in this chapter, the budgeting process involves using data from an organization's past performance to plan for the future. "Forecasting is predicting the outcome of events" (Shim et al., 2011, p. 4). Those skilled in the budgeting process are astute forecasters, and they have the ability to develop accurate plans for the future based on what they know about the past. Planning for the future at this step in the process involves examining past performance and then estimating (or forecasting) what will happen in the future. Forecasts for expected revenues and expected expenses are developed at this point. Because the forecasting process involves speculation, multiple forecasts that consider a variety of scenarios or variables may be developed. "Due to uncertainties inherent in planning, (several) forecasts may be projected: one at an optimistic level, one at a pessimistic or extremely conservative level, and one at a balanced, in-between level" (Shim et al., 2011, p. 8).

Estimation of Revenues

Organizations need revenue in order to cover the expenses associated with the work they do (and, in the case of for-profit organizations, to make a profit above and beyond the covering of expenses). The amount of revenue required depends on the organization's specific objectives. Some organizations plan to break even, which means the revenues generated only cover expenses incurred. Others plan for a surplus in revenue after expenses are calculated. Organizations rarely plan for a deficit, or less revenue than expenses; although, in some cases, organizations with sources of revenue that are seasonal may plan for deficits in some budget periods, which are balanced by disproportionate amounts of revenue in other budget periods (Busines Dictionary, n.d.c).

In order to estimate an organization's revenues, all sources of income should be analyzed and projections should be made as to how much income will be received from each source during the allotted budget period. In adult education organizations, revenue can come from a variety of sources. In some cases, tuition and fee payments for courses are sources of revenue. In others, such as nonprofit organizations, government subsidies may be primary sources of income. Some organizations depend on donations and fundraising, so these types of activities, along with the estimated income they will generate for the organization, should be noted here. Grant monies can also be considered sources of income if the organization is scheduled to receive money from a grant.

The estimation of these numbers is something that should be worked on carefully with special consideration of many variables. Consider a non-profit literacy organization, for example, that relies heavily on donations. When estimating donations for a budget time period, the budget committee must consider the organization's general history with regard to donations, past donations for the year and for that specific time period in prior years, seasonality of donations, economic conditions, status and financial condition of major donors (as the death of a major contributor can have devastating effects on an organization), and the potential for attracting new donors, among other factors. What appears as one line on a budget can involve a good deal of consideration and calculation. Sometimes an increase in revenue in one area can affect revenue in another. If an organization receives a large grant, for example, current donors may decrease their giving, believing that the organization is provided for by the proceeds of the grant.

These types of issues should be considered when forecasting each source of income for the organization. "These questions require knowledge of program plans, fundraising expectations, development activities, grant sources, and local and state laws. Accurate answers are essential and research may be necessary" (VSCPA, p. 3). The fact that these issues must be considered for every line item in the budget is a testament to the major undertaking that is the development of a budget. It also demonstrates the importance of a team approach in the development and maintenance of a budget.

Estimation of Expenses

Expenses include all of the costs incurred in the running of the organization. Expenses are forecast exactly like revenues, and there are a variety of types of expenses to consider when preparing budgets (Figure 4.4). Here are some terms related to expenses that are important to understand:

Fixed costs are costs that remain the same (or relatively stable) regardless of the activity of the organization (Investopedia, n.d.a). An organization's rent, for example, is fixed, as the same amount is paid each month, regardless of what the organization does during that month. Other types of fixed costs can include utilities, equipment, insurance, and salaries and benefits for full-time workers.

Fixed Versus Variable Costs

Fixed costs remain relatively stable regardless of organizational activity.

Variable costs change based on the number of people an organization serves. They are also known as "per person costs."

Figure 4.4 Fixed and variable costs.

Variable costs are costs that change depending on the number of people the organization serves. In adult education organizations, a major variable cost may be the cost of textbooks, supplies, and other materials for learners (Accounting Tools, n.d.). A community-based literacy organization might determine that textbooks and supplies cost $30 per learner enrolled in their programs, so the variable costs for any given budget period for learner supplies are $30 multiplied by the number of learners the organization projects it will serve during that period. If that organization pays instructors by the course, the variable cost for instructor pay will depend on the number of courses offered during that time period.

Direct costs are costs associated directly with the service provided by the adult education organization (Business Dictionary, n.d.b) (Figure 4.5). They are "funds actually spent that support specific program activities" (Caffarella, 2002, p. 306). Direct costs for the community-based literacy organization noted above would include all costs associated with the running of literacy courses and tutoring programs, including instructor salaries, books, and materials. Indirect costs are costs that cannot be tied directly to a program. They include things like rent, utilities, and office space. Caffarella (2002) notes that the categorization of direct costs and indirect costs is based on the organization and the program. "If a training program is held at the host organization's facilities, the space and equipment items are usually considered

---

Direct Versus Indirect Costs

Direct costs are associated directly with the service provided by the organization

Indirect costs cannot be tied directly to the services an organization provides

---

Figure 4.5 Direct and indirect costs.

indirect costs; if the program is housed at a motel or conference center, these same expenses are considered direct costs" (p. 306).

As explained earlier, most models for developing budgets suggest an examination of revenues and then expenses done separately (and later, combined into a budget). For some line items on a budget, income and expense forecasts can be developed together. An organization may rely on sales, raffles, auctions, or other types of fundraising activities as a source of revenue. In these cases, the questions noted in the previous paragraph can be used to forecast income from these activities. At the same time, expenses associated with these activities can also be forecast. Those expenses might be related to printing, advertising, costs for items to be sold or raffled, taxes, and other fees.

Step Four: Compare and Adjust

After revenues and expenses have been forecast, it is time to combine both sets of numbers together on an overall budget template. Sources of revenue should be listed on one side of the budget and expenses should be listed on the other. At this point, when numbers are examined all together, adjustments can be made. One of the main goals of the budgeting exercise is to make sure the organization has enough revenue to cover the expenses that will be incurred during the budget time frame and possibly earn income for the organization (depending on the type of organization). If, when revenues and expenses are compared, there is more revenue than expense, the budget committee is in good shape (determinations about how much income an organization should have in a budget period depend on many factors within the organization). If there is more expense than revenue, the budget committee has several options. It can review revenue figures and make adjustments if those on the committee believe additional revenue can be made. The committee can also look for items within expenses that can be cut back/reduced.

The process of reviewing and adjusting a budget can take a good deal of time. Often, when a budget proposal is complete, it will be sent to different stakeholders (outside of the immediate budget committee) for input. Several rounds of discussion and adjustment may take place before all parties agree on the budget.

Step Five: The Approval Process

Once a preliminary budget has been approved by the budget committee, it may be sent to higher-level stakeholders for approval. In the case of nonprofit associations, for example, the budget typically is approved by the organization's board of directors. These stakeholders may suggest revisions as well before final approval is granted.

Step Six: Budget Monitoring, Updating, and Adjusting

The approval of the budget is a major milestone, but, as explained earlier, budgets must be monitored, reviewed, and possibly updated depending on conditions within the organization. During step two of this process, the budget committee should have determined who was responsible for daily monitoring and updating of the budget, and they should have developed a timeline for budget review. Also determined at that time are the forms and systems to be used. From this point forward, monitoring updating, and adjusting occur, and these processes continue until the next budget is prepared.

Going forward from this point, actual numbers are compared with budget figures, and these comparisons can tell stakeholders about the organization's financial health at any given point in time. These reviews also involve discussions about why there are variances. Root causes or reasons for variances are determined (or at least discussed) so appropriate adjustments can be made (if it is determined that adjustments should be made). Common root causes for budget adjustments include changes in the external environment that affect the organization or because plans are deemed unattainable (Lalli, 2012).

In some cases, budget committees will build in "trigger points" when they prepare initial budgets. Trigger points specify actions to be taken if projections are not met. For example, if an organization budgets for $100,000 in donations in the first six months of the year, a trigger point may be attached to that figure at the end of that first six months. If $100,000 in donations isn't received by that time, the organization must decrease expenses for the rest of the year by the percentage equal to the difference between what was actually received and $100,000. These trigger points help the organization make ongoing adjustments to the budget and to its business.

Both systems and people involved can affect the success of this step in the process. "Inadequate software or a non-integrated accounting system can have a negative effect on the process. So can untrained or unmotivated employees. The human factor in any budget is as important as any quantitative statement the budget makes" (Rotundi, 1997, p. 51). Monitoring should be ongoing, and "numbers should be gathered as the process goes along and tracked against assumptions" (Sage, 2012, p. 5). Updating should be done on a weekly or monthly basis, or it should occur according to the specified budget period (annually, quarterly, etc.).

Budgeting Tips

Developing a budget is a bit like trying to predict the future, but in the case of budgeting, predictions for the future are based on a significant amount of information from the organization's past financial activity. Certain considerations can help make the budgeting process more accurate. First, be sure the budget developed is realistic and attainable (Shim, 2011). With regard to revenue, it is not good practice to hope for the best, and it is an even worse practice to spend first and hope for the best down the road. It is better to plan conservative estimates for revenues (although a variety of different scenarios can be developed and forecast). With regard to expenses, some organizations like to allow for "wiggle room" by budgeting for expenses at a higher level than actually anticipated. Sometimes vague account descriptions or generic and miscellaneous accounts are used to pay for unexpected expenses. While it may be beneficial to have some wiggle room to cover for unanticipated expenses, the accuracy of budget figures and the specificity of budget descriptions is even more important. Hartnett (2013) advises budgeters to "use the most accurate numbers possible so that the budget does not become distorted and therefore much less valuable for planning purposes" (p. 3).

Your budget should also be detailed enough to be beneficial to those who use it. Broad categories of budget items should be divided up into specific categories so accurate records can be kept. This will help those in the organization know precisely where revenues are coming from and exactly where expenses are incurred.

If you are involved with budgeting, be sure that notes and records regarding specific budget items are kept with the budget. These things will help the budget committee make decisions about budget modifications. For example, if an organization plans a major fundraiser for the month of February, the budget should note that February revenue estimates are based, in part, on this fundraising activity. If a February fundraiser is canceled and rescheduled for March, those on the budget committee will already have information about why both February and March budget revenue numbers need to be modified. Keeping notes and records regarding budget line items is important in ensuring that all involved understand what the budget numbers represent (and why circumstances may dictate their changes).

Ongoing communication with stakeholders in the organization is just as important as keeping notes and records on budget-related issues. Often, those closest to an educational program see trends or hear of valuable information that may affect an organization's budget. For example, an instructor in a nonprofit organization offering ESL courses to the community may hear (from his students) that the local community college is starting to offer free ESL courses to the general public. This is information that those on the nonprofit organization's budget committee need to know, as it may affect that organization's budget (as well as its educational programming). The more people in an organization who understand the importance of this type of communication, the more accurate the budget will be.

Finally, understand that budgets are living documents that are subject to change and modification. There is no shame in making adjustments to an organization's budget. The number of changes made to a budget is not related to the competence of the people involved in the budget process, but rather budgets are predictions, and as such they are made to be changed when necessary.

Taking Action

While it is true that budgets are continually being updated and changed, sometimes information gathered as part of the budget monitoring, updating, and adjustment process requires more than simply an adjustment to the budget. Sometimes information gathered as part of these processes requires a change in the way the organization operates. If an organization finds that one of its educational programs is continually losing money, it may determine that the program should be restructured, offered less often, or even discontinued. Alternatively, if a specific program is very popular, and is bringing in a good deal of revenue for the organization, that program may need to be expanded. It is one thing to maintain and adjust budget figures, but it is a totally different issue to take action and make changes to an organization's structure, programs, and course offerings. Making positive changes, such as expanding programs based on increases in revenue, can be exciting. Making cuts, however, based on revenue shortfalls, is another story. Decisions involving budget cuts are much more difficult, as they may involve instructors and learners that are served by the organization. They can be unpopular decisions to make. However, sometimes they have to be made, and organizations err when they do not take action based on trends they are seeing in their budgets (Maddox, 1999). Consider the following scenarios.

A community-based center for domestic violence offers courses on domestic violence prevention to local organizations and clubs. Their most popular program is one that costs them the most to organize and facilitate, and because it is offered free of charge to any group that requests it, it is draining the financial resources of the organization.

An AIDS resource center offers courses on AIDS awareness and prevention to students at high schools, community colleges, and universities in the area. The center has an amazing facilitator for its courses, but demand for those courses has declined, and attendance numbers for the courses has dropped substantially. The center charges the schools a fee for running the courses, and in the past, the fee has covered expenses and generated some revenue for the organization. However, the budget has shown that decreasing demand for the courses has decreased the organization's revenues.

The community health and wellness branch of a hospital offers weight-loss courses, which are open to anyone in the community. Attendees pay a flat fee and attend a series of 10 courses and workshops throughout a six-month period. The courses are very popular and provide a good amount of revenue for the organization. A new hospital has just been built on the other side of town, and one month ago, they started offering a similar program, but they are charging participants substantially less than this hospital is currently charging. As a result, both attendance and course revenues for this hospital have decreased.

In all of the above cases, information garnered as part of the budget maintenance process indicates that decisions on the organization's programs must be made. Those decisions can vary depending on the factors involved in the specific situation. In some cases, reducing expenses by cutting down on the cost of course materials may solve the problem. In other cases, the discontinuation of some programs and/or the replacement of unpopular programs with ones that may be more popular (and may generate more revenue for the organization) may be the answer. Sometimes, there are grants or other sources of funding that can be used to cover costs. Other times, increasing course fees can address the issue as well. In some cases, those in the organization may decide to gather more information about the issue during subsequent budget periods before making any decisions (although it is important to set realistic timelines and take action if problems persist). The important thing to take away from this discussion is that when there is a difference between budgeted figures and actual figures, budget adjustments must be made, and sometimes organizational adjustments must be made.

Two concepts to consider when making decisions on courses or programs based on budget information are return on investment and cost-benefit analysis.

"The term return on investment (ROI) describes the benefits (or savings) program activities provide in relationship to the total program costs" (Caffarella, 2002, p. 306). To determine a program's return on investment

Return on Investment (ROI)

The benefit or return on an investment to an organization divided by the cost of that investment to the organization

Benefit / Cost = ROI

ROIs should be positive (the more positive, the better)

Figure 4.6 Return on investment.

"the benefit (return) of an investment is divided by the cost of the investment, and the result is expressed as a percentage or ratio" (Investopedia, n.d.b). Positive ROIs mean the investment is a good one (the more positive, the better), and negative ROIs means the cost for the investment is greater than the benefit, so those investments should be reviewed and either discontinued or adjusted. The Figure 4.6 shows how ROI is calculated.

A cost-benefit analysis examines the ratio of costs associated with a program to the benefits the program provides (Figure 4.7). "The costs of education and training programs are related to the benefits they produce. These benefits are spelled out in monetary terms to determine their economic viability and efficiency of a program" (Caffarella, 2002, p. 307). Caffarella (2002) goes on to note that while costs can be calculated fairly easily, it is difficult to attach a monetary figure for the benefits an educational program can produce.

Chapter Summary

As a result of drafting (a) budget, the leadership will be expected to make educated assertions regarding the costs of its programming and services,

Cost Benefit Analysis

A ratio of costs associated with a program to the benefits that program provides.

From a budgeting perspective, the goal is to spend the least amount of money on things that will provide the most benefit to the organization

Figure 4.7 Cost benefit.

especially recognizing the real limits that exist on staff and volunteer availability, special skills, and other necessary resources. The budget plays a key role, forcing the organization to prioritize its activities so as to determine those that are most critical for fulfilling its mission (Hartnett, 2009, p. 4).

This chapter was designed to provide you with a basic overview of budgets and the budgeting process. As with most topics in this book, entire courses and programs of study can be devoted to the topics discussed in this chapter. The organization's "purse" is an important thing to monitor. A financially sound organization is in a much better position to fulfill its mission and serve its learners.

DISCUSSION QUESTIONS

1. Address the three scenarios described at the start of this chapter. What would you advise the people in each of the scenarios to do? Where would you advise them to start?
2. Consider an adult education organization you're familiar with. What are that organization's sources of income? What are its main expenses? When considering expenses, which are fixed and which are variable? Which are direct and which are indirect?
3. Consider an adult education organization you're familiar with (or one for which you work). Who is responsible for the organization's budget? Are there people who are not involved in the budget but should be involved?
4. How does the budgeting process work within your organization? What are the steps the organization follows when budgeting?
5. Consider some factors that might affect the budget at your organization. Which are the external factors? Which are the internal? Which have had the most significant effects on your organization's budget?
6. A for-profit organization offers one-, two-, and three-day-long computer courses and seminars. The courses are offered in classrooms at the organization's office, and they are taught by employees of the organization. Attendees receive course materials as well as lunch and food at break times for each day of the seminar. What are some of the fixed and variable costs associated with this organization? What are some direct costs and some indirect costs?
7. How often is the budget in your organization (or one with which you are familiar) reviewed and updated?

References

Accounting Tools. (n.d.). *Variable cost.* Retrieved from http://www.accounting-tools.com/dictionary-variable-cost

Beesley, C. (2013, January 7). Calendar or fiscal? Which tax year is right for your small business? *SBA.* Retrieved from https://www.sba.gov/blogs/calendar-or-fiscal-which-tax-year-right-your-small-business

Business Dictionary. (n.d.a). *Budget.* Retrieved from http://www.businessdictionary.com/definition/budget.html

Business Dictionary. (n.d.b). *Direct cost.* Retrieved from http://www.businessdictionary.com/definition/direct-cost.html#ixzz3e6lCa7d1

Business Dictionary. (n.d.c). *Estimated revenue.* Retrieved from http://www.businessdictionary.com/definition/estimated-revenue.html

Caffarella, R. S. (2002). *Planning programs for adult learners.* San Francisco, CA: Jossey-Bass.

Costello, T. (2011, September/October). Better budget planning. *IT Professional, 13*(5), 62–64.

Fiscal Management Associates (FMA). (2012). A five-step guide to budget development. *The Wallace Foundation.* Retrieved from http://www.wallacefoundation.org/knowledge-center/Resources-for-Financial-Management/Pages/A-Five-Step-Guide-to-Budget-Development.aspx

Government Finance Officers Association (GFOA). (1998). Recommended budget practices: A framework for improved state and local government budgeting. Chicago, IL: *Government Finance Officers Association.* Retrieved from http://www.gfoa.org/sites/default/files/RecommendedBudgetPractices.pdf

Hartnett, B. (2009, Summer). *The important role of budgeting in non-profit organizations.* Retrieved from http://www.sobel-cpa.com/articles_of_interest/whitepaper.budget.nonprofit%20(MR).doc

Investopedia. (n.d.a). *Fixed cost.* Retrieved from http://www.investopedia.com/terms/f/fixedcost.asp#ixzz3e6kitEux

Investopedia. (n.d.b). *Return on investment.* Retrieved from http://www.investopedia.com/terms/r/returnoninvestment.asp

Kung, F., Huang, C., & Cheng, C. (2013). An examination of the relationships among budget emphasis, budget planning models and performance. *Management Decision, 51*(1) 120–140.

Lalli, W. R. (2012). *Handbook of budgeting* (6th ed.). Hoboken, NJ: Wiley.

Maddox, D. (1999). Strategic budget cutting. *The Grantsmanship Center.* Retrieved from https://www.tgci.com/sites/default/files/pdf/Strategic%20Budget%20Cutting_0.pdf

Rotundi, A. M. (1997). Create a budget that works for you. *Nonprofit World, 15*(4), 46–41.

Sage ERP. (2012). *The budgeting process: Forecasting with efficiency and accuracy.* Retrieved from http://www.acutedata.com/pdf/sage-budgeting/The_Budgeting_Process.pdf

Shim, J. K., Siegel, J. G., & Shim, A. I. (2011). *Budgeting basics and beyond*. Hoboken, NJ: Wiley.

Virginia Society of Certified Public Accountants (VSCPA). (n.d.). Budgeting: A guide for small nonprofit organizations. Retrieved from http://www.vscpa.com/Content/Files/vscpa/Documents/2012/Budgeting2012.pdf

5

Funding and Support

Money Makes the World Go 'Round

So says the Emcee in a song from the Broadway musical *Cabaret,* and it is true that in order to do our work as adult educators, we do need sources of funding and support (although that support may not always be in monetary form). While some adult educators volunteer their time and services, and many providers of adult education operate on shoestring budgets, most organizations involved in adult education do need some types of resources in order to fulfill their missions. The types of funding and support needed depend on the type of organization and the organization's mission.

Think about adult education organizations with which you are familiar. In those organizations, does money make the world go 'round, in the sense that it allows the organizations to fulfill their missions? Or does the organization rely on a mix of monetary and nonmonetary funding and support? Either way, ensuring organization funding and support is an important job associated with the administration of adult education programs. Consider the following scenarios.

Organization and Administration of Adult Education Programs, pages 83–111
Copyright © 2016 by Information Age Publishing
All rights of reproduction in any form reserved.

Juan serves as an Associate Peace Corps Director (APCD), responsible for supporting and supervising Peace Corps volunteers serving in health education outreach. Malaria-prevention initiatives have really taken off, and he can see the potential for further development of education outreach initiatives. The current funding from the U.S. government and Ghanaian government is insufficient.

Alex is a human resource development administrator in a large manufacturing corporation in an urban location in the midwestern United States that produces small engines. He has hired an influx of production workers who speak Hmong and Spanish. Through a needs assessment of supervisors and Hmong- and Spanish-speaking workers, he has identified a need for cross-cultural training for supervisors and the production workers as well as English as a second language training for the production workers. In the economic downturn, money is tight for these types of initiatives, often viewed by upper administration as expendable soft training.

Maria serves as an administrator of a center serving nontraditional returning adult students at an urban community college. She is noticing an influx of military and veteran students and sees a need for her staff and the college as a whole to be better able to address the needs of this student population.

As you read through this chapter, consider how addressing issues of funding and support in creative ways could address the issues faced by those in the scenarios above. Creativity is important in addressing an organization's funding and support methods, so consider both traditional and innovative solutions.

Why Are Funding and Support Programs Important in Adult Education?

Securing funding and support for programs is an essential role for administrators of adult education programs. Often organizations are energized by good ideas, and teams and individuals put a great deal of effort into program development; however, good ideas are not always funded or supported. Even good ideas that are implemented can find themselves victims of failure if they are not sustainable financially. Administrator knowledge, skill, and vision inform the processes associated with program funding and support.

Funding, or cash income, can come in a variety of forms, and support for programs may come in forms other than cash. It is important for the administrator to think creatively about the types of funding and support needed, how to create new streams of funding and support, as well as how to leverage existing resources. Whether you are an HRD administrator in a large for-profit corporation or an administrator in a small, grassroots adult basic education initiative, securing funding and support for programs is essential if the organization is to survive.

Chapter Overview

As an administrator, strategizing about how to support programs and maintain that support involves systems thinking (Senge, 2006). Each input into funding and support impacts other systems in the organization. Administrators need a vision for identifying, securing, and maintaining that "mix" of funding and support as well as an understanding of how each input impacts structures within the organization. This chapter will be divided into two sections: content on the funding and support mix, which includes information on sources of support, and proposal writing, relevant to both for-profit, nonprofit, and higher-education adult education administrators. The chapter concludes with questions for discussion and reflection that build from concepts discussed in the chapter.

The Funding and Support "Mix"

Adult education administrators share fiscal responsibility for their organizations. This may be one of the more stressful roles administrators play, but the more they educate themselves on their fields or industries, trends, budgets, and financial management, the more tools they will have to inform this aspect of their jobs. Both funding and support are necessary for a fiscally sound organization. Funding refers to sources of income. Caffarella and Daffron (2013) discuss eight income sources for adult education programs:

- parent organizational subsidy,
- donations and other sponsorship funds,
- participant fees and tuition,
- auxiliary enterprises and sales,
- grants and contracts,
- government funds, and
- profits from the education or training unit. (p. 296)

Support also can be financial income, but, in this chapter, it refers to nonmonetary types of backing, such as bartering, in-kind donations, and lobbying. Typically, administrators need a mix of funding and support to see that

---

Funding and Support Categories

- Line item in an organization budget
- Bartering and reciprocity
- Financial donations and sponsorships
- In-kind donations
- User fees
- Products and services
- Lobbying
- Grants

Figure 5.1 Funding and support.

the organization, unit, or division is able to operate. As you read through the elements of a funding and support mix, reflect on the details that might be important in order to create a similar mix in your organization. Funding and support areas will be addressed in the categories shown in FIgure 5.1.

Note that there may be some overlap in categories; however, rather than thinking in strict categories, think about how specific organizations may use these categories to inform the creation of their own unique mixes of funding and support.

Funding and Support Categories

Line Item in an Organization Budget

HRD practitioners working in business or industry typically rely on budgets that are provided to their departments or units. If your unit or initiative is given a line item in a budget, it means that your unit is funded through a planned amount of money and in the parent organization's annual budget. For example, in large companies, the HRD budget may be a piece of the overall organization's human resource division budget. If a line item is given to your unit or initiative, it usually means the larger organization views the allotment as a long-term commitment, although the sum given may change, for example, based on government funding or overall corporate fiscal health. Within a line item in a larger budget, there may be several subcategories. HRD-related personnel salaries, supplies, equipment, programs, space, and other items may be given specific line items in an overall HRD budget. Being given a line item in a budget is something that some units or initiatives strive for, because it usually indicates more permanence and organizational support.

As noted above, even though a department (such as an HRD department) is budgeted funds by its parent organization, that doesn't mean the amount of funds budgeted will stay the same throughout the fiscal time period. If an organization is having difficult financial times, it may revise budgets throughout the year and ask individual departments to "return" funds or budget less than previously planned. In these cases, departments must review the states of their current budgets, revise priorities, and make adjustments. In some cases, if the organization is doing well, an individual department may request, and receive, additional funds.

Bartering and Reciprocity

Bartering and reciprocity are both means of obtaining support for your organization. Bartering involves an organizational exchange of products, services, or resources that serve as an equal trade in a similar way that you would use money. Bartering and reciprocity are different from donations in that they involve an exchange of goods or services. Donations involve the giving of goods, services, or funds, with no expectations of getting something in return from the organization. For example, a community-based organization interested in moving to a larger facility might barter for discounted rent in exchange for fixing up the facility by painting, rewiring, and remodeling the facility. Think about services that organizations may provide. There may be trades they can arrange with other organizations that can benefit both groups. In bartering, the exchange usually is relatively equal so that the outcome for each organization monetarily is about the same.

Those involved in reciprocity view program support as a mutually beneficial relationship: They help another organization and that organization, in turn, helps them. Think about the internal and external partnerships your organization has developed or would like to develop and how partnerships with other organizations might be mutually beneficial. Many actions of support or reciprocity may not originally have a price tag attached, but they can contribute to the bottom line for your organization. Buying lists of magazine subscriptions or an organization's membership list costs thousands of dollars. However, having access to a partnering organization's membership or contacts list (or having the partnering organization send your messages out to those on their lists) and being able to get the word out about your adult education programs and outreach initiatives can be very valuable. In return, you may offer to list the organization as a co-sponsor of the event you are promoting, have their literature available at your program, and offer to send out a message on your listserv when the partnering organization needs to promote something. Other points of reciprocity might include the use of space, such as classrooms or meeting rooms, cross-marketing in course catalogs (when each organization has something unique to offer and will not compete for the same students), and a reduction in fees for members or supporters of each organization.

Bartering and reciprocity should not only be measured in financial terms. There are many types of intangible benefits and synergies that bartering and reciprocal arrangements provide, including the establishment of goodwill and collegiality. Bartering and reciprocity also can benefit learners and other stakeholders at each organization involved in these types of arrangements. They may not work for every aspect of programming, but they may help the bottom line in some areas. It is wise to think about the reasoning behind your decision for bartering and reciprocity in advance. Being able to justify bartering and reciprocity, and being able to explain both costs and value of these types of arrangements is helpful for everyone in the organization, including those who report to you and those to whom you report.

Financial Donations and Sponsorships

Financial donations and sponsorships are monetary contributions made by individuals or groups of individuals to your organization and its educational programs. Many individuals reading this book are probably donors to, or sponsors of, some kind of adult education program or initiative. Anyone who has graduated from any institution of higher education is regularly called upon to make financial donations to that school. Donors and sponsors range from individuals who give a few dollars to foundations that give thousands of dollars.

There is a difference between donations and sponsorships, although there can be overlap in the two terms. Financial donations are funds given to support an organization's mission and there is no expectation that the organization will pay back or compensate the donor in any way. Donating is a one-way exchange: The donor simply gives money (or other financial consideration) to the organization. That money can be given for a specific initiative or project or it can be designated for the organization's general operating fund.

Sponsorships are more formal agreements that involve the supporting of specific initiatives or projects. They are also two-way exchanges. In exchange for sponsoring a specific event, that sponsor receives compensation of some sort, and both the financial support from the sponsor and the ways in which the sponsor is formally compensated are drawn up in a sponsorship agreement. For example, a sponsorship that is secured from an individual or company may underwrite a specific educational program or outreach effort, such as a series of educational sessions on acting and play therapy for returned combat veterans. That sponsor may be recognized in promotional and marketing materials for the event and in course-related materials used in the event. Donors may also sometimes be recognized in some way, but sponsors are recognized in formal ways that are specified in a sponsorship agreement.

In-Kind Donations

In-kind donations are donations of services or products. They may be internal (from other areas of your organization) or external (from organizations outside of your own), and they typically involve items and services your organization needs to support an adult education program or initiative that the organization would normally have to purchase. Examples of in-kind donations may be printing for brochures, refreshments for an open house, accounting services from a board member, or airplane tickets for guest speakers. In-kind donations often involve formal procedures for recordkeeping, as donors may want receipts that indicate the value of their donations. Organizations receiving in-kind donations should also keep track of the value of in-kind donations received as part of the bookkeeping processes. Like sponsorships, the organization receiving in-kind donations usually provides some recognition so that the company or firm providing the in-kind donation is publically acknowledged for their contributions. Different from sponsorships, though, in-kind donations are usually in the form of products or services (as opposed to money). Examples of recognition for in-kind donations may include branding on the organization's website, logos or listings on promotional materials and program brochures, and verbally, at events like fundraising dinners or public programs.

User Fees

User fees, including learner tuition fees, are often a significant source of income for adult education organizations. Tuition and fees are charged to students who enroll in adult education courses. Sometimes tuition and fees are paid for directly by the student, and other times a sponsor or donor will pay tuition and other fees for students. In some cases, the tuition and fees charged for educational programs go directly to the organization and that organization uses the money to pay program-related expenses. In formal education, government, and in larger for-profit and nonprofit organizations, however, that is not always the case. In these examples, sometimes the parent organization takes a portion of the tuition and fees brought in and sends a percentage of what was earned to the unit or department that ran the program. It is important for program administrators to understand how the funds raised by providing educational programs are allocated (and to whom they are allocated). Consider public higher education as an example of how tuition and fees are distributed. There may be multiple fee structures for different situations. Distance education tuition and fees may be calculated differently from fees for face-to-face programs. In-state, out-of-state, and foreign-participant tuition and fees may all be calculated differently. Often a portion of a student's tuition and fees are taken out for registration, student organization support, or other overhead. State government entities also have a say in how much money generated from student tuition and fees is kept by the institution. This is an example of how money generated from tuition and fees does not always go directly to the organization that provides the educational service. Program administrators should consider these types of issues when calculating revenue from tuition and fees.

There are other ways tuition and fee can be managed. For example, in some businesses, when an employee takes an in-house training course, that employee's department is charged a participation fee by the department running the training session (often the HRD department). This is how some corporate training departments fund themselves.

Selling Products and Services

Adult education organizations may sell products and services their organizations have created, such as textbooks, learning materials, or other resources, or they may sell a service such as consulting. The profits from these products and services can be part of the organization's funding mix. Administrators must calculate the costs associated with these types of initiatives to make sure that they are actually profitable to your organization.

Lobbying

Lobbying is the act of trying to influence lawmakers and policymakers' opinions on local, state, federal, and international levels. Lobbying is defined as "public policy advocacy activities" (Maskell, 2005, p. 2). Lobbyists are individuals who advocate for these interests. Lobbying sometimes has negative connotations because of its association, at times, with illegal or unethical practices. However, organizations involved in adult education on topics such as domestic violence, adult literacy, retraining for employees, and malaria prevention in Africa (and other topics that are current, controversial, or the focus of rules, regulations, and policy), may consider getting involved in lobbying to influence policy.

Why is lobbying included in a chapter on funding and support? The purpose of lobbying for advocacy on issues such as those mentioned above is to increase awareness on those topics. One of the ways that can be done is through adult education—so part of lobbying for an issue may involve requesting funds or suggesting opportunities for education that the administrator's organization could provide, and that might be funded by the entities being lobbied.

The degree to which an organization can lobby depends on the type of organization it is. Before doing any lobbying, investigate the ways your organization may be involved with lobbying. In government and other public organizations, lobbying may be strictly forbidden, but administrators working in nonprofit organizations may be able to lobby.

Lobbying can be done on informal levels in many different types of organizations as well. In a broader sense, lobbying means drumming up support for your educational programs. Those who work in HRD in for-profit organizations, for example, may find their budgets increased if they have influential employees in the organization who believe in their efforts enough to do so.

Grants

Grants are monies that an organization applies for with a specific idea and organized plan to address a certain need. Unlike a donation, organizations applying for grants must specify what the money will support, and they must provide specific information about the project and its costs. If the organization offering the grant is in favor of your proposal for constructive use of their money, they will award you the grant.

External grants can come from government or private sources, such as foundations. Internal grants come right from within the organization. In higher education, for example, an internal grant might provide start-up or seed money for the development of workshops, educational outreach, and research. Understanding how to write a grant proposal is a critical skill for an administrator to master, especially if their organization depends on grants and "soft" money to make up a significant part of its operating budget. Even if you, as an administrator, are not the person writing the grant, it is essential to have an understanding of what grants are and how they might be used. Later in this chapter, we will look at the typical components of a grant proposal or application.

When we talk about funding sources such as grants, the terms *soft money* and *hard money* are often used. Grants are an example of soft money sources, because grant money comes from outside the immediate organization, it needs to be pursued (often competitively), and it is awarded to an organization on a limited (perhaps one-time) basis to be used during a specific time period (Barinaga, 2000). In contrast, hard money refers to more permanent and ongoing sources of income for the organization, such as tuition (Stein & Candler, 2007).

Positions and initiatives in organizations that are funded by soft money are those that are paid from the source of that soft money (often a grant) (Barinaga, 2000). When the grant time period ends (and/or when the grant money is spent), the position or initiative also ends (unless the grant is renewed or another grant is found in the meantime). However, if a position or an initiative is funded by hard money, it is paid for by a standard line item in the organizational budget, independent of whether or not the organization receives any grants. As such, hard money positions and initiatives tend to be more permanent, or longer-term, in the organization, such as an administrative assistant's salary or money to pay for electricity (Stein & Candler, 2007).

Summary of Funding and Support Categories

Some of the above funding and support categories discussed here may be more relevant to some administrators than others. For example, an administrator within an HRD unit may receive a line item in an organization budget as its unit's sole source of funding (so the other types of funding described above may not be applicable in this situation). Administrators in nonprofit organizations may find that all of these categories are relevant. Most adult education organizations rely on a mix of funding and support to ensure that the organization, unit, or division is financially stable. Identifying potential sources of financing is only one piece of the equation. Figuring out the proper mix for a particular organization is the next essential step.

How to Determine the Proper Mix

How does an administrator determine the proper mix of funding? There is not a one-size-fits-all approach or a magic formula for determining the right mix of funding for an organization; however, there are guideposts that can serve as checkpoints to help inform the decision-making process. Start by creating contextual strategies, or strategies that fit the organization or unit, that address financing and funding. Then learn about the processes associated with obtaining each source of revenue the organization relies on. Don't forget that new potential sources of revenue become available every day, and sometimes existing sources of revenue dry up or disappear. That is why an organization's financing and funding strategies must be dynamic and flexible.

The strategies an administrator chooses should be related to the age and history of the organization. These variables are important because they can determine the options available for the organization. For example, if the organization has not been in existence long enough to have an established, proven track record, it might be difficult to gain financial donations or grants; however, it might be helpful to think about bartering and reciprocity, in-kind donations, and small sponsorships for specific initiatives. However, if an organization has a history and a track record of successful well-established partnerships, it may be appropriate for the administrator to write a proposal for a large grant.

Timing of the year is also important. An educational organization's strategy may be determined by when its learners are ready to learn. Summer is the time when more people travel, so an organization may need more financial resources in the fall, when potential learners are more focused on educational opportunities. Strategy may also be determined by considering times potential donors are willing to give. Some organizations raise money around holiday seasons or major events, as those are times when donors are willing to give to the organization. Also, for memberships or donations, solicitation may occur before the end of the calendar year when individuals are considering making charitable donations for tax purposes. Alternatively, strategy may focus on specific donors, and activity might occur during a time period when a potential donor starts the beginning of its fiscal year (with a new year's budget). Strategy may also involve activity during a designated heritage or awareness month.

Funding strategy may also depend on internal factors. At some point in time, an administrator may have access to more revenue from product sales because the organization may be offering a new educational DVD or book for sale. Product sales may peak and then wane.

Current events may affect an organization's strategy as well. When an important story comes out about community gardens and education, this might be the time to meet with potential benefactors to discuss support for the organization's educational programs that deal with these topics. When a news story is aired about workplace bullying, and an administrator has been trying to get a workplace bullying educational program off the ground for months, it might be the time to move the initiative forward.

Planning a strategy for funding and support connects to organizational strategic planning, marketing, and budgeting. In thinking about new areas of support for your organization, keep in mind that each area of support needs support! Every potential source of funding and support is accompanied by the need for internal resources dedicated to manage it. For example, if an administrator decides to create a membership structure, databases need to be created, membership support services need to have backing and staffing, and efforts must be placed on soliciting memberships and encouraging existing members to renew their memberships. Administrators may find that great sources of support cannot be managed within the organization, and in those cases, it's important to really think about the value of pursuing that source. A project may look exciting, but resources needed to support and manage the opportunity may be greater than the value received by the organization. Be sure to consider cost versus value when planning strategy related to funding and support. Future funding and support opportunities can dry up quickly for an organization that gets a reputation for squandering or mismanaging its funds, not keeping its promises, and not following through on its commitments.

Although there is no one general rule for the number and variety of sources of funding and support an organization should rely on, one thing is certain: Not all sources can be relied on forever. Most organizations should focus on a variety of diverse sources so the effects of one source drying up are minimal to the organization. If the organization is a department in a larger organization (such as the HRD department in a larger corporation), this may not be an issue. However, organizations that do not have "parent" organizations they can rely on for support must seek funding from a variety of different sources in order to maintain themselves in the long term.

Figure 5.2 is a summary of factors to consider when developing an organization's funding and support mix.

Funding and Support Mix Variables

- The phase of an organization's growth
- Season or annual programming
- Calendar of fiscal year timing
- Introduction of new products/services
- Current events
- Organizational infrastructure

Figure 5.2 Variables that affect funding and support.

One common variable is important regarding funding and support, regardless of your type of organization and your options for funding and support. In order to receive internal and external support, you must be able to effectively and concisely communicate reasons to internal and external stakeholders why your organization should receive that support. This is especially important in times of scarce resources and competing demands. It is also especially important in writing proposals for grants, which is the focus of the next part of this chapter.

Proposal Writing

As noted above, grants can be part of an organization's funding and support mix. Typically, in order to receive a grant, an organization prepares a proposal, which is submitted to the organization offering the grant. The grant-offering organization then evaluates the application and decides whether or not a grant will be awarded. When grants are awarded, they are usually accompanied by periodic requests for records and information regarding how the money is being spent. The organization receiving the grant must understand, up front, what type of information the grant-providing organization needs so they can fulfill their obligations to the grant provider. The organization applying for the grant is also informed if a grant is not awarded. In those cases, the grant writing organization can use the exercise as a learning experience for the next time a grant proposal is developed.

This section will highlight important areas of proposal writing relevant to adult education administrators. It starts with a discussion of grant sources, followed by content on the many types of written proposals that these sources may request. Key questions to consider when developing grant proposals and steps in the proposal process are then presented.

Funding Sources

There are a variety of sources for grants, including foundations, governmental organizations, associations, companies, and individuals (see Figure 5.3). Each of these entities works differently with regard to how grants are handled, and each will be discussed in this section.

Foundations are nongovernmental funding organizations supported by an endowment, or a permanent amount of money (or other assets) that are used to provide grants (Gitlin & Lyons, 2008). Some foundations have specific missions and provide grants for specific things, such as cancer research, clean water access, or the arts. Others may focus on certain areas

---

Potential Funding Sources

- Foundations
- Government Organizations
- Associations
- Companies
- Individuals

Figure 5.3 Funding sources.

such as communities, regions, and states, and consider grants of all kinds that involve initiatives in those areas. There are so many sources for grants that an important factor is ensuring there is a match between what your organization does and what the grant-funding organization is looking for. *The Philanthropy Journal*, Guidestar, The Center for Civic Partnerships, and the Community Foundation Locator are places to look for potential foundation matches. The Foundation Center also provides lists of funders. Additionally, look for state or city organizations that connect those who are seeking funds and those who are looking to support funding proposals. These can be found by doing a keyword Internet search for "giving foundations" by state to find potential funding sources.

Local, state, and federal governments (and even international governing bodies) are another potential grant source. Grants.gov in the United States is a search engine that can be used to find government grants. "Grants and sponsored projects" are keywords used to identify potential sources by state. In addition, look at specific commissions or departments such as a commission on higher education or the Department of Labor, which may have particular funds available that relate to your organizational mission.

Associations can serve as important sources of funding as well. Consider the associations those in your organization belong to. Those associations may offer grants, and, by virtue of membership, chances are that there is a good match between your association's mission and grant guidelines set forth by the association. Remember to consider local and state associations, world trade associations, and chambers of commerce too.

For-profit companies of all sizes often have funds designated for philanthropy. Some of these funds may be managed by a separate organization and others may be managed in-house. There is typically a person or a department in each company who reviews requests for funding. The company's website may even describe the process of applying for funds, along with the types of initiatives the company prefers to support. As noted above, if the company has grant information on its website, be sure to review that information so you understand the parameters of the organization's funding, including requirements for applying for and using funds. Sometimes there is a matching fund requirement, meaning that an organization awards a grant based on the premise that additional funds from other organizations will be secured for the same project. For example, a neighborhood literacy organization may be awarded a $2,000 grant from a business in the neighborhood with a matching fund requirement. That means that the literacy organization would have to raise $2,000 from other sources (for the same initiative) in order to receive the grant from the business. Also be sure that there is a match between the requirements of the funding organization (with regard to how the grant funds are spent) and what the organization hopes to do with funds being requested. As with all of potential funding, the process involves more than just "the ask."

Individuals also may support specific initiatives in the form of grants. For example, an administrator in an organization who focuses on refugee support and education may learn of a member in the organization who may have the interest and the resources to fund a community education program on refugee needs. Perhaps an individual may wish to underwrite (provide funds and support for) (Strover, 2003) programs on computer literacy courses or suicide prevention. There are often very personal reasons individuals have for underwriting a specific program, so it is important to understand those personal motivations and their life stories. In working with individual funders, frequently there is not the bureaucracy and paperwork associated with working with foundations, government entities, and companies. However, understand that individual's needs, motivations, and issues, some of which may be personal and/or sensitive, are important.

A program administrator may have resources within their organizations to help them locate grants or potential funders. Sometimes, grant-funding organizations solicit requests for grant proposals (also known as RFPs). There are many online databases that consolidate RFPs. These databases make searching for appropriate funders relatively easy. Don't wait for an RFP, however, to search for potential grants. Develop contacts at foundations and associations, and with potential individual funders as well. Pitch ideas to these contacts and obtain feedback. Ask about past grants that were funded to get an idea of what a successful application to that organization looks like. Even if contacts made are not directly helpful, those contacts may know others who could be helpful.

When potential supporters, such as individual donors or family foundations, are found, it is important to make sure that initial contacts are positive. Realize the importance of relationship building in the grant process. Building relationships takes time and requires nurturing. Once a potential donor or supporter can see the good work an organization is doing, that organization is more likely to receive support. The administrator should do all they can to communicate the value of the work their organization is doing and the results that are achieved. Invite a potential supporter to be a special guest at programs and events. Add potential donors to newsletter mailing lists.

Program administrators in for-profit organizations should seek out those in the organization who are willing to support their initiatives. Those people may be within the administrator's department, or they may be outside of it. Remember that in any organization, there are formal and informal networks of power that can influence decisions made about the organization's training function. Regardless of the type of organization, administrators must dedicate time to building supportive relationships with a variety of stakeholders.

Over time, a program administrator will build a network of potential funders and supporters. After having done research and making potential contacts, a grant opportunity may present itself. The next section of this chapter deals with the various types of proposals that potential funders request.

Types of Funding Proposals

Proposals for funding can take many forms depending on the organization or unit seeking a grant and the organization offering the grant. Some proposals may be as simple as creating and sending an email message or a request letter. Others may be as complex as a 25-page written narrative with several different appendices (Yang, 2005). The audience for whom the proposal is intended may be varied as well (Rosenberg, 2010). The educational program administrator (who also may function as grant writer) may be seeking outside donations from a foundation, or they may be pitching an internal proposal to someone in the organization to secure additional funding or a "line item" in a budget for the upcoming year. Examples of types of written proposals for funding and support are noted in Figure 5.4.

Types of Written Proposals for Funding and Support

- A letter to a potential donor
- An email to a supervisor
- A PowerPoint presentation to a board of directors
- A government grant proposal
- An internal grant proposal for project start-up money
- A grant application to a private foundation

Figure 5.4 Types of proposals.

Although all of these proposal types are different, they have one thing in common: Each is a request for funding or support, and each requires the communication of a clear message as to why that funding or support is needed. How the grant writers communicate that message depends on the type of proposal and type of funder or supporter. Also important, as previously noted, is an understanding of the motivations, needs, requirements, and interests of the entity offering funding, so the grant writer can match their proposal to those needs (Karsh & Fox, 2014). Doing significant research helps to make sure time is not wasted on the development of proposals that are of no interest to the funder.

When completing requests for funds, be thorough and provide all of the information requested. A grant proposal is a reflection on both the writer and on the organization. Incomplete and vague proposals will rarely be considered; neither will proposals containing grammatical and/or mathematical errors. When a proposal is subpar, those evaluating the proposal may question the organization's ability to effectively manage grant funds requested.

Questions to Ask Yourself and Steps in the Proposal Writing Process

As explained above, most funders and supporters require requests for proposals (RFPs) as part of the process of applying for a grant from that organization. Information required in RFPs varies depending on the funder or supporter and the situation.

While there is little standardization among RFPs, there are themes and key questions that can inform the proposal-writing process. Consider the questions in Figure 5.5. Take notes on each question and think about how

---

Key Questions to Inform the Proposal Writing Process

- Where do I see the organization in five years? In 10 years? To what does the organization aspire?
- What information and resources do I have to support my proposal or the grant writing process?
- What are my organization's parameters, or the parameters within which I need to work?
- What is my idea and why is it important?
- Who might be my partners?
- How do I communicate my message concisely?
- How do I get in the loop?
- Who are my adult learners?

Figure 5.5 Key questions.

those notes can be used in the proposal. For new proposal writers, these questions may be beginning points for investigation, and for more experienced proposal writers, the questions may prompt reflection. Each is discussed in more detail below.

Where Do I See the Organization in 5 Years? In 10 Years? To What Does the Organization Aspire?

Asking these questions is critical. There are many opportunities for funding and sponsorship, but they have to fit with what your organization does and with what it aspires to accomplish. Understanding the answers to these questions is critical to finding good fits. Consider your organizational mission and vision, and consider what is necessary for the organization to grow and prosper. In which ways (and in what areas) do you see your organization making a difference and filling a need? If you do not answer these initial questions, you can get sidetracked soliciting money only tangentially related to your organization's mission. This can pull the organization off track, no matter how tempting the funding opportunity may be. The key is in understanding the organizational vision.

What Information and Resources Do I Have to Support My Proposal or Grant Writing Process?

By now you probably understand the importance of doing proposal-related homework (or prework). Doing this homework also means learning about the contexts in which you are writing the proposal. Research in your field can be used to justify your request and support your case. Trends and conditions in your area, whether that area is a neighborhood, community, state, or region, also are important to consider. Understanding your organization (as noted in Figure 5.5) is critical, but so is understanding your discipline, your environment, and your stakeholders. Keep in mind that all of the aforementioned are continuously changing, so staying up-to-date on these types of things is important in this process.

Another initial question to consider deals with the type of organizational support you have for submitting grant proposals efficiently and timely (Walden & Bryan, 2010). Walden and Bryan (2010) cite the perception of a lack of system of support for submitting grants as a barrier to pursuing them. Before becoming overwhelmed with an RFP, investigate the resources your organization has (and whether those resources can support your focus on grant writing). Consider others in your organization who have grant writing experience—employees, volunteers, or other stakeholders. For example, nonprofit organizations may have an association or board members willing to provide grant writing expertise. You may be able to organize a working group and delegate tasks to pull the project together by tapping into those resources. Determine internal and external resources available to help you in the proposal writing process; but do this before you start writing RFPs in order to make the process flow smoothly.

What Are My Organization's Parameters or the Parameters Within Which I Need to Work?

What are the rules governing who in your organization can request funding? Can any department within an organization request funding or is there a coordinated effort through one department? What policies, rules, and guidelines do you have to follow when investigating potential funding sources and requesting funds. Who (within the organization) needs to know when you complete and submit an RFP? Various people within your organization may need to read through your proposal and sign off on it before it is submitted, so that should be considered in the RFP development time frame. Sometimes parent organizations will take a percentage of funds awarded through grants as overhead, and this must be considered as well. It is important to investigate all of these policy- and procedure-related questions during this process. Addressing these issues will help you to avoid making mistakes and stepping on toes as you move forward.

If your organization regularly receives money from donors and sponsors, you probably have structures, policies, and procedures in place. If you are an administrator of a unit within a larger organization, be sure to understand what system is in place to handle "the asks." An organization never wants one unit to ask a large corporation for $1,000 to underwrite a public program when the organization is asking that same corporation for millions to underwrite cancer research. It undermines the entire organization if the fundraising effort looks disorganized, and that negatively impacts credibility. Understand your unit's place within the system prior to seeking financial support and embarking on fundraising efforts. Identify with whom you need to connect to positively contribute.

Some organizations have rules that govern the types of funders and supporters they will and will not accept money from. Funders and supporters sometimes expect their organizations to be promoted, or at least mentioned, in exchange for their support. Be sure that the funder or supporting organization you're investigating is not one that is outside of the mission and scope of your organization or one that may be in conflict with the work your organization does. Also, be sure that the funder or supporter is not a competitor of a different funder or supporter of your organization, as sometimes exclusive funding and support arrangements are made with specific organizations. Understand your organization's policy for how grant money can be used (within the organization) and what type of reporting is required. Be clear on things like the amount of influence a supporter can have on how you use the funds you receive from that supporter. For example sometimes a funder may feel entitled to exert control over educational program content, and this may be a concern for your organization. How much influence a funder should have over content is a financial and ethical dilemma. Having clear policies about these issues (and knowing about them up front, before writing any RFPs) helps all involved in the process.

Funders or donors may be members of your organization. If your organization offers memberships, be clear on what benefits are provided in exchange for membership. These types of things add another dimension to the infrastructure needed in the organization, and they require a system of policies and procedures.

What Is My Idea And Why Is It Important?

These are the "so what" questions: Why are you looking for funds, and why is that reason important? As administrators, we often are so entrenched in the problems and needs within our organizations that it is difficult to articulate them! Consider these questions, and then communicate your responses to both people who are familiar with your field and people who are not familiar with it. Convince them that your program is important and your idea for funding matters, and ask them for feedback on how you can improve your responses to these questions. Through this type of communication, you may realize things you hadn't previously considered, such as the kind of data that may be important to a funder, statistics that might help sway funders, and stories that may be impactful on your RFP. Asking these questions will help you make a compelling case in the RFPs you write.

In considering these questions, investigate whether your idea has already been funded (and if so, by whom)? If it has already been funded, how can you find niches that differentiate your requests and build on what has been done in the past? For example, perhaps your agency does work in an urban area, but outreach education in a specific kind of health prevention has only been attempted in a rural area. This type of differentiation would be important to potential funders.

Who Might Be My Partners?

Often, funders like to see collaborations and partnerships with community groups, institutions of higher education, and businesses. In for-profit organizations, it may be important to stakeholders (supervisors, managers, or executives) to see collaboration between units or subsidiaries. Sometimes, partnerships and collaborations are requirements within an RFP. Funders can usually tell if these partnerships are thrown together at the last minute for the purposes of providing information in an RFP. Therefore, be proactive in identifying partnerships and in fostering collaborations. In written grant proposals, letters of support are often required from each partnering organization (with roles and contributions clarified), so find partners with whom you can work and build relationships and trust. You may find, in this process, that you have some common goals and can partner on many grant proposals. Work together to identify potential funding sources and to cultivate relationships with potential funders and supporters.

How Do I Communicate My Message Concisely?

The biggest piece of advice regarding communicating your message is to stay positive and concise. Even when requesting funds to aid in the most dire of human rights circumstances, you can communicate the need for your project and optimism about how your organization can best address that need. If the situation seems completely hopeless/apparent problems appear insurmountable, donors or supporters may not think anyone will be able to positively impact the situation.

Just as administrators should be able to communicate the mission of the organization in an "elevator speech," you should be able to do the same. What is absolutely necessary for people to know if you have only three to five minutes on a board meeting agenda to state the importance of your case/situation? What will you tell people in a 20-minute presentation? As administrators of adult education programs, how will you sell your idea? We may not like to think of gaining funding and support in such a way, but this frame of mind is critical. Develop positive messages about your idea that can be used in a variety of situations, including everything from an elevator speech to a board presentation.

How Do I Get in the Loop?

It seems like everyone knows someone, and who you know is critical as a grant writer. The "people who know people" do so only because they took the time to build networks of contacts. Think about the types of entities that are important for you as well as the people important to you. Professional associations, local, state, federal, international, and supranational organizations all have levels in which to network—maintain old relationships, and create new networks and partners.

Who Are My Adult Learners?

Keep your adult learners in the forefront of your mind. If you're involved in grant writing in an adult education organization, your learners are the reason why you are writing an RFP in the first place. While it is important to pay attention to the details, it also is easy to get caught up in politics, policies, and procedures, and to get discouraged by what may be an arduous process. If you can keep your learners in mind, you can reenergize yourself throughout the process. Stay connected with your learners even if (as an administrator/grant writer), your job is very removed from "the front lines." Take care to step into trainings, classes, or workshops periodically, so you are reminded of why you are doing what you are doing. Grant writers who know the needs of their adult learners will be better able to tell their stories when it matters the most. Focus on your learners as your motivation for getting through the grant writing process.

Your answers to the questions above should inform how you develop an RFP. These questions and steps continually need to be revisited. For example, you may be in the process of revising a strategic plan or organizational vision. New partners interested in addressing timely issues may emerge. As an administrator, use your listening skills to make sure you are open to hearing the input of multiple stakeholders throughout this process. The questions and steps together can provide an important road map as you begin writing.

Proposal Writing and Structure

With regard to structure, each proposal is different, and each RFP will require different information. However, there are general categories of information that are typically found on RFPs. Those categories are outlined below.

1. **Proposal Abstract or Summary:** This is a "snapshot" of your proposal. Very briefly, state the problem, what you are planning on doing about it, why your organization is best suited to addressing the problem, and how much money you are seeking.

2. **Introduction of the Organization Seeking Funding:** Why should someone trust you with the money he/she seeks to contribute? This section should establish credibility, and it should provide evidence that your organization has proven success and the ability to properly administer the kind of proposal you are suggesting.

3. **Problem or Needs Statement:** Who cares? This is the "so what?" section. It should provide supporting information for the problem. Be careful not to state the absence of your proposed initiative as the problem (Foundation Center, 2012). In other words, the fact that your drug prevention education program does not exist is not the problem. Decide which statistics best support your problem and decide how to tell the story. This section should provide the reader the ability to get a clear understanding of the problem.

4. **Project Objectives:** What do you want to accomplish? This section should state clear aims of your initiative.

5. **Design:** How are you going to accomplish your objectives? This section should state how you propose to structure the initiative and why. Be sure to justify your design-related decisions.

6. **Evaluation:** How will you know that you are succeeding within your proposed initiative? This section should indicate how you will measure success. Formative and summative evaluations should connect to the project objectives you have outlined.

7. **Future Funding:** What are the chances of this project continuing with other funds after this project is over? This section should articulate how you see this project situated within the organization's future and how you view the potential for future funding so that the project continues in its current form or continues to the next phase.

8. **Project Budget:** This section should outline expenses and how funds requested will be supplemented or matched by your organization, other grants, or donations.

9. **Staffing:** Who will be involved with the project and why do they have the expertise required to carry out the project?

10. **Timeline:** How long will it take you to complete this initiative from start to finish? Remember to include all of the "lead time" it will take to establish the project or the effort it will take to get it off the ground (not only the time of the actual training or workshop), for example.

11. **Appendices:** Are there any documents you think might be helpful to the reader (charts, graphs, or supporting reports) that do not quite fit within the narrative? You can include these documents in the appendices.

While the type of information required will differ from one RFP to another, an important guide for proposal writing and structure can be successful past proposals that were funded by the organization offering the current funding opportunity. There is no need to "reinvent the wheel" by trying to second-guess what will be successful. Look at/consider what has worked in the recent past (the more recent, the better) to get an idea of what the funding organization is most interested in funding in the future.

Both writing style and structure are important as you begin to put together a proposal. As noted above, get help and advice from people familiar, and not familiar, with your topic and proposal. Insiders, or those familiar with your topic, can help you with details and facts. An outside reviewer is one who may not be familiar with the area of the proposal within which you are writing. Outside reviewers are beneficial because people at funding organizations may not be as familiar with your topic as you are. Outside reviewers can ensure that you are communicating at an appropriate level.

Some administrators have a hard time writing grant proposals because the kind of writing they have learned to master to make them successful in their professions does not lend itself to successful grant writing (Porter, 2007). Writing RFPs is not the same as writing or developing educational materials. You may need to adapt the kind of writing you have learned to master in your profession or practice to the grant or proposal writing process. Figure 5.6 illustrates some style-related tips to keep in mind when writing RFPs.

Submitting Requests and Waiting for Responses

Once an RFP is finished, it is ready for submission. Don't lose sight of the necessary details during the submission process. Also, note that there are things that can be done during the waiting or "in-between" times.

Make careful note of how (and to whom) potential funders would like requests submitted (Foundation Center, 2012). Individuals at advanced

---

Tips for Proposal Writing

- Connect your writing to the potential funder's or supporter's goals.
- Write in an action-oriented style.
- Be focused on a specific project or idea.
- Write to persuade the reader.
- Be reasonable and enthusiastic about your idea.
- Focus on the importance of teamwork.
- Write concisely and use accessible language.

Figure 5.6 Proposal-writing tips.

levels in the organization may wish to have documents submitted to an assistant to vet before they read them. Some funders may have an online portal submission process, whereas others may prefer electronic submissions, and others may require hard copies be sent to the attention of a representative via priority mail or a parcel delivery service. Some may wish to have both electronic and hard copies submitted. After having done the work of developing an RFP, demonstrate your attention to detail in the submission process by providing the funder exactly what they request exactly in the manner they request it.

It is a great feeling to have submitted a completed proposal. Having submitted a proposal provides a feeling of relief, but it also involves stressful feelings about what will happen next. After submission, grant writers typically receive a record of receipt from the funder (Foundation Center, 2012). Before asking about timelines for decisions or about when documents will be reviewed, make sure that this information is not already available to you. Locating this type of information is part of doing your homework (Karsh & Fox, 2014). If the information is not listed anywhere, gauge when (and how) to best contact the funder to check in. Consider all variables, and be proactive, but do not be a nuisance. During this waiting time, think about other sources of funding and support. Don't wait for one stream to come through before thinking about another one. Continue to pursue multiple streams during the waiting process.

Although it is logical to think there are two possible outcomes as a result of submitting a proposal, there are actually three possible outcomes: "Yes," "in between," and "No."

If a "Yes" response is received, start planning for the management of the funds. Also, an "in between" response may be received. When this kind of response is received, the funder or supporter may indicate they are interested in supporting certain aspects of your proposal, but not all of it. When this occurs, look at how to modify the project and look at the possibility of using alternative sources of funding to underwrite other aspects of the proposed project. It is important to determine whether or not it is in the best interest of the organization to accept the funding for a piece of the project (or the pieces to be funded) or whether it is better look at other potential sources of support for the entire project.

If you receive a "No" in response, consider the process a learning experience and note lessons learned from the process that can be used for the next RFP. Remember that everyone who writes grants receives "No" responses, so it is not uncommon at all. Take a deep breath before responding and talk to collaborators and partners about the best ways to follow up. Thank the funder for the opportunity to apply and ask if there are suggestions for things that could be done differently within a request the next time around. Inquire about the next funding cycle if that is appropriate. Sometimes reviewers' comments are forwarded to RFP writers, which can help inform future requests. Also remember that a "No" response does not necessarily mean that there was something wrong with the proposal. For example, it may be that the funder's budget is tighter than initially anticipated, so fewer grants than anticipated were awarded. It may also mean that many worthwhile RFPs were submitted.

No matter what the response, express appreciation for the opportunity and for the potential funder's time (Karsh & Fox, 2014). Regardless of the response you receive on one RFP, don't stop looking. It is important to keep focusing on future opportunities.

Managing the Funds

If you are awarded the support for your initiative, rejoice! And then immediately think about the systems that need to be in place to manage and report on the use of these funds. Each organization or unit that is awarded funds should have a system to manage those funds and report progress as required by the funding agency or parent organization. Established organizations typically have built-in processes for reporting and managing funds. If an organization or unit is just starting out, processes will need to be created so that the management and reporting process is complete. Continually revisit what you included in your original proposal and the guidelines for fund use set forth by the funder. Also, remember to provide anyone involved with the grant with a "big-picture understanding" of how the grant money fits into the organizational mission. Those responsible for any type of expenditures should also understand the parameters for how the money may be used.

Plans for reporting on initiatives funded by grants are typically requested in RFPs. Remember that when reporting this information, things don't always go as planned, and make note of abnormalities and unusual situations. Communicate with the funder about issues that may impact how funds are used. For example, perhaps there was a snowstorm the night of an outreach education program and the snowstorm reduced the number of people who were able to participate in the program. While it is unwise to bother a funder with every small "bump in the road," it is important to keep the lines of communication open so the funder understands how your efforts are going. Open communication with a funder, as part of an ongoing effort to build a long-term relationship will be beneficial if you request support from that funder in the future.

Summary

Money may not make the world go 'round, but it does help organizations fulfill their missions. As this chapter has explained in detail, there are many ways organizations can secure funds in order to achieve their missions. Administrators of adult education programs should continually be mindful of their funding and support mixes. As funding or support gets tight in one sector, they may need to think of creative ways of finding support from other sources. Staying current with regard to funding and support-related challenges and trends as well as continuing to be proactive in securing funds will help the organization to move ahead smoothly.

Although the proposal-writing process is not a linear one, there are some commonalities within it, and many of those were described in this chapter. Guidelines presented here can set the foundation for creating and submitting a solid proposal. Specifics on each proposal may vary, but the style-related tips for proposal writing presented in this chapter should be considered throughout the process. Remember as well that the process does not end with the submission of an RFP. Follow-up work will depend on the response received from the funder, but everything learned in the process of developing and submitting one RFP can be used to continuously improve your proposal writing skills.

DISCUSSION QUESTIONS

1. What types of bartering or reciprocity happens both internally and externally within your organization? How are these forms of reciprocity helpful to your funding and support mix? In what ways are they challenging? How might you build additional relationships involving bartering and/or reciprocity to add to your funding and support mix?
2. If your organization takes donations, who is responsible for identifying potential donors and fostering relationships? What are the types and levels of donors in your organization and how does each level contribute to your funding and support mix?
3. What kind of in-kind donations are given or received by your organization? What are ways in-kind support is (or could be) beneficial to your organization?
4. Ask to see the current budget for your unit, division, or center.
   - What is the current funding and support mix in this organization, program area, unit, or division?
   - If you work in a multilevel organization, how does the form of support from smaller programmatic areas fit into the larger organization's support structure?

    – What environmental factors impact funding and support?

    – Where do you see potential for new ideas in areas of funding and support?

5. Review the key questions to inform the proposal writing process section in this chapter. After reading through the questions, which ones resonated most with you? Why did they?

6. What processes exist for managing funds received in your organization or unit? What is your role in managing those funds as an adult education administrator?

7. Address the three scenarios described at the start of this chapter. Identify and discuss strategies that may be useful to the people in the scenarios. Identify possibilities for funding and support.

8. In each of the scenarios below, research, identify, and discuss strategies and next steps. What might be a possible source of funding and support? To whom would you direct your inquiries? What might you include in a proposal?

    – You serve as the administrator of a library at a tribal college in New Mexico. Government sequestration has significantly impacted your ability to provide services and keep employees.

    – You serve as an administrator, program planner, and educator of a small, grassroots organization in a rural county in the southern part of the United States. Your organization focuses on education and prevention of gender-based violence. The organization is composed of you, a part-time secretary, and a small board of directors. You are exhausted and putting in 60-hour weeks. Your organization has had requests from law enforcement and health care to help with training. All the organizations asking for requests are also strapped for money.

    – You serve as an administrator for the travel programs in the division of continuing education for a large university. Most of the travel programs are intended for enrichment and involve domestic and international excursions. Ability to pay is the only criteria for the programs.

    – You are a human resource administrator for an international information technology corporation. You have noticed a significant turnover in employees after they are sent on extended expatriate assignments. After conducting quantitative and qualitative evaluations, you discover that many employees feel they failed in their overseas assignments and feel unsupported upon their return.

References

Barinaga, M. (2000). Soft money's hard realities. *Science, 289*(5487), 2024–2028.

Cafarella, R., & Daffron, S. (2013). *Planning programs for adult learners: A practical guide.* (3rd ed.). San Francisco, CA: Jossey-Bass.

Foundation Center. (2012). *The Foundation Center's guide to proposal writing* (6th ed.). New York, NY: Foundation Center.

Gitlin, L. N., & Lyons, K. M. (2008). *Successful grant writing: Strategies for health and human service   professionals* (3rd ed.). New York, NY: Springer.

Karsh, E., & Fox, A. S. (2014). *The only grant-writing book you'll ever need* (4th ed.). Philadelphia, PA: Basic Books.

Maskell, J. (2005). Lobbying regulations on non-profit organizations. CRS Report for Congress 96-809 *American Law Division*. Retrieved from research. policyarchive.org/18985.pdf

Porter, R. (2007). Why academics have a hard time writing good grant proposals. *Journal of Research Administration, 38*(2), 37–43.

Rosenberg, G. (2010). *The artist's guide to grant writing: How to find funds and write foolproof proposals for the visual, literary, and performing artist* (1st ed.). New York, NY: Watson-Guptill.

Senge, P. (2006). *The fifth discipline: The art and practice of the learning organization* (2nd ed.). New York, NY: Double Day.

Stein, D. G., & Candler, A. G. (2007, May). Hard money/soft money: The two cultures. *The Academic Exchange, 9*(6). Retrieved from http://www.emory. edu/ACAD_EXCHANGE/2007/may/steinessay.html

Strover, S. (2003). Remapping the digital divide. *The Information Society, 19*(4), 275–277.

Walden, P. R., & Bryan, V. C. (2010). Tenured and non-tenured college of education faculty motivators and barriers in grant writing: A public university in the south. *Journal of Research Administration, 41*(3), 5, 7, 85–98.

Yang, O. (2005). *Guide to effective grant writing: How to write an effective NIH grant application.* New York, NY: Springer.

6

Marketing

The Language of Marketing

Throughout this chapter, several marketing-related terms and concepts will be used and discussed. When we talk about marketing, in a general sense, we talk about "producers" and "consumers." Producers are those people or organizations that make or offer products (or services) in a marketplace. Consumers are the purchasers, and often the users, of those products. They are the customers of the producers. Customers can be individuals or they can be organizations (Business Dictionary, n.d.a).

When we talk about products in the context of this book, we are talking about the educational courses offered by the organization. These may be seminars, training sessions, semester-long courses, and even entire degree programs. The term *product* means any type of learning activity or event organized and offered by the "producer" for "consumers" (Business Dictionary, n.d.c).

There can be many types of producers of educational programs, including colleges, universities, nonprofit organizations, community groups, educational consultants, and businesses that provide educational opportunities

Organization and Administration of Adult Education Programs, pages 113–144
Copyright © 2016 by Information Age Publishing
113

for adults. Consumers, in these cases, are students or learners who participate in the educational programs offered by these entities.

Producers can also be departments within a larger organization. The human resource development department in an organization can be considered a producer as well, as this organization offers training and development opportunities for the employees of the company. In this case, the consumers are the employees of that company.

There is generally agreement on the idea that providers of adult learning activities are producers. However, should learners be seen as consumers? Many would argue that there is a difference. Let's look at higher education as an example. In a free-market economy, consumers with the most money have more choices over their purchases. Those with more money can buy nicer homes and cars, for example, than those with less money. However, to attend college or university, one has to meet academic qualifications as well, so even consumers with the most money can't buy their way into the best institutions of higher education if they don't meet academic standards (at least ideally, this is the case). Also, educational programs have expectations for their learners in a way that is different than the traditional producer/consumer relationship. In higher education, if the learner does not meet those expectations, they do not pass the course. The old adage "The customer is always right" may not be applicable to this situation either. Some customers may expect to pass every course they take without doing any of the coursework. We all know that should not happen. Because a customer pays to attend a course does not mean that the customer will successfully complete the course, regardless of the money the customer paid to attend.

What do you think? Consider this issue as you work your way through this chapter on marketing. Because this is a chapter on marketing, the terms *producer, consumer* and *product* will be used throughout the chapter. Whether or not you would like to use the terms beyond this context is up to you.

In this chapter, Producer = Provider of Learning Experience; Product = Learning Event or Activity; and Consumer/Customer = Learner. Consider the following scenarios.

Carla works in human resource development for a large U.S.-based company. She was excited to be transferring from her company's office in Montgomery, Alabama, to the corporate headquarters in Boston, Massachusetts. She immediately scheduled a training program for the employees at the Boston office that had been very popular at the Montgomery office, but there was very little interest in the program among Boston employees.

Joe teaches English at a nonprofit organization whose mission is to help non-English-speaking people in the community. The organization offers a variety of workshops at no charge to attendees. His workshops have always been very popular, but recently he has held several workshops that were not as well attended as those same workshops were the year before.

Thomas works in administration at a small private 4-year college. Recently, an online university has started advertising in his area, and he is concerned that his potential students may be more attracted to the online university rather than his college.

Why Is Marketing Important to Adult Educators?

Maybe you have faced situations similar to those described in the above scenarios. Or maybe you know people who have faced similar situations. Something that all of these scenarios have in common is that they may involve marketing as a potential solution in one way or another. Marketing is a powerful tool that is often misunderstood. Used correctly, marketing can help promote the educational services you offer to the most appropriate people for those services. It can help your organization become more well-known in the community or area you serve. It can spur interest in your educational programs and can ultimately help your organization to increase revenues.

On the flip side, when marketing is done incorrectly, it can be costly and time-consuming and can result in little benefit for the organization. Marketing can even result in unintended negative consequences for organizations. Marketing activities can fail, plans can go askew, and the best intentions of marketers can be foiled by a host of variables. The difference between success and failure of marketing depends on the planning that goes into marketing efforts up front, the execution of the marketing plans, and the appropriate follow up.

Educators sometimes wonder why marketing of any type is necessary for education. They have the "If you build it, they will come"-type mentality, meaning that they believe all that's necessary for educational programs to succeed is to develop a quality program. In some cases, this is true, and some educational programs can be very successful with limited or no marketing efforts. However, in this day and age, that's not always the case, and even if it is the case today, it may not be so tomorrow. Organizations of all types, including educational institutions, are facing increased competition, and educational customers now have many more options from which to choose when they make education-related decisions. The traditional brick-and-mortar college, for example, now faces competition from a host of national universities that offer online courses and entire degree programs. These national institutions attract students through extensive marketing campaigns that feature television ads, billboards, and Internet advertising directed specifically at potential learners. Additionally, traditional universities are expanding their degree programs to different cities, states, and countries; sometimes in the back yards of existing educational institutions in those markets. In doing so, they are increasing the competition for student tuition dollars.

Educational marketing is relevant not only to institutions of higher education, though. For-profit organizations are finding that the same educational programs they offer may be available, at lesser or no student cost, through nonprofit organizations. Nonprofit organizations must continue to justify their adult learning opportunities to donors and benefactors by demonstrating their worth, and that worth is often measured in terms of numbers of learners in seats. Consultants and private companies specializing in training and development must continue to cultivate relationships with existing clients and must always be looking for new clients. All organizations, regardless of their type, must work to ensure that their potential learners are aware of their programs, that their programs meet the needs of the individuals they seek to attract, and that it is financially feasible for learners to enroll in their course offerings.

Even HRD professionals must be aware of the basic principles of marketing. Marketing educational programs to employees in an organization may be the responsibility of those working in human resource development. Internal marketing can promote awareness of an organization's employee learning opportunities, and can result in increased attendance at employee training events and higher visibility for the HRD function in an organization. This visibility is especially important given the ever-increasing emphasis organizations are placing on value-added activities and accountability. Internal marketing can help HRD professionals demonstrate the value of their work to a variety of stakeholders in an organization. It is something that HRD professionals cannot ignore.

Chapter Overview

This chapter will delve into the concept of marketing as it relates to adult education programs. Marketing-related terms will be defined and discussed, and concepts, such as marketing strategy, the marketing mix, product life cycles, and advertising and promotion, will be presented and examined through the lens of adult education organization and administration.

An important aspect of marketing is examining what drives consumer decision making. Consumer behavior and the decision-making process will also be discussed, again, in the context of decisions regarding adult education opportunities. By the time you complete this chapter, you should have a better understanding of the role of marketing in adult education.

What Is Marketing?

To start this chapter, several definitions of marketing will be presented. Many people think of marketing in terms of advertising, but marketing is much more than advertising. The American Marketing Association (AMA) defines marketing as follows: "Marketing is the activity, set of institutions, and processes for creating, communicating, delivering, and exchanging offerings that have value for customers, clients, partners, and society at large (AMA, n.d.b, para. 1).

Lamb, Hair, and McDaniel (2011) add to the AMA definition of marketing noted above as follows:

> Marketing entails processes that focus on delivering value and benefit to customers, not just selling goods, services and/or ideas. It uses communication, distribution and pricing strategies to provide customers and other stakeholders with the goods, services, ideas, values, and benefits they desire when and where they want them. (p. 3)

Merriam-Webster defines marketing as "the process or technique of promoting, selling, and distributing a product or service" (n.d.a). They continue by noting that marketing is the overall process of moving a product or service from a provider to a consumer. Kotler and Bloom (1984) have researched the marketing of professional services, including educational programs. Their definition of marketing, presented in a service-related tone, is as follows:

> Marketing is the analysis, planning, implementation and control of carefully formulated plans designed to bring about voluntary exchanges of value with target markets for the purpose of achieving organizational objectives. It relies heavily on designing the organization's offerings in terms of the target markets' needs and desires, and on using effective pricing, communication and distribution to inform, motivate, and service these markets. (p. 4)

What do you think of when you read these definitions of marketing? What similarities among the definitions do you notice? What differences? What types of things are associated with the definition of marketing that you had not considered?

Most definitions of marketing indicate that it is a process or that it involves a set of activities. Those activities are typically associated with efforts to get products or services from organizations to people (or sometime from organizations to other organizations) and include things such as selling, promoting, pricing, and distributing. While marketing activities are many and varied, the goal of marketing is fairly straightforward. It is to get products or services to people who need them. Marketing creates a benefit called utility in that it satisfies a customer's need for something when that customer purchases the product or service. In doing so, it also creates a desired effect for the organization that is developing or distributing that product or service, as that organization depends on the learner in order to survive (Linton, n.d.).

Marketing is an exchange process. Marketing is successful when the customer is happy with the products or services they receive from an organization and the organization receives some sort of value that they desire from the customer (Linton, n.d.). This value may be in the form of tuition, fees, or payment for courses taken by the customer.

In some cases, the actual purchase of a product or service is not involved in the exchange. Many types of adult education opportunities are offered by organizations at no charge, as part of the organization's mission to serve the community, for example. Personal enrichment courses offered by a community library, a local college or university, or a community service–type organization may be free and open to the public. Utility is still created in that attendance at these types of learning activities satisfies a learner (or customer's) need for enrichment or knowledge, but no money changes hands. That does not mean that marketing efforts do not need to take place in these situations. Organizations that offer free adult education opportunities as part of service to the community still need to promote those opportunities to potential learners. Creating awareness through marketing efforts can help boost attendance and create interest (which can ultimately result in better-educated community members). It can also promote the goodwill and benefit the organization provides to the community (Lamb et al., 2011).

Equally as important is to examine what marketing is not. A common misconception about marketing is that it is used to coerce consumers into making purchases they do not need or cannot afford. Marketing is sometimes associated with schemes and tricks used by deceitful companies to separate people from their money. You might have heard the expression that someone is such a good marketer that they "could sell ice to an Eskimo." In reality, marketing is about focusing efforts on people who actually need your product. A good marketer would understand that this group does not need to purchase ice and would change their product and service offerings to things the group does need (Harrington, 2014).

Marketing is also not typically one activity, nor is it a series of random activities done to increase business. The best marketing plans are coordinated efforts that are developed based on an organization's overall marketing strategy. That organization might be an entire business or it may be a department within a larger organization, such as an HRD department (as marketing can take place on many different levels in an organization). Every organization, large or small, should have a marketing strategy. It is the overall strategy that drives individual marketing efforts (Lamb et al., 2011).

Why Do We Market?

Based on what you now know about marketing, you may see its importance in educational settings. Educational programs are marketed so potential learners know that programs exist and can possibly meet their needs. Through marketing, organizations can differentiate themselves from others who may offer the same types of products or services and give potential customers reasons for choosing that particular organization's educational programs. While some people do seek out opportunities for learning, there are many others who intend to do so but don't have the time or resources to investigate those potential opportunities. Some don't know where to begin to look for them. Marketing provides potential learners with information that may be of value to them. It may encourage them to contact the organization for further information, to sign up for a program or class, and maybe to tell their friends and acquaintances about the organizations and its programs.

Marketing Strategy

As noted above, often marketing efforts are piecemeal. An organization may advertise in a publication on a random basis. It may do some type of direct-mail marketing or occasionally send out email marketing messages to a list of existing customers. It may sponsor a local event of some sort. While all these may be good things to do, the best type of marketing is based on an overall marketing strategy. That strategy is derived from the organization's overall mission and organizational goals (Figure 6.1).

A market is defined as "the set of all people and organizations (that) have an actual or potential interest in a service and the ability to pay for it" (Kotler & Bloom, 1984, p. 58). Markets can be broad or narrowly defined or segmented. For example, a university's market for a graduate degree

Figure 6.1 Organizational mission and marketing.

program in adult education may be all adults in a certain geographic area who have undergraduate degrees, who work in the field of adult education, and whose household income is above $50,000 per year. The market for an ESL course for recent immigrants in a large city may be people ages 18 and older who do not speak English, who live within a 20-minute commute of the sponsoring organization, and who have been in the country less than one year. The market for an employee training session dealing with the organization's benefits may be all employees who have been with the organization for less than six months. The market for an educational consulting organization may be businesses with more than 50 employees that have small internal training departments.

Target markets are select markets or groups an organization has identified as potential customers for their products or services (Lamb et al., 2011). These are the markets that marketing efforts focus on.

Based on an organization's mission, a series of specific goals is developed for the organization. Following are some examples of goals educational organizations might have:

- Increase new student numbers in a particular course by 10% each year for the next three years.
- Increase student credit hours by 5% in adult education master's program courses over the next four semesters.
- Decrease attrition rates by 20% in a basic skills math course this month.

▪ Remain consistent in the number of students enrolling in an organization's diversity training course this calendar year when compared to last calendar year.

You can see that organizational goals can be stated in terms of increases, decreases, or status quo. Sometimes goals involve new products and new customers and sometimes they involve repeat customers and existing products. They may involve any combination of these variables as well. All of this work is part of the strategic planning process. Once those variables have been identified, the marketing planning process can begin.

An organization's marketing strategy is the way the organization will go about reaching those customers in the aforementioned target markets in order to meet the goals of the organization. Marketing strategies involve planning activities, and the activities focus on how to expose the organization's products or services to the target market. There may be several activities associated with each goal or there may be a few. The number of activities depends on several things.

- **New or existing target market:** It often takes more activities, and a greater variety of activities, to reach new markets than existing markets (as those markets already know about the organization).
- **New or existing product:** New products also typically require more activities than existing products, as it takes more work to introduce a new product.
- **Size of target market:** It can take less effort to reach a large target market than a smaller one.
- **Size of goals:** Meeting larger goals can require more activities than meeting smaller goals, or goals that involve remaining at current levels.

The marketing mix is a critical element of marketing. It should be used when developing marketing activities to meet organizational goals. The marketing mix is "the tools that are used together to create a desired response among a set of predefined consumers" (Solomon & Stewart, 2000, p. 9). The marketing mix is also known as the four Ps of marketing: product, price, place, and promotion (Lamb et al., 2011) (Figure 6.2). In other words, those tools are the organization's product, the price of the product, the place in which it is available, and the promotional efforts undertaken to introduce potential customers to the product (which, hopefully, causes the potential customer to purchase the product). All four Ps of the marketing mix should be considered in an organization's marketing plan and "all four

Figure 6.2   The four Ps of marketing. Adapted from Lamb et al. (2011).

must be blended to create optimal results" (Lamb et al., 2011, p. 47). Each of the four Ps of the marketing mix will be discussed individually in the next section of this chapter.

The First P: Product

The first P in the marketing mix, product, is fairly straightforward. In the case of organizations that provide adults with educational opportunities, the products are the courses, training sessions, or degree programs that the organization is offering. In the world of marketing, these types of products are considered intangible products, because there is not a physical product that the consumer purchases (as opposed to tangible products, such as bread, cars, and soap). Rather, they purchase admission to something or an opportunity to experience or participate in something. Other examples of intangible products include travel, health care, accounting, and insurance (Levitt, 1981).

An organization's products are typically developed based on the mission of the organization, the organizational resources available, and the needs of a particular market of people. A product mix is "the full sets of products offered for sale by an organization. The product mix includes all product lines and categories" (AMA, n.d.d). Product mixes can be broad or narrow as well. Some educational organizations can be very successful offering one or two courses or seminars on a particular subject, while other organizations have multiple courses on many different topics. Some organizations offer the same courses for many years, while others continually update and change their course offerings.

Within the parameters of the mission and goals of the organization and the organizational resources available, how do educational organizations determine what specific types of courses to offer their learners or potential learners? This is typically done through some sort of needs analysis. Based on the results of a needs analysis, educational programs can be developed and then marketed to those people the organization wishes to target. Needs analyses also help programmers identify the correct number of courses to offer on a given topic. For example, an organization that is involved with educating new parents on child-rearing skills may find that they have more potential students in some months than others. During those busier times, more sessions of this course are offered, and at times of less demand for that particular course, other types of courses are run instead.

Conducting a needs analysis is not a one-time event. People's needs are continually changing and evolving. Market variables, such as competition from other providers, continually change as well. A needs analysis conducted a year ago may not be valid today, so needs analyses should be conducted regularly. Needs analyses do not have to be formal nor lengthy. They can be informal, and can be done in a variety of ways. Regardless of the method, understanding the needs of those in an organization's target market should be a priority.

The Product Life Cycle

The product life cycle is important to examine when discussing the concept of product in the marketplace. Products in any marketplace are like people in that as they age (or spend time on the market), they go through definite stages or periods of their lives. The product life cycle "represent(s) the nature of time effects in product markets" (Weitz & Wensley, 2002, p. 96). It is "a highly stylized representation of the product sales patterns of most products during their lifetimes" (p. 96). Stages in the product life cycle are as follows: Introduction, Growth, Maturity, and Decline. The product life cycle is represented in graph format in Figure 6.3.

In Figure 6.3, sales are displayed on the "Y" axis of the graph, while time is on the "X" axis. Most organizations measure the success of their products in terms of sales and profits (in dollars), however, providers of adult education do not always do the same. Some measure success in terms

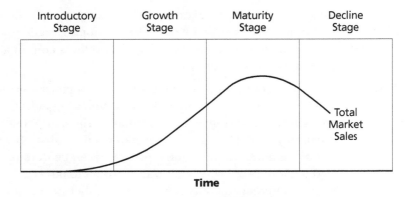

Figure 6.3 The product life cycle. Adapted from Weitz & Wensley (2002).

of numbers of students served, student credit hours generated, student retention, or a host of other ways. These other types of measures are equally appropriate on the "Y" axis. HRD departments may also measure success in terms of employee interest and participation in a particular learning event. When reading about the product life cycle, consider that the word *profit* may be measured in a variety of ways.

Stage 1: Introduction

Introduction is the first stage of a product's life. During this stage, the organization is working to introduce the product to the desired target market(s). This stage can be difficult, as the goal is to make consumers aware of the product's existence, so marketers are typically starting at the ground level. Organizations typically spend a good deal of marketing-related resources simply to introduce products in the marketplace. This is done to ensure that the next stages in the product life cycle are long and profitable for the organization.

In this stage, the consumer is exposed to the product and gets a first opportunity to learn about the product. They also now have the opportunity to purchase the product, which, from an educational standpoint, means signing up to attend a training session or enrolling in a course. Because the product is new at this point, the producer may have to be flexible in order to increase awareness and acceptance. For example, a community-based agency that holds educational courses on neighborhood-related issues may not run courses for fewer than five learners at a time. The agency recently introduced a new course on environmental issues in the neighborhood and three people enrolled. The agency may want to make an exception and run the course with three people in order to help the course gain traction in the neighborhood. In doing so, the agency is betting on the fact that those three learners will have a positive experience in the course and will tell their neighbors about the experience. This may help increase enrollments when this course is offered again (Inc., n.d., paras. 1–2).

The length of this first stage of the product life cycle depends on a few things. How quickly those in the target market are attracted to the product is one factor. The faster the product is accepted in the market, the quicker it moves to the next stage in the product life cycle. The amount of resources the organization wants to put into the product is also key. In the case of a day-long course, the organization may want to run the course regularly for several months before making decisions about the future of the course. In the case of a university course offered only once per year, it may take several years for the course to move to the next stage. It's important to remember that not all products move out of this first stage. Some simply fail and organizations discontinue them. Some are changed or revised and become pieces of other products (Lamb et al., 2011).

Stage 2: Growth

The next stage in the product life cycle is the growth stage. By this time, the product has been introduced in the market, and it has been accepted by enough of the target market for it to become profitable. Demand for the product continues to rise throughout this stage, and the job of marketers is to continue to encourage consumers to purchase the product. Sometimes at this stage, an organization's competitors, seeing the interest in the product, introduce similar types of products, so the job of marketers is also to promote the fact that consumers should choose their product over those offered by the competition (Lamb et al., 2011).

Stage 3: Maturity

The maturity stage of a product is often the longest (Solomon & Stewart, 2000). During this stage, demand for the product, along with profit on the product, levels off and can even start to decline. Often by this time competitors have realized that there is value in offering similar products, so there is more competition in the marketplace. Getting new customers may mean attracting them from a competitor. At this point, producers may change the product to stimulate interest. They may offer new features, updates, or improvements to the existing product. They may also try to attract new customers in different markets (Solomon & Stewart, 2000).

Stage 4: Decline

Decline is the final stage of the product lifecycle. In this stage, overall demand for the product decreases. New products may have been introduced that make the existing product obsolete or customers simply do not need the product anymore. At this point, competitors may leave the market and revise their strategies to focus on other products or markets. At some point, the product may be a burden for the organization, so it has to decide whether or not to continue offering it (Lamb et al., 2011).

The Product Life Cycle and Educational Programs

Do educational programs follow the product life cycle the same as other products and services in the marketplace? To some degree they do, and in other respects, they do not. Let's consider the educational programs offered by a nonprofit organization, a community college, and a business.

Colleges and universities may offer the same core courses for many years. There will always be demand for courses in English, math, and science, for example, and that demand will be consistent for many years (unlike the typical demand for products in a product lifecycle). Those courses typically will not change a great deal with regard to content either. So we could say that they are in a permanent stage of maturity. However, instructors or program developers may change or tweak the courses based on new research or developments in their respective fields. Basic literacy courses offered by a nonprofit organization may stay the same for many years. The HRD department of a business may offer a course on workplace communication to its employees. Some parts of that course, such as those dealing with face-to-face communication, may stay the same for long periods of time. Other parts, such as those dealing with electronic communication, may change regularly as electronic communication methods evolve.

Many courses offered by formal educational institutions fall into the product maturity stage. They are revised and tweaked based on new developments in the field, but their basic topics remain the same for many years. Most formal educational programs do add courses based on significant developments in a field, changing priorities in a field, or on new ways to examine existing topics.

Other types of courses may follow the product life cycle more closely. There was a time when not every office workspace had a computer on the desk. Computers in the workplace started becoming more common in the 1980s, and their use in business rose in popularity very quickly. As a result,

HRD departments found that they had to provide courses on basic computer skills, such as keyboarding, to their employees. Consultants and educational organizations, including community and technical colleges, seeing the demand for such courses, were quick to jump on the computer training bandwagon, and businesses found they had many options for computer training for their employees. Some training could be done by HRD departments. Others could be done in-house by hiring temporary consultants, and still others could be done by sending employees to seminars and workshops. Demand was great, and it continued to rise. Training was effective in reaching the many employees who were computer illiterate and providing them with the skills and abilities necessary to use their desktop computers.

Because of these efforts, a few years later most people in the workplace had basic knowledge of computers and computer systems. Basic computer courses were no longer necessary because the use of computers in the workplace, at home, and in primary and secondary education became a common part of everyday life for most people. People were learning how to use computers at younger ages, and computer knowledge became a prerequisite for many jobs. The courses that consultants and HRD departments had offered on basic computer skills were no longer necessary. They had reached the end of the decline stage of the product lifecycle, and were eventually discontinued.

There are many reasons why educational programs are introduced in the marketplace (Mahmoud, 2007). As demonstrated above, programs developed to meet consumer demand is one reason. Legal, professional, and licensure requirements are others. An increased emphasis on safety is the reason why many community colleges are offering motorcycle safety courses. Changes in licensure are behind an increase in continuing education programs offered for school counselors and childcare providers. Human interest in the Internet has spurred demand for courses in web design and a host of other topics.

Likewise, there are many reasons products are discontinued. An organization may find it does not have the resources (instructors, physical space, or other resources) to support the number of training programs it could offer, for example. An organization may find that a course they are offering is farther outside the mission and scope of the organization than originally thought, so the course is discontinued. Also, an organization may determine that it is not cost efficient to offer a particular course anymore. Sometimes changes in society in general result in the discontinuation of products. Advances in technology have meant that organizations offering face-to-face training find they are competing for learners who can access those same training programs online. As a result, some face-to-face programs are being discontinued or replaced with online versions of the same training (Mahmoud, 2007).

The product is arguably the most important of the four Ps of marketing. Without the product, the three other Ps—price, place, and promotion—are irrelevant.

The Second P: Price

Any economic system is based on the exchange of goods or services for something of value. Often that value is money, which is directly related to the second P in the marketing mix—price. Price is what the seller charges for a product and price is what the consumer pays in exchange for the product (Lamb et al., 2011). In the case of educational programs for adults, that price may be in the form of tuition paid for a course, seminar, or educational program. As noted earlier in this chapter, however, price can be looked at in a broader sense. Price can also refer to the price of one's time spent in a workplace training program (when that employee could be doing other things at his or her desk). It can be examined in terms of "opportunity cost," or "the cost attributable to doing a thing caused by foregone opportunities that are sacrificed in order to do this one thing" (AMA, n.d.c).

Price is an element of the marketing mix that is becoming increasingly important to all providers of adult education programs. In the past, colleges and universities relied heavily on subsidies from local and state governments to supplement tuition charges paid by students. Lately, however, governments are cutting funding for institutions of higher education, meaning that these organizations must rely to a larger degree on tuition dollars from learners. As a result, institutions of higher education are focusing more on running profitable programs. Educational programs that are not profitable may find themselves changing to maximize profitability or even being eliminated. Changes may include larger class sizes, heavier reliance on adjunct faculty, and fewer course offerings per semester.

Nonprofit organizations that provide educational opportunities for adults also must pay attention to price. Decisions as to whether to charge adults for educational programs may affect the survival of the organization. If a price is charged, the correct or optimal price must be calculated in order for the program to be successful. A price that is too high will discourage potential students from attending. A price too low will result in the organization not meeting its financial goals or sustainability requirements.

The workplace is not immune to decisions regarding price either. Employee services, such as training and development, must justify their existence by demonstrating their value to organization, and that value is often in the form of employee training programs that are efficient and effective. Employees must find these programs value added, and worth the time spent in them in order for the HRD department to justify its existence.

When we talk about decisions regarding price, two equations are important:

Revenue is the total amount taken in as a result of learners paying for an educational opportunity, such as a course or seminar (Merriam-Webster, n.d.c).

Number of Students × Price Each Student Paid = Total Revenue

Profit is the amount an organization earns when all expenses associated with the learning event are deducted (Merriam-Webster, n.d.b):

Total Revenue − Total Expenses = Profit.

If expenses are more than revenue, there is a negative profit, or a loss. The goal of most organizations is to take in more revenue than they have expenses for a course or learning activity. This results in a profit for the organization. The goal of some organizations, namely, nonprofits, may be to take in at least enough revenue to cover all expenses, resulting in a zero-sum gain (no profit or loss).

Keep in mind that revenue may come from fees associated with a course, and it may come from other sources as well. Grant monies and donations, for example, may provide nonprofit organizations with enough to cover the expenses on courses they run without having to charge students fees to attend those courses. Businesses typically do not charge employees to attend training courses (although sometimes, individual departmental budgets are charged when employees in that department participate in training opportunities). Rather, the HRD budget is a part of the overall organization's budget, which comes from the overall organization profits. This type of training is viewed as a service to employees, with the broader goal of helping employees to become more effective and efficient, so it is considered a cost of doing business, or an expense.

Some who work in the organization and administration of adult education programs do not have to deal with issues of price at all. In some cases, prices are set by boards of directors or individuals higher up in the organization. In some organizations, educational programs are free, paid for by grants or donations instead of through participant fees. In business and industry, as noted above, educators are teaching employees at their own organizations, so price is not an issue. However, if a price for an educational program is to be set, there are several factors to consider (Lamb et al., 2011).

- What are your expenses for the course? If making a profit is important, prices can be calculated by figuring total expenses, dividing those expenses by the optimal number of students in the course, and then adding a markup to that number (which will be the profit).
- What are others doing? As part of strategic planning efforts, it is important to understand what similar organizations are charging for similar courses. This will give you an idea of what your pricing structure should look like. It will also give you an idea of how much competition is already in the market for a particular course.
- What will learners pay? A survey of potential learners for a particular course will give you an idea of what learners are willing to pay to attend such a course.
- At what stage in the product lifecycle is the product? As noted above, you may have to take losses on courses being introduced to the market in order to stimulate demand in the longer term.

Consider that there are ways to attract customers by offering price-related incentives. Things like coupons or discounts help to stimulate demand for courses. Some educational programs offer quantity discounts for students who register for multiple courses, for example. Some basic skills courses charge a small tuition fee, but that fee is refunded upon successful completion of the course.

The Third P: Place

The concept of place may seem obvious to you: In order to provide educational opportunities to adults, you have to do it in a place they can attend. There are a few additional factors that are part of place, when viewed from a marketing perspective, however. In marketing terms, place means having the product available at the time and place the customer wants it (Whalley, 2010). Also to be considered is the length of the learning event, which is something marketers of traditional products do not have to consider to the same degree.

Place can be looked at on several levels. From a larger geographical standpoint, the educational services you offer to potential target markets must be offered in a place that is convenient for the learner to access. In some areas, that means offering the course or seminar in a place that is a reasonable driving distance for the learner (provided learners have the transportation to get to the learning event). In larger cities and urban areas, public transportation should be considered as well, and the place at which the learning event occurs should be readily accessible to potential learners using public transportation.

Key to providers of services (such as educational-related services) is the element of time as well. Not only does the place have to be appropriate for the learner, but the timing of the learning event must be considered. If you are running a program for learners who work during the day, the most optimal time for courses may be in the evenings. People who work in the service industry, which involves substantial evening and weekend work, may be more likely to attend courses offered during the day. Decisions involving time also should include the length of the learning event. People who work all day may find it difficult to attend a three-hour course in the evenings. After a full day of work, attention spans are short and interest in learning may wane. In these cases, several shorter courses may be more appropriate. If your potential learners have children, they may find it difficult to attend courses in the evening, when issues of childcare must be considered.

How do you choose the best place and time for your learning event? These types of decisions should be based on what you know about the target market for your learning events.

Learner perceptions of place are important to consider. There may be some stigma associated with taking basic skills courses at a neighborhood literacy center, for example, as potential learners may feel embarrassed to be seen by their neighbors attending courses at a literacy center. So in these cases, a more neutral venue for these types of courses may be more appropriate. Likewise, ESL courses may be better attended if they are offered at churches, because churches are assumed to be safe places, and a potential audience for an ESL course may include undocumented individuals or those who are in the country illegally. Courses or learning events of a personal nature, having to do with topics like domestic violence or living with and managing medical-related issues, for example, may also be better attended if held in neutral locations.

Use of the Internet in adult education has had a profound effect on the concept of place. Online educational opportunities are now available to adults in the privacy of their own homes. In these cases, the physical location of the educational provider does not matter. There are plusses and minuses associated with this change. On the one hand, there are many more online learning opportunities available to adults who are interested, and those opportunities are on a wide variety of topics. Potential students for whom education was not an option due to their geographic distance from educational providers now have opportunities to participate. Online learning may be much more convenient for your target market as well. Educational providers may find that it is cheaper to offer online courses than face-to-face (although costs to develop and maintain online courses can also be substantial). Blended learning options, which involve both face-to-face and online components, are also viable options for learners who may want the benefits of each method. Trainers in HRD departments may find that employees are more willing to learn via online training programs that can be taken around their own schedules, as opposed to traveling to a specific venue at a specific time for a face-to-face course. Savings on travel-related expenses is a benefit as well, especially for organizations with employees at different sites around the country or world.

While the concept of place may not be as important now as it was in the past, if you are considering offering courses online, it is important to know whether or not your target market has access to the Internet and where that access is. You might find that many in your target market do not have Internet access in their homes and that finding access to the Internet may be more difficult than attending a face-to-face course. You may find that the learners in your target market may prefer face-to-face instruction and the benefits that come with a face-to-face learning experience. Some learners are more motivated to attend face-to-face courses and to complete coursework if they have deadlines and due dates developed around those face-to-face sessions.

Online learning has also brought more competition to some educational markets. Traditional colleges and universities are finding that their competition is now online degree programs offered by schools based in many geographic areas around the globe. Online learning has meant that learners have more options and there is more competition for them in the marketplace. Unfortunately, some of the online learning "opportunities" now available to students involve high tuition and fees for less-than-reputable courses and degree programs. Learners in the educational marketplace have to make smart, well-researched decisions, lest they fall victim to high-priced, low-quality, and sometimes unaccredited organizations.

In summary, there are many decisions about place that must be considered when offering educational programs. Even though the Internet has made the concept of place less relevant for a lot of potential learners, this is not always the case. A thorough understanding of your target market will lead to the best decisions regarding place.

The Fourth P: Promotion

The fourth P of marketing, promotion, is probably the most familiar to the general public. Promotion is "the advancement of a product, idea, or point of view through publicity and/or advertising" (Business Dictionary, n.d.d). When people think of the concept of marketing, they typically associate it with advertising and promotion. As we now know, there is much more to marketing than advertising, but promotion is an important component in the marketing mix.

Just as the marketing mix consists of the four Ps of marketing, there is a promotional mix that consists of the different ways in which products or services can be promoted. The promotion mix is defined as "the various communication techniques, such as advertising, personal selling, sales promotion and public relations/product publicity available to a marketer that are combined to achieve specific goals" (AMA, n.d.e). Each of the four components of the promotional mix should be considered and used, to varying degrees, as part of a promotional strategy. A common mistake made by marketers is to focus on only one technique and ignore the others. A more appropriate and more balanced approach to promotion is one that employs multiple techniques.

Each of the four major components of the promotional mix (Figure 6.4)—advertising, personal selling, sales promotion, and public relations—will be discussed in the sections that follow.

Figure 6.4 The promotional mix.

Advertising

The American Marketing Association defines advertising as follows:

> The placement of announcements and persuasive messages in time or space purchased in any of the mass media by business firms, nonprofit organizations, government agencies, and individuals who seek to inform and/ or persuade members of a particular target market or audience about their products, services, organizations, or ideas (n.d.a).

As noted above, advertising is probably the most visible part of both the marketing mix and the promotional mix. Consider how many advertisements you are exposed to on a daily basis. Advertising is everywhere. Advertisements air on TV and print advertisements are in newspapers and magazines, as well as on busses, taxis, and in subway trains. Advertisements appear on websites and are on billboards and in store windows. More subtle forms of advertising are common as well. Look at the backs of cars in a parking lot and notice how many dealership name stickers you see on those cars. Or look at yourself in the mirror and notice how many brand names or brand identifiers that you see on your clothes. Both of these are examples of more subtle ways of advertising.

There are plusses and minuses associated with the use of each aspect of the promotional mix. One of the benefits of advertising is its ability to reach large groups of people in a relatively inexpensive way. Through advertising, organizations can "control their message" and communicate exactly what they want to say to potential customers. Advertisements can be done in multiple ways, which is also advantageous. They can be in print form, online, or live action. Advertising can also be segmented to reach exactly the market in which the organization is interested. The number of different newspapers, magazines, websites, and television networks makes it possible to focus advertisements on a specific population, which is a great advantage to the marketer (Lamb et al. 2011).

Advertising can be done within an organization as well. What types of advertisements do you see within your own organization? Consider ads on employee websites, in internal emails you receive, and in employee newsletters. These types of advertisements may be placed by other departments in the organization, promoting their services to employees. Seminars on retirement planning, for example, may be advertised to all employees within an organization.

The sheer number of advertisements we are exposed to on a daily basis is a disadvantage of advertising, however. We see so many advertisements in a day that they are easy to tune out; so it is easy for the advertisement you place to be ignored by the population you wish to attract. Costs for developing and placing advertisements may be high as well. Advertising can also have negative connotations associated with it. The general public can be skeptical of claims made in advertisements. Advertisements for products that promise miracle cures for common ailments, easy weight loss, hair growth, instant sex appeal, and related things cause the average consumer to discount claims made in all advertisements.

Sales Promotion

When was the last time you tried a free sample of food available at the grocery store? How about the last time you clipped a coupon for a discount on a product you often use? These are two examples of sales promotions. Sales promotions are defined as "the media and nonmedia marketing pressure applied for a predetermined, limited period of time at the level of consumer, retailer, or wholesaler in order to stimulate trial, increase consumer demand, or improve product availability" (AMA, n.d.g). Product or service information booths at trade shows and consumer fairs, discount or frequent-buyer cards, contests, sweepstakes, and give-aways are also forms of sales promotion. From an HRD standpoint, informational tables at employee events or in common areas like an employee cafeteria are methods of promoting an organization's training and development opportunities.

Unlike advertising, which is focused on the masses, sales promotion is more focused on the individual and is more direct—the individual consumer at the grocery store, the show or expo attendee, or the coupon clipper. Sales promotion is also focused on immediate action (as opposed to advertising, which is more passive). The goal of an effective sales promotion is to get a customer to immediately make a purchase or register for a course. Often sales promotion focuses on incentives—a cents-off coupon or a discount on registration, for example. Sometimes organizations offer discounts to customers who register for a series of courses. This type of promotion, a "quantity discount," encourages repeat business. The more personalized approach is a benefit in that it involves direct contact with a potential customer, as is the emphasis on immediate action. A disadvantage of sales promotion is that a great deal of time may be spent with potential customers who do not end up buying or enrolling (Nielsen, n.d.).

Public Relations

Public relations is defined as follows:

> That form of communication management that seeks to make use of public-
> ity and other nonpaid forms of promotion and information to influence the
> feelings, opinions, or beliefs about the company, its products or services, or
> about the value of the product or service or the activities of the organization
> to buyers, prospects, or other stakeholders. (AMA, n.d.f)

One of the keys to public relations is the idea that it is a nonpaid form of
promotion (unlike advertising and sales promotion, which both involve payments of some sort). Consider an organization that is sponsoring an event
to raise money for the building of a library, for example. That organization
works with the library board to organize a children's fair with rides, games,
and other activities, and has employees of the organization volunteer to work
at the fair. All of the money raised at the fair goes to the library. The organization then sends a series of press releases, with details about the event, to local
media (newspapers and TV stations), inviting them to attend the fair and
cover the event in the news. When the story is covered by a local TV station,
the organization receives publicity for its efforts on behalf of the library. The
news generated from this event is an example of public relations.

Public relations tools focus on methods of communication with key
stakeholders. These may include things like media alerts and press releases
(as noted in the example above), and annual reports for shareholders.

The goal of public relations is typically to have others provide information on your organization (the press, for example, covering the children's
fair in the example above). Information about the organization is presented by a newscaster or a reporter, and because of the "messenger," public
relations can be seen as more credible by the general public. The downside
of this dependency is that organizations don't have any say in how the press
cover the event or interpret the story. So the message ultimately provided to
the stakeholder may not be exactly what the organization hopes for.

Personal Selling

Like sales promotion efforts, personal selling is an individual, one-on-
one way of promoting a product or service. The process of personal selling is probably familiar to everyone. It involves direct interaction with a
potential customer, addressing the customer's needs or concerns directly,
and ultimately (if all works as planned) having the customer purchase the
product (Business Dictionary, n.d.b). A benefit of personal selling is that it
can be customized to meet the needs of each individual potential customer.
However, a lot depends on the skills of the salesperson. A downside is that
personal selling may be of higher cost than other methods.

Additional Methods

There are several other methods of promotion that can be considered as part of the promotional mix. These methods do not fall neatly into one of the above four categories. Direct marketing combines elements of sales promotion and advertising. It is the sending of brochures or advertisements to a specific list of potential customers. This can be effective in providing people who meet your target market with the information you wish to send them. Direct mail can be done via USPS mail, telephone (telemarketing), and also online using email. The downside of direct mail is that often people see it as junk mail or spam and ignore it.

Sponsorship of events and activities is another method of promotion that combines elements of advertising and public relations. "With a sponsorship, a company spends money to support an issue, cause or an event that is consistent with corporate objectives, such as improving brand awareness or enhancing corporate image" (Lamb et al. 2011, p. 580). Under a sponsorship agreement, an organization pays to put on the event, and in exchange, has their name associated with the event. For example, Macy's Department Store is known for the sponsorship of a Thanksgiving Day parade in New York. The sponsorship of college football bowl games and sports stadiums is another example. So is a placard on an easel at an event or a listing in a program given out at an event. Sponsorship is a way for organizations to promote their names and brands. However, sponsorships typically do not allow organizations to go into detail about their products or services. An organization's name may be exposed to many people, however information about that organization, beyond the name, may not reach the desired customer.

Promotional Mix: A Summary

As noted above, a mix of promotional efforts is important in an effective marketing campaign. One aspect of the promotional mix should not be relied on at the expense of others. Often elements of the promotional mix work together. If an organization raises money for a charity by donating a percentage of a day's sales to that charity, they may advertise the event in a local newspaper. They may also use sales promotion–related efforts, such as coupons, to get people to purchase on that day. They may also use press releases to alert the media that this event is going on, so it is covered on the news.

Product, Price, Place, and Promotion: Working Together

"A simple definition of marketing would be: The right product in the right place at the right time at the right price" (Whalley, 2010, p. 13). The reason that product, price, place, and promotion are called the marketing mix is because they all work (or mix) together and affect each other. This is why all involved in the marketing efforts of an organization must work together and be on the same page with regard to the marketing efforts being made. For example, if an organization decides to increase its promotion efforts for a particular course, they first must make sure that the organization can handle an increase in student demand as a result of the promotion. This means working with the program planner to ensure that additional sections of the course could be added, if necessary. If an organization wants to expand to a new geographic area, they should first make sure there is demand for the product in that area. If new courses are to be offered, pricing must be examined to make sure the course can be run profitably, and promotional efforts should feature this new course in order to stimulate demand.

As noted several times throughout this chapter, keys to marketing success are an understanding of the organization and its mission, an understanding of the marketplace, and careful management of the elements in the marketing mix.

Marketing and Consumer Behavior

It is helpful for those who develop marketing plans to understand how consumers make decisions. In every market that an organization targets, some people in that target market do purchase the organization's product and others do not. What makes some purchase and other ignore or decline? Understanding consumer motivations and behaviors helps marketers to plan more effectively. Consumer behavior is the study of how individuals, groups, or organizations make decisions on how they "select, secure, use and dispose of products, services, experiences or ideas to satisfy needs" (Hawkins & Mothersbaugh, 2012, p. 6).

Regardless of the product or service being purchased, customers typically go through a similar process when making decisions (Figure 6.5). The process always starts when the consumer realizes that he or she has some type of need that is unfulfilled and must be addressed. In the case of educational programs, that need may revolve around learning something new for personal interest, improving one's skills or abilities for a current or future job, or expanding one's area of expertise on a particular subject area. Regardless of topic or level of knowledge the consumer already has, the need is the "seed,"

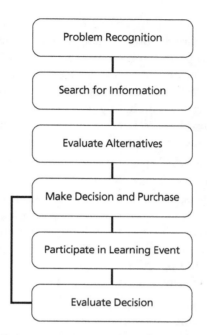

Figure 6.5 The buying decision process (modified for education-related decisions).

or the basis for what will become the quest to fulfill the need. It is what motivates the consumer to take action (Hawkins & Mothersbaugh, 2012).

That action typically starts with some type of search for alternatives. This step in the process can be brief or extensive, depending on the type of need to be fulfilled. In fact, sometimes there is not any type of search for alternatives. If the consumer has a need to learn more about a particular hobby, for example, the search for alternatives may only involve the consumer's decision that the easiest and most efficient way to do so would be through self-directed learning on an Internet website. On the other hand, the search for graduate programs in a particular discipline may involve the examination of many alternatives and may take an extensive amount of time.

Once alternatives have been identified, the consumer evaluates those alternatives against the criteria established when the need was realized (in Step 1). This step may also be brief or extensive depending on the alternatives discovered by the consumer. Many options require more time to evaluate than fewer options. Decisions of higher consequence also require more time to evaluate than easy or routine-types of decisions.

When a decision has been made, the consumer proceeds to purchase the product. In the case of adult education programs, this is when the potential learner enrolls in the course or the program. This step also involves the learner's participation in that program. This is where enrolling in an educational program is somewhat different than simply purchasing a product. Purchasing a consumer product such as a newspaper or magazine may be a quick, one-time event that results in the need being fulfilled and the customer moving on. Purchasing an educational product means that the consumer will also have to participate in the learning activity, and participation involves time commitment.

We can look at cost in a few different ways as well. Purchase decisions always involve some type of cost. That cost is often expressed in terms of money—tuition or fees, for example. Cost also can be represented in terms of time commitment. In a business, for example, an employee may sign up to participate in a course offered by the organization's HRD department. In this case, the purchase decision involves the commitment of the hours necessary to attend the program. The cost may be measured in terms of time away from the employee's job while that employee attends training.

Enrolling in an educational program may help the consumer to feel as if the need were starting to be met. If the program is a one-time learning activity, that need may be met relatively quickly. For an employee who enrolls in a day-long course on a specific computer program, the decision to purchase, participate, and evaluate could happen one time, in the course of a few hours. However, learning-related needs may not be met until the conclusion of the course, semester, or even degree program. The learner may evaluate the decision process (typically the last step in the model) after each course period, class, or entire program level. In this way, the purchase, participation, and evaluation processes can be seen as an ongoing loop that the learner is engaged in throughout the time period of the larger learning event.

Consumer Influences

None of the steps in the purchase process for any consumer happens in a vacuum. There are variables that influence the decision process at all levels. All influences are important for marketers to understand when developing strategies for reaching members of a potential target market for that organization's services.

There are three major types of influences on buyer behavior (Figure 6.6). Internal influences are things internal to the consumer. They include that consumer's self-esteem, personality, needs, attitudes, and motives for making the purchase decision. Social influences include the consumer's culture,

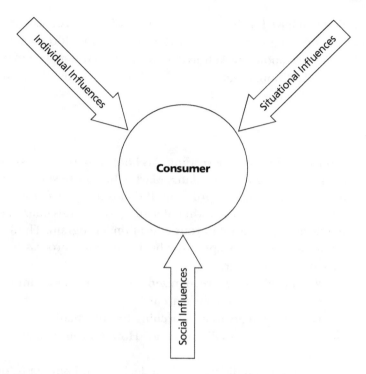

Figure 6.6 Consumer influences.

social status, social class, and reference groups. Situational influences include the physical location where the decision is made and how much time the consumer has to make the decision (Solomon & Stewart, 2000).

All of these influences have an effect on the purchase decision, however with regard to making decisions about educational program participation, internal and social influences are probably the most critical. Situational influences are more related to other types of purchasing decisions.

Chapter Summary

After having read this chapter, you should have a better understanding of what marketing is and how it can be used in the field of adult education. You should also understand how marketing strategies can relate to an organization's overall strategic plans and goals. This chapter on marketing started with a big-picture view of the concept and then drilled down into more specifics, including the marketing mix, product lifecycle, consumer behavior, and decision making.

Now that you have finished this chapter, revisit the three scenarios presented at the opening of the chapter. How would you address them now? What did you learn about marketing that would help you make more effective decisions? Additional marketing-related questions for discussion and debate are noted below.

DISCUSSION QUESTIONS

1. It is possible that you are reading this book as part of an assignment for a course you are taking. Maybe the course you are taking is part of a larger degree program. If that is the case, consider the decision process you used when deciding to take this course, or when deciding to enroll in your educational program. Think about each of the following steps in the buying decision process (for your course or degree program):
   – What problem was recognized, or what need was unfulfilled when you started your search?
   – How did you go about searching for information?
   – What alternatives did you find? How did you evaluate those alternatives?
   – At what point did you make a decision and purchase (or enroll)?
   – How do you feel about your decision to purchase or enroll?
   – What will you do in the future as a result of your evaluation of the current learning event? For example, will you continue in the same program, or consider other alternatives?
2. Consider an education-related decision you made. Maybe it was the decision to take a course, to attend a training session, or to enroll in a program of study. What were the internal, social, and situational influences that affected your decision-making process?
3. Consider the courses offered by your organization, or an organization with which you are familiar. What courses are in each of the four stages of the product lifecycle? Provide support for your decisions.
4. Consider the courses offered by your organization, or an organization with which you are familiar. Research the four price-related bullet points noted on page 130 of this chapter to learn the following:
   – What are expenses for the course?
   – What are others doing?
   – What will learners pay?
   – At what stage in the product lifecycle is the product?

5. What would your promotional mix be for each of the following (be sure to address all aspects of the promotional mix when addressing each scenario):
    - A nonprofit literacy center in a large urban environment
    - An organization in a midsized urban area focused on community health and wellness
    - The HRD department of a business interested in promoting a series of computer courses to its employees
    - A statewide association of adult educators looking to increase its membership

6. Revisit the three scenarios at the start of this chapter. From a marketing standpoint, what issues are problematic in each case? How would you address these issues?

7. Find a recent story in the news or in your industry or field related to marketing in adult education. How do the concepts in this chapter apply?

8. Debate the following topic: Viewing the learner as a customer is a necessary mindset to establish an effective marketing plan.

References

American Marketing Association. (AMA). (n.d.a). *Advertising*. Retrieved from https://www.ama.org/resources/Pages/Dictionary.aspx?dLetter=A

American Marketing Association. (AMA). (n.d.b). *Marketing*. Retrieved from http://www.marketingpower.com/_layouts/Dictionary.aspx?dLetter=M

American Marketing Association. (AMA). (n.d.c). *Opportunity cost*. Retrieved from https://www.ama.org/resources/Pages/Dictionary.aspx?dLetter=O

American Marketing Association. (AMA). (n.d.d). *Product mix*. Retrieved from http://www.marketingpower.com/_layouts/Dictionary.aspx?dLetter=P

American Marketing Association. (AMA). (n.d.e). *Promotional mix*. Retrieved from https://www.ama.org/resources/Pages/Dictionary.aspx?dLetter=P# promotion

American Marketing Association. (AMA). (n.d.f). *Public relations*. Retrieved from https://www.ama.org/resources/Pages/Dictionary.aspx?dLetter=P

American Marketing Association. (AMA). (n.d.g). *Sales promotions*. Retrieved from https://www.ama.org/resources/Pages/Dictionary.aspx?dLetter=S

Business Dictionary. (n.d.a). *Customer*. Retrieved from http://www.business dictionary.com/definition/consumer.html#ixzz3XsFDnmnl

Business Dictionary. (n.d.b). *Personal selling*. Retrieved from http://www.business dictionary.com/definition/personal-selling.html

Business Dictionary. (n.d.c). *Product*. Retrieved from http://www.business dictionary.com/definitin/poroduct.html

Business Dictionary. (n.d.d). *Promotion.* In Retrieved from http://www.business dictionary.com/definition/promotion.html

Hawkins, D., & Mothersbaugh, D. (2010). *Consumer behavior: Building marketing strategy.* Boston, MA: McGraw-Hill.

Harrington, K. (2014). On your mark...get set, market! *Forbes/Entrepreneurs.* Retrieved from http://www.forbes.com/sites/kevinharrington/2014/04/07/on-your-mark-get-set-market/

Inc. (n.d.). *Product life cycle.* Retrieved from http://www.inc.com/encyclopedia/product-life-cycle.html

Kotler, P., & Bloom, P. N. (1984). *Marketing professional services.* Englewood Cliffs, NJ: Prentice-Hall.

Lamb, C. W., Hair, J. F., Jr., & McDaniel, C. (2011). *Marketing.* Mason, OH: South-Western Cengage.

Levitt, T. (1981, May). Marketing intangible products and product intangibles. *Harvard Business Review.* Retrieved from https://hbr.org/1981/05/marketing-intangible-products-and-product-intangibles

Linton, I. (n.d.). What are the four types of business marketing utilities? *Small Business Chron.* Retrieved from http://smallbusiness.chron.com/four-types-business-marketing-utilities-20698.html

Mahmoud, O. (2007). The operation was a success but the patient died. Why research on innovation is successful yet innovations fail. In P. Mouncey & F. Wimmer (Eds.), *Market research best practice.* Hoboken, NJ: Wiley.

Merriam-Webster. (n.d.a). *Marketing.* Retrieved from http://www.merriam-webster.com/dictionary/marketing

Merriam-Webster. (n.d.b). *Profit.* Retrieved from http://www.merriam-webster.com/dictionary/profit

Merriam-Webster. (n.d.c). *Revenue.* Retrieved from http://www.merriam-webster.com/dictionary/revenue

Nielsen, L. (n.d.). The effect of sales promotion on sales volume. *Small Business Chron.* Retrieved from http://smallbusiness.chron.com/effect-sales-promotion-sales-volume-5051.html

Solomon, M. R., & Stuart, E. W. (2000). *Marketing: Real people, real choices.* Upper Saddle River, NJ: Prentice-Hall.

Weitz, B., & Wensley, R. (2002). *Handbook of marketing.* Thousand Oaks, CA: Sage.

Whalley, A. (2010). *Strategic marketing.* London, England: Bookboon.

7

Human Resources

The Importance of People

The following quote from the 2001 Harley-Davidson Motor Company Annual Report discusses the importance of people in organizations.

> At Harley-Davidson, our most valuable asset has always been our people—in fact, they represent our greatest sustainable competitive advantage in the marketplace. So we've created an environment of lifelong learning in which employees can develop the skills, knowledge and creativity that will allow them to grow as employees and as people. (p. 20)

Most organizations today maintain that same philosophy about the people who are involved in the work of the organization. If you were to review just about any corporate or organizational mission statement, you would see references to the importance of the organization's employees. People are an organization's most important asset, and they have great influence over the success (or failure) of the organization. In adult education organizations, those people may be employees and work for the organization full or part time. They might also be volunteers who are involved with the organization

Organization and Administration of Adult Education Programs, pages 145–167
Copyright © 2016 by Information Age Publishing
All rights of reproduction in any form reserved.

in varying degrees. They may work directly with learners or they might serve in administrative functions. People play many different roles in adult education organizations, and the management of people, or the organization's human resources, is a function that must be discussed in a book of this nature. Consider the following scenarios.

Jack was hired to fill a position in human resource management in a small nonprofit organization staffed by a combination of volunteers and a few salaried employees. The organization offers basic skills training to members of the community. One of his first duties is to develop a policies and procedures manual for the organization. During his preliminary investigations, he finds that some of the organization's current policies and procedures are written and formal, and others are unwritten and informal.

Robin is employed in the human resource management department of a large corporation. The human resource department of that organization is in charge of new employee orientations, but lately, survey data they have received from new employees attending the orientation has indicated that most believe the training is a waste of time. Robin is charged with investigating the issue.

Sarah recruits volunteer literacy trainers for her organization. Lately, she has had trouble recruiting qualified volunteers, and she thinks that her typical recruiting methods, including recruiting efforts at the local community college and through several church organizations, should be reviewed and new possibilities for recruitment should be identified.

Why Are Human Resources Important to Adult Educators?

In order to operate successful adult education programs, organizations must have the correct people with the correct knowledge, skills, and abilities, doing jobs that they are capable of doing (and hopefully jobs that they enjoy and are motivated to do well). Those people must also be in the right places at the right times in order to provide service to learners. Getting the right people in the right places with the right skills at the right times does not just happen. It takes preparation, focus, and hard work, and that is why human resource management (HRM) must be a focus of program administrators.

As noted earlier, people involved in working in adult education programs may be volunteers or they may be employees (or some combination thereof). HRM-related duties, policies, and procedures should not apply only to employees of the organization. Organizations that rely on both employees and volunteers may have separate policies and procedures for each group. There may be many different levels or categories of volunteers to be accounted for in HRM-related policies and procedures as well. Consider the manager of community health and wellness programs for a healthcare system in a largely rural area. That manager may have a small staff of program planners and instructors who facilitate health and wellness-related programs for those in the communities in which the healthcare system has clinics and hospitals. These may be paid employees of the healthcare system. The manager may have a core group of 5–7 volunteers that dedicate several hours each week to the organization, and work alongside the organization's paid employees. That manager might also have developed a group of volunteers within the community that she can call upon several times per year to help with major initiatives such as wellness fairs and larger community events. Other volunteers may be physicians and subject-matter experts who work for the healthcare system but who volunteer to teach classes in the program. While it may not be necessary to develop separate HRM policies and procedures for each of these groups, it is easy to see where the HRM function can become complicated in adult education organizations.

Chapter Overview

This chapter presents basic human resource functions that those in adult education–related organizations should understand. It begins with an overview of the topic of human resource management and moves into discussion of five main human resource functions. Each of those five main functions is then presented in more detail.

What Is Human Resource Management?

"Human resource management (HRM) refers to the policies, practices, and systems that influence employees' behavior, attitudes, and performance. Many companies refer to HRM as involving 'people practices'" (Noe, Hollenbeck, Gerhart, & Wright, 2010, p. 4). "Human resource management is the general term for all of the functions encompassed in the acquisition, retention, development, and administration of a company's employees (Holihan, 2006, p. 13). Sometimes the terms *human resource management* and *human resource development* (HRD) are confused. Human resource development is an aspect or subsection of the overall human resource management concept. It encompasses the training and development of individuals in an organization. As such, human resource development employees and departments can often be found within larger departments of human resource management.

There are a lot of specific subject areas that fall under the larger umbrella of HRM. Many different programs of study in higher education, as well as thousands of books, articles, and websites, are devoted to the various aspects of HRM. Despite the wide variety of works published on the subject, there are core categories or functions of HRM that most in the discipline agree upon, although various authors present those main functions in different ways. The Small Business Chronicle identifies six core functions: recruitment, safety, employee relations, compensation and benefits, compliance, and training and development (Small Business Chron, n.d.). Rao (2010) identifies five core functions, including employment, human resource development, compensation, and employee relations. Sims (2007) identifies eight: strategic management, recruiting and selecting employees, training and development, performance appraisals, career development, compensation, safety, and labor relations. We have arranged the core functions of HRM into five categories (Figure 7.1).

The core functions of HRM that will be discussed in this chapter as follows:

1. **Policies and procedures:** The development of policies for the organization, including policies related to hiring, compensation, performance review and appraisal, discipline and termination, and safety fall into this category. Also included here are employee benefits such as vacation and sick time policies and services such as employee assistance programs.
2. **Recruiting and hiring:** This function includes the analysis of work-related needs and the development of positions and job descriptions. Also included in recruitment and hiring are résumé screening, interviewing, and making hiring decisions.
3. **Orientation and training:** Once a candidate has been selected, that candidate must be provided with an orientation to the organization as well as job-specific training. Ongoing training and development for existing employees also fall into this category. Most of you who

---

Core Functions of Human Resources

1. Policies and Procedures
2. Recruiting and Hiring
3. Orientation and Training
4. Records Maintenance and Legal Compliance
5. Strategic Planning

Figure 7.1 Human resource functions.

are reading this book are involved in adult education in one way or another, so this part of the HRM function may be familiar to you.

4. **Records, maintenance, and legal compliance:** Records related to employees, including personnel files, are included here. Also included in this section is information about compliance with legal requirements, including safety, employment law, and tax law.

5. **Strategic planning:** The HRM function of an organization must be focused on the human resource-related needs of the organization today, but they also must be involved in the strategic planning process of the overall organization so it is prepared to serve the organization effectively in the future.

While the above list is extensive, depending on the size of the adult education organization, many of these duties may be carried out by one or two people. The degree to which the five items noted above are formal or informal does depend to some extent on the size and scope of the organization. Smaller organizations may not formalize some of the items listed above (although even informal policies and procedures and standards can be documented). Some adult education organizations have only one or two employees, so those functions can be easily managed. Other organizations may have an employee or a group of employees who work on HR-related issues. The number of people involved and the formality of the documentation depends on a variety of factors related to the organization itself.

Policies and Procedures

Policies and procedures are designed to influence and determine all major decisions and actions, and all activities (that) take place within the boundaries set by them. Together, policies and procedures ensure that a point of view held by the governing body of the organization is translated into steps that result in an outcome compatible with that view. (Business Dictionary, n.d.)

An organization's policies and procedures help set guidelines for how people perform their jobs and for what they can and cannot do while they are working at the organization. An organization's policies and procedures provide the framework for action within the organization. Well-documented policies and procedures save time and eliminates the necessity of continually having to explain what an organization does in a given situation. They also provide for consistency from one person to the next and hopefully prevent situations in which people in an organization are treated differently in response to the same issue.

Policies Versus Procedures

Policy—a statement, rule, or guideline

Procedure—A series of steps or a process

Figure 7.2 Policies and procedures.

Those working in the field of HRM may not only be responsible for the development of policies and procedures, they may also be responsible for implementation of policies. For example, a policy involving employee relations can involve the administration of a yearly survey to all employees of the organization. This survey may be administrated by an employee in the HRM department. Or, based on an organizational policy, someone in HRM may be in charge of mediating disputes between employees and supervisors.

Policies and procedures may apply to an organization's volunteers as well as its employees. Some policies and procedures may be the same for both employees and volunteers, or they may be different for each group. Both are important, as Pynes (2013) notes: "Managing volunteer programs requires the development of HRM policies and procedures to assist with the integration of volunteers into the agency's everyday operations" (p. 378). Policies and procedures are often discussed together, but in numerous ways they are different. Therefore the two will be examined separately in the section that follows.

Policies

"A policy is a statement of how an organization intends to deal with an issue. A key element of a policy is that it is a predetermined guideline providing a specified course of action for dealing with prescribed circumstances" (Hubbartt, 1992, p. 4). Policies can include information that relates to many different topics. Human resource-related policies can cover specific topics such as recruitment and hiring, benefits, job classification, compensation, conditions of employment, discipline, dispute or grievance resolution, diversity, employee leave, performance management, employee separation, training and development, and work records and reports. Formally written policies can be as brief as one sentence or they can include numerous details and span several pages. A policy relating to hours of operation may be as simple as the following: "The Neighborhood Literacy Society is open for business from Tuesday through Sunday between the hours of 12 noon and 5:00 p.m." Additionally, an organization's policy on employee pay may read like the following: "Employees are paid on the first and the 15th day of each month." Other policies may be more extensive than the examples above. Some policies, especially those relating to employment, may be based on certain laws, while others may be based on standards the organization has created itself. Many policies evolve from ongoing practice that becomes standard operating procedure (Hubbartt, 1992).

As noted earlier, an organization may have differing policies for multiple classifications of people who are involved with the organization. Some policies for employees may be different from those for volunteers within the organization. A policy regarding volunteers may read as follows: "All volunteers must successfully complete three hours of training before they are allowed to work with clients." The same organization may hire employees with the skills necessary to work with clients, so the aforementioned training policy for volunteers may not be necessary for the organization's employees. Some policies are applicable to all employees (or all volunteers) in an organization, and others can be specific to all personnel who work within a certain department or division of the organization.

While an organization's policies are, by their nature, stable, they are not necessarily set in stone or unchangeable. A policy may change based on changes/amendments to laws, changes in best practices for the organization's industry, changes in the organization's operating environment, or changes in the organization's structure. Policies may change based on societal trends as well. For example, many organizations are altering their benefits policies in direct response to the specific needs of transgender employees. As the number of people working or volunteering for an organization grows, so too does the need for a set of organizational policies. Also, the larger an organization gets, the more need there may be for a manual or handbook that includes all of its policies. Hubbartt (1992) notes that a comprehensive policy handbook includes the following topics:

1. Hiring, promotion, and other employment policies;
2. Work hours, employee schedules, and attendance;
3. Leaves of absence;
4. Pay, performance, and other compensation;
5. Discipline, discharge, retirements, and other separations;
6. Holidays, vacations, and other employee benefits;
7. Electronic communication, telephone, dress code, and related administrative issues;
8. Safety and security; and
9. Substance abuse, disability accommodation, and similar topics.

The process of developing policies starts at the top, or senior levels of the organization. "It is crucial to have senior management support, especially where policies relate to employee behavior. The endorsement and modeling of the behavior by the CEO, senior managers, and supervisors will encourage staff to take the policies seriously" (NSW Industrial Relations, 2013, p. 2). Planning potential policies involves careful consideration about how and when they may be applied. As part of that planning process, benchmarking other organizations, examining best practices, and conducting research on the topics themselves are critical. When writing drafts of potential policies, be sure key/important terms are carefully defined, and be clear which individuals the policies apply to. Also consider contingency plans for situations in which policies cannot be adhered to, and consider ways violations of policies should be addressed. Policies should be clear and written simply in plain language. Also, they might have to be translated into multiple languages for employees or volunteers for whom English is a second language.

Implementation of a policy involves communication with employees and/or volunteers. Information on each policy should be readily available to those within the organization it affects. After implementation, ongoing review of the policy should take place, and ongoing efforts should be made to ensure compliance with the policy (NSW Industrial Relations, 2013).

Procedures

While procedures are related to policies, they are different from policies in several ways. Procedures are "the steps a team takes to complete an action" (Peabody, 1996, p. 24). "Procedures are the specific methods employed to express policies in action in day-to-day operations of the organization" (Business Dictionary n.d.). Several concepts are important in this definition. Procedures are steps that are taken toward a goal or final point (as opposed to policies, which are rules or guidelines). Actions on procedures start with a "trigger," which indicates that the procedure should start. They end with a "target," which is the last step or ending point in the procedure (Peabody, 1996). As stated previously, some procedures involve multiple people in multiple departments or areas of an organization, whereas others are limited to one person in one area of the organization. Like policies, standardized and documented procedures can help make an organization more efficient, and they can help save valuable time and resources. Policies often include procedural steps and processes. A health and wellness organization, for example, might have a policy on vacation time for its employees. Within that policy may be a procedure for requesting vacation time that employees complete when they want to take vacation days. A policy on continuing professional development also might include forms employees or volunteers may need to complete to request time and resources for those types of activities.

Procedures are necessary in organizations for the same reasons policies are necessary. They provide a map or layout of a task so each person in the organization subject to following the procedure comes to a common end. They allow for efficiency, consistency, and equal treatment of people in organizations.

In order to be effective and consistent, procedures must be documented properly. The documenting of procedures is something many of us in adult education are familiar with, as that type of documentation is often used for training purposes. Documenting procedures starts with compiling the individual steps or activities that, together, compose the procedure. This may involve observing steps in the process, interviewing those involved, probing for detail, clarifying ambiguities, examining data, mapping and diagramming, and making conclusions. The end result is the documentation of a procedure that can be used by all individuals within the organization going forward.

The development of procedures also includes information supplementary to the procedure itself. The responsible person or department may be included in the documentation of a procedure. Time frames and time limitations for the completion of steps in the procedure may also be included, as may be forms, tools, equipment, or other resources necessary for the completion of the step in the procedure. This documentation is often done created using flowchart software.

Policies and Procedures in Program Administration

Administrators of adult education programs may have several responsibilities related to the organization's policies and procedures. They may help develop those policies and procedures, and they may be charged with documenting them. The development of policies and procedures may take a substantial amount of time, energy, and skill. That development "requires strong decision-making skills, the ability to think ethically, and a broad understanding of business activities that will be covered (by the policies and procedures)" (Noe et al., 2011, p. 11). Developing a set of policies and procedures can be well worth the time spent doing so.

Program administrators may also be charged with the communication of those policies and procedures to new employees and/or volunteers. This may be done using social media, by giving presentations at meetings, by posting documents online and on employee bulletin boards, and in other ways (Noe et al., 2011, p. 11). Policies and procedures manuals can be given to new employees on their first day of employment, only to be put in desk drawers and never referenced again. That's why the way in which policies and procedures are presented to the employee should be in line with the number of each and the needs of the employee. There are many creative ways to communicate policies and procedures to employees. While there should be a central place in which all are located, the ways in which policies and procedures are communicated can be varied.

Recruiting and Hiring

When the average person thinks about human resources, they probably associate it most closely with the recruiting and hiring of employees. Recruitment and hiring is only one function of human resource management, but it is an important one. Also, recruitment and hiring is more complex than simply placing ads, interviewing people, and hiring those deemed most qualified. The hiring process is one that starts long before the search for candidates begins. It starts with planning for the needs of the organization. There are many different models that illustrate steps in the hiring process. Following is an example of one series of steps that we have developed (Figure 7.3). It can give you an idea of how the process might work.

Most organizations have a series of policies and procedures regarding employment and recruiting (one of the reasons why policies and procedures were discussed in the beginning of this chapter). If the program administrator's organization does not have them, they should consider developing some policies and procedures regarding the hiring of employees and the recruitment of volunteers as well.

All organizations have (or should have) strategies, plans, and objectives that form the basis for their short- and long-term operations. This is true for businesses, nonprofits, and even volunteer-based organizations. That plan, whether simple or complex, can form the basis for people-related decisions. In other words, an organization's business plan should be the basis for the organization's work plan. The work plan determines the workforce needed (Cascio, 2013).

Based on the organization's plans, decisions or forecasts about the "people needs" of the organization can be made. Those decisions may include the number and types of people needed, the qualifications of those people, and the time frame for which they are needed. Other issues to be

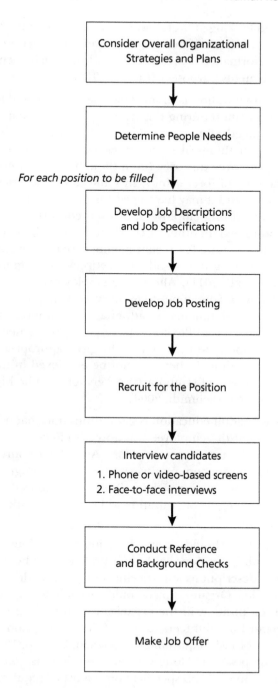

Figure 7.3 The hiring process.

considered when looking at overall workforce needs include how positions interact and work with each other, how training for each position is conducted, how performance is measured, and how much each job is worth (for salary and benefits purposes) (Cascio, 2013).

Unless the organization is brand new, the existing workforce must be taken into consideration during this type of planning. That means that in addition to new needs, forecasters must look at their existing workforce. They must consider things like employees who will be retiring, and they must allow for employee turnover (even though they may not have definitive data at the time of forecasting). In some cases, the organization may find itself growing, and it may have need for new employees (or they may offer overtime to existing employees, or even convert part-time positions into full-time positions). In other cases, when organizations are downsizing, they may find they require fewer staff members than they current employ. In these cases, reducing hours and early retirement programs may be investigated (Noe et al., 2011). Alternative employment arrangements can be considered as well. Sometimes temporary workers can be brought in to work on short-term assignments. An advantage of temporary workers is that the organization has more flexibility to respond to the needs of customers. However, temporary workers have to be given appropriate training for their positions even though they may not be employed in those positions for long. Also, turnover of temporary workers tends to be higher than for permanent employees (Schmidt, 2004).

In many cases, adult education organizations find that using volunteer help to complement the employee workforce is effective. Literacy organizations, for example, use volunteer tutors. An AIDS resource center may use volunteer trainers for community-based awareness programs. Volunteer needs can be examined as part of the staffing analysis as well. Once this type of analysis is complete, the organization will have a good idea of its staffing needs for the future.

The organization should already have job descriptions and job specifications for existing positions (although updates may be required), and at this point job descriptions and specifications can be developed for new positions to be filled. Organizations should have job descriptions and specifications for each position in the organization. It is helpful to have both of these on hand for volunteers as well. A job description is "an overall written summary of task requirements" (Cascio, 2013, p. 169) that are associated with the position. Along with job descriptions, job specifications may also be developed. A job specification is a list of requirements for the person who fills the position. An emphasis on minimum qualifications (for the position) are important to note here. "Job specifications should reflect

---

Elements of a Job Posting

1. Job Description Summary
2. Job Specification Summary
3. Application Instructions

Figure 7.4 Job postings.

minimally acceptable qualifications for job incumbents. Frequently they do not, reflecting instead a profile of ideal job components" (Cascio, 2013, p. 169). Job descriptions and specifications can be created by those who know the most about the position(s). Those people may include the position's supervisor, people already doing portions of the job, and human resource specialists.

Both job descriptions and job specifications can be used during the hiring process. Typically, job postings consist of elements of both the job description and specifications (Pynes, 2013). The job posting is what is used to attract potential employees as part of the recruitment process. The posting also instructs potential candidates how to apply for the position. Some organizations require that all applicants complete an application form, while others require only the submission of a résumé. Some require both. For some positions, examples of previous work may be required also (Figure 7.4).

The Recruitment Process

The process of recruiting employees can start when the job posting is complete. "Recruiting consists of any practice or activity carried on by the organization with the primary purpose of identifying and attracting potential employees" (Noe et al., 2011, p. 143). Recruitment "demands serious attention from management because any business strategy will falter without the talent to execute it" (Cascio, 2013, p. 200). At this point, an organization has several options for recruitment. The organization may focus on internal methods such as postings on employee bulletin boards or organization websites. They may consider existing employees or existing volunteers to fill open positions. Sometimes existing employees or volunteers may refer external candidates for open positions. External methods of recruitment are also used. They may include ads in periodicals, trade journals, online job sites, employment agencies, and college and university recruitment websites (among others) (Noe et al., 2011).

The process of recruitment should result in a pool of qualified applicants for the position. At this point, the selection process starts. The goal of the selection process is to narrow down the pool of applications to a point at which one candidate is selected for the position. Selection begins with an initial screening of all applications.

There will undoubtedly be people who apply who are not at all qualified for the position being advertised despite how clear the requirements within the job posting are. During this initial screening process, those applications are eliminated. The initial pool is narrowed down to qualified applicants. Applications that have passed the initial screening process are then examined more carefully, often by several people in the organization. Those reviewers typically come up with a list of people who are to be interviewed for the position.

There are several types of interviews that can be conducted at this point. If there is a large number of applicants at this stage of the process, the organization may want to consider telephone or Skype interviews as the next step. These types of interviews can be short—10 to 15 minutes each—and they may provide additional information that is helpful to those in the organization filling the position. Sometimes a candidate's résumé or application does not address an important point or qualification for the position. Other times the content on the application may cause one of the reviewers to further question something about the candidate. If someone in the organization has a few key questions for a potential job candidate but does not want to bring that candidate in for a formal face-to-face interview, the use of telephone or Skype interviews is a good intermediary step.

Application reviewers may also wish to examine examples of an applicant's previous work. If they are not requested as part of the initial application process, reviewers may ask for work samples at this point in the process. A review of work samples and short interviews with applicants via phone or Skype can help reviewers determine which candidates to include within the next step in the process.

After telephone/Skype interviews are completed and several people in the organization have reviewed applications, the pool can be narrowed even further. At this point, face-to-face interviews can be scheduled. The number of face-to-face interviews scheduled for any given position depends on the number of qualified candidates who have gotten to this step in the process and the time constraints of those in the organization who will be conducting interviews. How many candidate interviews is enough? That's a difficult question to answer. For some positions, three to five candidates is optimal. In other cases, interviewers may want to bring in seven or eight candidates. All those involved in the process should be comfortable that they have enough interviews scheduled so they can pick the best candidate for the job from those they interview.

Legal Aspects of Recruitment

As noted earlier in this section, organizations typically have policies and procedures that deal with the recruitment and hiring of employees. It is important to remember that there are also many laws (at many different levels) that govern the recruitment and hiring processes. Organizations that hire employees must be aware of all of these laws and legal standards, and they must pay close attention to be sure they are in compliance with them throughout the hiring process (and when dealing with issues regarding potential and existing employees, in general). The chapter on legal and ethical issues discusses these topics in more detail.

The Interview Process

In order to be fair and accurate in assessing candidates, the same process should be used when interviewing all candidates for a particular position. The same overall set of questions should be asked, the same people should be involved, and the same general schedule should be used. As part of the interview process, some organizations ask candidates to perform tasks, such as in-box exercises and prioritization-type activities, which demonstrate how the candidate may perform in certain situations. Aptitude tests and/or personality tests may also be required. The same exercises or activities should be given to all candidates. The same information should be provided to each candidate as well (Pynes, 2013). Remember that the interview process is a two-way street. The organization is looking for the best candidate for the job, but the interviewee is also looking for the best organization for which to work. A good match between interviewee and organization is one in which both are happy with the outcome of the interview.

Job interviews can be nerve-racking, so it is important to put the candidate at ease during the interview process, especially at the beginning of the process. Having a few general questions prepared to break the ice is a good way to start. It may be best for the interviewer to start with some general information about the company and the position and then work into a discussion of specifics as they relate to the job.

Interview questions should be open-ended, and they should allow for the candidate to respond in detail about his/her qualifications. Remember that the person being interviewed should be the person talking the most. Interviewers sometimes have a tendency to dominate conversations in interviews, which makes it difficult to learn about the candidate. Be sure questions that address the candidate's knowledge, skills, and abilities are addressed. Interviewers should pay attention to both verbal and nonverbal cues as well. Did the candidate arrive on time? Was he/she properly dressed for the interview? Did the candidate seem interested in the position? All of these things should be considered as part of the hiring process.

Be sure to allow the candidate time to ask questions. Remember that the interviewer is selling his/her organization to the candidate as much as the candidate is selling him/herself to the organization. Sometimes the questions asked by the candidate can tell the interviewer a lot about the candidate's interest in the position. Be prepared to share the next steps within the process with each candidate. Discuss timelines so the candidate has an idea of when to expect to hear from the interviewer (Entrepreneur, 2013).

After each interview, compare notes with the others in the organization who participated in the interview process. If multiple candidates are being interviewed throughout several days or weeks, make notes that will ensure all candidates are evaluated using the same criteria (Pynes, 2013). It is easy to forget what a candidate said several weeks ago, so taking notes during the interview is crucial.

After the interview process is complete, reference checks and background checks should be conducted. Based on all of the information gathered to that point, all involved with the hiring process should meet, and a decision should be made regarding the best candidate for the position. Ideally the process does result in a best candidate (or candidates, as it may be the case that there is more than one good candidate). Unfortunately, sometimes the recruiting process does not result in any consensus about the best candidate for the position. In these cases, it is important to review the process and the documentation surrounding the position (such as the job description, job summary, and job posting) to determine where mistakes were made or where the process fell off track. Appropriate fixes can be made and the process can be repeated if necessary.

When the best candidate for the position is identified, a formal job offer can be made. When (or if) it is accepted, details regarding the candidate's employment can be addressed and negotiated. After a candidate accepts the job, remember to contact the other candidates to let them know the position has been filled. Too often, this step in the process is ignored, which does not portray the organization in a positive light. Remember that applicants who were not good fits for one position may be excellent candidates for another. Do not burn any bridges at this point in the process.

Volunteer Recruitment

There are many similarities between recruiting employees and recruiting volunteers. Just as the organization's strategic plan guides the hiring and recruitment strategies for employees, it should be considered when assessing and planning for an organization's volunteer needs. Many organizations do not consider the planning of volunteer needs at the strategic level, but efficient and effective use of volunteers starts with an examination of the organization's overall mission and strategic plan (Tsruda, 2014).

Once volunteer need has been assessed, job descriptions and specifications can be developed for volunteer positions. Volunteers can be recruited using similar channels as recruitment for employees. However, the employer/employee relationship is different than the organization/volunteer relationship. Volunteers, by definition, do not receive payment (in the form of salary and benefits) for their work. Because of this difference, an organization has to market itself to potential volunteers. That entails first developing job descriptions and specifications so the qualifications for the volunteer positions are clear. This helps the organization look for people who have the proper knowledge, skills, and abilities for the position. Once volunteer job descriptions and specifications are developed, the organization can begin marketing itself to potential volunteers. This involves understanding what the organization has to offer to potential volunteers and then marketing those benefits. "Volunteer positions—and the marketing of them—should specify the unique benefits of working with your organization, particular benefits that correspond to people's motivators" (Tsruda, 2014). There are many reasons why people volunteer at organizations. They include "the need for experience, connections, achievement, personal rewards, social approval, and expression of personal values" (Tsruda, 2014). How the organization can meet these types of needs should be considered when recruiting volunteers. To be considered as well are specifics about the particular organization that potential volunteers might find appealing. Working with fun and interesting people, being part of a larger team, and doing meaningful work are all benefits that can be presented to potential volunteers as part of marketing efforts to attract volunteer help.

Recruitment of volunteers should also involve communicating the organization's obligations to volunteers while they are working. For example, volunteers are typically covered under an organization's liability insurance and they are covered under the organization's workers compensation policies as well (Pyne, 2013). This type of information should be understood by all volunteers.

Orientation and Training

The orientation and training components of the human resource function involve working with employees and volunteers to make sure they know their roles and responsibilities in the organization. Both initial job training for new employees and volunteers and ongoing training and development for existing employees and volunteers falls under this broad function.

Employee and Volunteer Orientation

It is natural to talk about the human resource function of orientation and training after a discussion of the recruitment and hiring processes, because soon after a new employee is hired, the employee should be provided with a new-employee orientation. However, some organizations, even those involved in adult education, fail to provide new employees with the orientation they need in order to be successful on the job. Sometimes orientations are unstructured and are conducted on the fly, or they are conducted by employees who do not have the educational background or communication skills required to conduct an effective orientation. In some cases, there is a gap between the ideal and the actual, and the "rosy picture" painted within an orientation does not reflect the realities of the workplace. In some cases, new employees arrive at their first day on the job only to find that existing employees do not have the time to orient or train them. The results of poorly conducted orientations can be such that the new employee feels more confused after the orientation than before it. Lack of any sort of orientation is also problematic. A new employee excited to begin a new job can become disillusioned with the organization very quickly with improper treatment in his or her first few hours on the job (Schmidt & Akdere, 2007).

New employee orientations, regardless of the size of the organization, should be conducted in a deliberate and organized manner by employees with the skills to do so. Everyone who will be interacting with the new employee should be made aware of the date the new employee starts work. Introductions should be made early in the orientation, and the new employee should be made to feel comfortable and welcome. Orientation is also an appropriate time for new employees to complete HR-related paperwork, including tax forms, insurance forms, and other personnel forms.

The same is true for new volunteers in an organization. While volunteer orientations may not be exactly the same as new employee orientations, it is important to remember that volunteers are part of the organization, just like paid employees. The people who the adult education organization serves may not know the difference between that organization's employees and volunteers. Anyone associated with the organization represents that organization, and he or she should have the knowledge and skills to be able to do so. Orientations are important first steps in the development of that knowledge and those skills (Schmidt, 2004).

Employee and Volunteer Training

While orientation for new employees or new volunteers is conducted at the start of that employee or volunteer's working relationship with the organization, training and development-related activities for current employees and volunteers should be ongoing. While new employee or volunteer orientations may be similar regardless of the position being filled by the employee or volunteer, job-specific training should be customized for each position in the organization. All organizations should have plans in place for the training of new employees and volunteers within all positions. Plans for ongoing training and professional development should also be in place, although those plans may be more flexible than initial training, as they may depend more in the individual needs of each employee or volunteer (Schmidt, 2004).

Because this is a book on the organization and administration of adult education programs, you probably already understand the importance of employee and volunteer training. As noted earlier, however, many organizations' internal practices may be inconsistent with their overall missions. Some organizations focus so much attention on the learners or customers they serve they neglect those employees or volunteers who consistently serve the learners. As administrators of adult education programs, it is important to provide opportunities for learning and growth to employees and volunteers so they can continually improve how they provide service to the organization's learners.

Records Maintenance and Legal Compliance

Records maintenance and legal compliance is appropriate as a next step in the discussion of core HRM functions for administrators of adult education programs, because those topics are related to both orientation and training as well as policies and procedures. Employee and volunteer records for training and orientation are among many types of records that HRM departments keep for an organization's employees. HRM also involves the keeping of records to show that the organization is in compliance with laws at all levels.

Records Maintenance

A main component of human resource-related records maintenance deals with the employee personnel file. An employee's personnel file should include all job-specific records pertaining to that employee from the time the employee applies to the organization to the time the employee leaves the organization. While contents may vary, personnel files typically include the employee's initial application form, tax and employment records, records of employee reviews, information about disciplinary action, pay information, and training records (SHRM, 2015). Items not specifically related to the employee's job should not be kept in a personnel file:

> Any record that includes protected and/or non-job related information such as date of birth, marital status, dependent information, SSNs, medical information, immigration status, national origin, race, gender, religion, sexual orientation, criminal history, financial history, subjective statements or accusations, etc., should be filed separately from a personnel file. (SHRM, 2015)

Because much of this information is confidential, personnel files should be stored in a secure area, and they should be accessible only to those authorized to see them. Volunteers may also have a human resource file, although the information included in volunteer files may be different from the information for employees.

Legal Compliance

A variety of laws on many different levels governs the types of law-compliance records kept by those in HRM. For example, the US Department of Labor requires organizations to keep records on employees. Failure to comply with legal regulations (and the recordkeeping associated with these regulations) can have serious consequences for an organization. Compliance with the law is covered in more detail in the Legal and Ethical Issues chapter of this book.

Strategic Planning

The fourth key function of HRM is involvement in the organization's overall strategic planning process. As noted earlier, the organization's strategic plan should drive the HRM efforts of the organization. This means that those involved with HRM should be directly involved with overall strategic planning efforts. The strategic planning process is covered in more detail in the Strategic Planning chapter.

Chapter Summary

The importance of people to an organization was highlighted at the start of this chapter. The HRM function of an organization deals with the people-related issues that organizations must be prepared to manage. By now you should have a good understanding that these functions go far beyond the hiring process and that they involve both the organization's employees and volunteers.

Some adult education program administrators deal with HRM issues more than others. This is especially true of education departments that are part of larger organizations. Consider the manager of community health and wellness programs for a healthcare system that was discussed in the opening pages of this chapter. That administrator might not deal much with HRM issues, as those issues may be managed by the hospital's HRM department. The same can be said for HRD professionals in business and industry. A separate department may handle all of the organization's HRM-related issues. In some smaller organizations, such as a nonprofit community-based organization that provides English lessons for non-English speakers, the HRM function might be managed by the organization's director, who may also be in charge of administering the organization's educational programs. In these cases, volunteers can be charged with some HRM-related duties, such as orientation and training of new employees or volunteers (although it is important to note that some HRM issues, including those related to personnel and legal topics, should not be handled by volunteers).

The five core functions of HRM—policies and procedures, recruitment and hiring, training and development, records management and legal compliance, and strategic planning—have direct effects on the employees and volunteers of the organization. If these functions are designed and administered fairly, the result can be satisfied employees and volunteers. Alternatively, if they are inconsistent or poorly designed and executed, they can cost the organization a great deal.

QUESTIONS FOR DISCUSSION

1. Address the three scenarios noted at the start of this chapter. Put together a plan of action for each of the three people in the scenarios.
2. Which of the five core HRM functions are you most familiar with? Which are new to you? Which of the four core HRM functions does your organization do well? Which need improvement?

3. Discuss some policies in your organization. What areas or topics are covered by those policies? What areas are not covered? How formal are the policies in your organization?

4. If your organization depends on volunteers to function, does it have policies for volunteers? What makes up those policies? How are they different from policies for employees?

5. Consider some of the procedures in your organization. What are the policies that correspond to those procedures?

6. How are procedures at your organization documented?

7. What types of procedures is your organization lacking?

8. How does your organization manage and conduct new employee orientations? What are the specific elements of a new employee orientation at your organization?

9. What type of orientation for volunteers does your organization provide? How is it similar to or different from employee orientation?

10. What types of plans does your organization have in place for the job-specific training of new employees and volunteers? What does that training entail?

11. What types of records does your organization keep for its employees? What types of records does your organization keep for its volunteers?

12. What (if any) special issues regarding legal compliance does your organization have to manage?

13. How might HRM functions in an organization that relies mostly on volunteers be different from those of an organization staffed mostly by paid employees?

References

Business Dictionary. (n.d.). *Policies and procedures.* Retrieved from http://www.businessdictionary.com/definition/policies-and-procedures.html

Cascio, W. F. (2013). *Managing human resources.* New York, NY: McGraw-Hill/Irwin.

Entrepreneur. (2013). *How to conduct an interview effectively.* Retrieved from http://www.entrepreneur.com/article/225960

Harley-Davidson Motor Company. (2001). *Annual report.* Milwaukee, WI: Author.

Holihan, M. B. (2006). *365 answers about human resources for the small business owner.* Ocala, FL: Atlantic.

Hubbartt, W. S. (1992). *Personnel policy handbook.* New York, NY: McGraw-Hill.

Noe, R. A., Hollenbeck, J. R., Gerhart, B., & Wright, P. M. (2010). *Fundamentals of human resource management.* New York, NY: McGraw-Hill.

NSW Industrial Relations. (2013). *Workplace policies and procedures.* Retrieved from http://www.industrialrelations.nsw.gov.au/biz_res/oirwww/pdfs/workplace_pp.pdf

Peabody, L. (1996). *How to write policies, procedures, and task outlines.* Lacey, WA: Writing Services.

Pynes, J. E. (2013). *Human resource management for public and nonprofit organizations* (4th ed.). San Francisco, CA: Jossey-Bass.

Rao, P. S. (2010). *Human resource management: Text and cases.* Mumbai, India: Himalaya.

Schmidt, S. W. (2004). The relationship between job training satisfaction and overall job satisfaction among employees in customer contact positions (Doctoral dissertation). University of Wisconsin, Milwaukee.

Schmidt, S. W., & Akdere, M. (2007). Measuring the effects of employee orientation training on employee perceptions of vision and leadership: Implications for human resources. *The Business Review, Cambridge, 7*(1), 322–327.

Sims, R. R. (2007). *Contemporary human resource management.* Charlotte, NC: Information Age.

Small Business Chronicle. (n.d.). *Six main functions of a human resource department.* Retrieved from http://smallbusiness.chron.com/six-main-functions -human-resource-department-60693.html

Society for Human Resource Management (SHRM). (2015, March 17). *Personnel records: What should, and what should not, be included in the personnel file.* Retrieved from https://www.shrm.org/templatestools/hrqa/pages/includedinpersonnelfile.aspx

Tsruda, L. (2014, February 13). Preparing your nonprofit to recruit volunteers. *Third Sector New England.* Retrieved from http://www.tsne.org/site/c. ghLUK3PCLoF/b.6367587/k.AF95/Articles_Preparing_Your_Nonprofit _Organization_to_Recruit_Volunteers.htm

8

Strategic Planning

Is All Planning Strategic?

Strategic planning has become a common practice in business for a variety of reasons. Most businesses exist in competitive environments that are continually changing and adapting to conditions in the marketplace. New products and services are introduced to the marketplace every day, and customers continue to have an ever-expanding variety of choices and options available to them. New businesses are opening and existing businesses are expanding and focusing on new customers as well. Conversely, many businesses close/shut down every day for a variety of reasons. Some close because their products are no longer in demand, and others go out of business because owners elect to do something else. Sometimes businesses close simply because of poor planning. The Bureau of Labor Statistics' data showed that less than half the new businesses started between 1994 and 2005 remained open past six years (Bureau of Labor Statistics, n.d.).

There are many things that separate organizations that succeed from those that fail. Planning is one of those things. Strategic planning

Organization and Administration of Adult Education Programs, pages 169–199
Copyright © 2016 by Information Age Publishing
All rights of reproduction in any form reserved.

does not guarantee success, but it can help organizations be successful (Bryson, 2011).

Notice in the above paragraph, we progress from using the term *business* to use of the term *organization*. Strategic planning today is not limited to the business world. Some organizations that provide adult education are businesses or are divisions of a larger business (such as a department that focuses on human resource development [HRD] in a manufacturing company). Many types of organizations, including those that provide adult education, benefit by engaging in the process of ongoing strategic planning. Volunteer-based organizations, such as clubs, service organizations, and various associations, should be planning strategically in order to ensure long-term survival as well.

To get back to the original question, and the heading for this section, it makes sense to ask, Shouldn't all planning be strategic? The contrary would imply that some types of planning are not strategic, and this might imply that nonstrategic planning is synonymous with poor planning. In reality, while all plans should be strategic in nature, not all planning is strategic planning. Strategic planning is different from the type of planning inherent within day-to-day organizational decisions. Those differences will be discussed in the next section. Consider the following scenarios.

Pamela manages a community-based literacy organization. She was recently promoted to manager of her organization when the former manager left. That manager wanted to do some strategic planning, but he never found the time to get started. Pamela believes the organization would benefit from going through the strategic planning process, and she does not want to procrastinate. However, she is not sure how she should organize and implement that process.

Margie works in the community health and wellness department of a regional hospital. Recently, a new hospital has opened and that hospital is offering educational programs for the community that are similar to those that Margie's hospital offers.

Vicki works in HRD in a large corporation. She has learned that many employees interested in learning advanced computer skills have been taking computer courses from external vendors, and she wonders how her department might better meet the needs of these employees.

All of the above scenarios involve organizations engaging in some type of strategic planning. As you read through this chapter, think about how each person in each scenario above might use the strategic planning process to address her concerns.

Why is Strategic Planning Important to Adult Educators?

Program administrators should be actively involved in planning strategically for their respective organizations. All organizations operate within continually changing environments and all are continually changing internally as well. As discussed often in this text, organizations today have to continually add value to their specific objective(s) or they risk becoming obsolete or ultimately becoming eliminated. The strategic planning process can help educational organizations thrive and grow, just as it can for businesses. Strategic planning is a good way to plan for evolution and growth to meet both learner and organizational needs.

As an administrator, you are in a position to manage, or be involved in, the strategic planning process. Strategic planning requires knowledge of internal and external factors that others in the organization may not have. Administrators work on levels that allow them to see those factors (as well as the interplay among them). Administrators also have decision-making power, and because they typically work at managerial levels, they have the ability to implement and manage strategic plans that are developed.

Chapter Overview

This chapter begins with providing definitions of strategic planning, followed by content on why strategic planning is important. Strategic planning can be utilized in many different types of organizations, and it also can be used on several different levels within a single organization. A large corporation may engage in the process of strategic planning on a corporate level. Within that corporation, departments and divisions may also be engaged in the process of strategic planning. The HRD department in an organization, for example, may create and utilize some sort of strategic planning at the department or division level. The benefits of engaging in the process on several levels will be discussed in this chapter.

The timing of strategic planning may affect the planning process and the implementation of strategic plans. Times when planning should (and should not) be undertaken are discussed as well. Before strategic planning can begin, preplanning should take place; within this chapter, a list of prerequisites for strategic planning will be presented.

Once preplanning has concluded, the strategic planning process can begin. A process for strategic planning will be presented, and each step in the process will be discussed separately. The chapter concludes with content that explains how to integrate the strategic planning process into the ongoing work of the organization. You may not have encountered the strategic planning process before, but this chapter gives you the tools you need to understand and conduct it.

Strategic Planning Defined

Strategic planning is "a disciplined effort to produce fundamental decisions and actions that shape and guide what an organization (or other entity) is, what it does, and why it does it" (Bryson, 1988, p. 5). A strategy is "a plan that aims to give the enterprise a competitive advantage over rivals through differentiation. [It] is about understanding what you do, what you want to become, and—most importantly—focusing on how you plan to get there" (Harvard Business Essentials, 2005, p. xiv). Porter (1980) provides a more succinct definition of strategy as "a broad formula for how a business is going to compete" (p. xxiv).

Mittenthal (2002) defines strategic planning to include additional details about how the process works: "A strategic plan is a tool that provides guidance in fulfilling a mission with maximum efficiency and impact. If it is to be effective and useful, it should articulate specific goals and describe the action steps and resources needed to accomplish them" (p. 2). Mittenthal continues by noting that strategic plans should be reviewed and revised regularly—approximately every 3 to 5 years.

Some definitions of strategic planning include use of the word *business*, which may indicate that businesses are the only types of organizations that engage in strategic planning. As discussed earlier in this chapter, however, that is not the case. Bryson (1988) lists the types of organizations that can benefit from strategic planning:

1. Public agencies, departments, or major organizational divisions;
2. General-purpose governments, such as city, county, or state governments;
3. Nonprofit organizations providing basically public services; and
4. Special functions, such as transportation, health, or education, that bridge organizational and governmental boundaries.

Some common themes emerge from the definitions noted above. First, strategic planning is planning that focuses on ways the organization plans to implement its objectives. It focuses on the heart of the organization (the organizational mission), and it takes its direction from that mission. It is a process designed to guide the organization forward in purpose and scope. It also defines how an organization will position itself within the marketplace, that is, what will make the organization stand out and differentiate itself from other similar organizations?

In addition to the above explained principles for use(s) of strategic planning, it is important to note that strategic planning focuses on specific attributes of an organization and conditions within the organization's environment. It can be reflective in nature, as participants in the process should examine core beliefs and assumptions about the organization. In order to move ahead, people in organizations have to understand the current state of their organization(s). Creating an effective strategic plan requires participants to be honest in assessments about organizational strengths and weaknesses.

Strategic planning is action oriented. It first requires participants in the process to assess and examine organizational processes on an overall (comprehensive) level; then, it also requires them to develop actions and plans, and finally it requires implementation of those actions and plans. It can be longer term in nature, but is not necessarily long term. Strategic planning should allow for flexibility. As noted in the definitions above, strategic plans must be continually reviewed and revised based on the organization and the environment.

Strategic plans are different from other plans that an organization may develop, but many other types of plans may be based on principles within

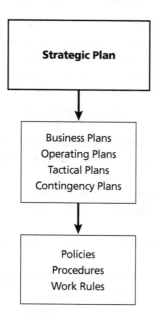

Figure 8.1   Hierarchy of plans.

an organization's strategic plan. Business plans, operating plans, action and contingency plans, for example, all may be based on an organization's strategic plan (however they are not classified as strategic plans but rather plans based on the strategic plan) (Lake, 2012). Then, from those types of plans, policies, procedures, and rules can be developed.

Why Plan?

Some believe the strategic planning process is simply an exercise to complete in order to produce a document. Others engage in strategic planning because other organizations are doing so. Strategic plans are created without appropriate introspection—they create a plan simply for the sake of having one. In some cases, the strategic planning process ends with a document that is never used. While a strategic planning initiative may result in the production of a finished planning document, that document should then be used; strategic plans should be implemented if an organization takes the time to create one. Remember, in the definitions of strategic planning, taking action is an important component of the process. Strategic planning that ends with a document that is never used is an incomplete process. If the planning process ends with such a document, it may as well not have been created in the first place, and the time, money, and other resources spent on the creation of a strategic plan are therefore wasted.

The purpose of strategic planning is to provide vision and focus for the organization. Also, it is to assess a variety of factors that the organization can influence and factors that can influence the organization. It is an opportunity to chart the course of the organization—to put plans together that will move the organization forward (Lake, 2012). Following is a summary of some of the many benefits of strategic planning.

- Helps clarify the future direction of the organization;
- Helps focus on issues that are truly important in the organization;
- Establishes organizational priorities;
- Improves decisions made in the organization by providing a basis for decisions;
- Improves understanding of the organization's customers or learners;
- Helps establish differentiation in the marketplace, which could lead to new customers or learners;
- Provides a point of reference when dealing with changes in environmental conditions; and

▪ Builds teamwork within the organization (Bryson, 1988; Cook, 1994; Kaufman, Oakley-Browne, Watkins, & Leigh 2003).

Despite its undeniable benefits, there are some who scoff at the idea of strategic planning. Others create reasons why a strategic planning process may not be helpful to them or their organization. Chief among these negative perspectives is the idea that the process takes resources; namely, time and money (Kaufman et al., 2003). This is certainly true. The strategic planning process does take both time and money in order to be successful. However, the process can pay off. For those involved in adult education, those payoffs can be in the form of increases in learner participation, course revenues, and overall awareness and interest in the organization. Sometimes people do not plan because they feel they will be stuck with the plan going forward, or that the end result may be incorrect, therefore sending them/ their organization in the wrong direction. Fear of change is also a barrier (Kaufman et al., 2003). It is true that decisions based on strategic plans can involve some degree of risk. However, there is risk associated with any type of movement within an organization. In fact, not making any change involves risk. Strategic plans are designed to be flexible ("living documents") in the sense that they don't force an organization to move in a direction that later may not be deemed appropriate. The strategic plan should be continually reviewed, consulted, and altered, as necessary, when key decisions are to be made. It can also change when key stakeholders deem it appropriate.

It is easy for administrators to get stuck in the daily work of their organizations and to lose sight of the bigger picture. Strategic planning can help those in the organization to see that bigger picture. It can help remind employees, volunteers, and other stakeholders why they are there. It can reinvigorate the organization and help everyone to move forward on a common page, toward common goals. Along the way, it can help those in the organization develop a clearer picture of who they are (as an organization) and what they do. Strategic planning, if done correctly, can be a vehicle to motivate and move the organization forward. In order to be effective, though, strategic plans have to be used. This is often where organizations fail. Strategic plans must result in action plans, and those action plans must be carried out (Kaufman et al., 2003).

When to Plan

There is not a set time frame or "right" time frame to use in the strategic planning process. There are sometimes, however, when it may not be wise to engage in the strategic planning process. Some argue that those who go through the process at regularly scheduled times are missing the point of strategic planning, as it is not an activity that should (necessarily) be done every 3 or 5 years on a regular schedule (Latham, 2012). If the organization's existing strategy is working and the strategy looks appropriate for the foreseeable future, it may not be time for another round of strategic planning. An organization should go through the strategic planning process when those in the organization begin to question existing strategies. Timing is very important here, as it is important to not wait until something changes dramatically in the marketplace or in the organization before strategic planning is done. In fact, Bryson (1988) argues that strategic planning is not a good option at times of financial crisis in an organization or at times of turnover of key positions in the organization. He recommends waiting until the organization stabilizes before undertaking strategic planning. Ironically, it is at times of financial crisis that most organizations turn to strategic planning. "Some companies leap to action only when performance falls off a cliff or projections miss their mark in a big way. Some scramble, chasing every appealing idea to get back on track" (Latham, 2012, para. 7). The time for strategic planning is long before these events happen. Hopefully, strategic planning at the appropriate time will prevent them from happening in the first place.

Prerequisites for Strategic Planning

"Strategic planning is never conducted in a vacuum. There is always an organizational and cultural context within which it occurs and this context plays a central role in the success of [an organization's] efforts" (Russell & Russell, 2005, p. 17). Simply put, strategic planning does not simply happen. It takes a good amount of preparation in order for a strategic plan to be successful. In this section, we will look at what must be done to lay the groundwork for successful strategic planning efforts. We will look at four components necessary to lay the groundwork for successful strategic planning: leader support, key project champions, open environments, and a clear plan of action (Figure 8.2).

Leader Support

Organizations must be ready to take on the strategic planning process. This readiness starts at the top, with support from key leaders in the organization. Leaders must demonstrate their commitment to the process, and they must demonstrate a mindset open to learning, reflection, and the possibly of taking risks. They must be as involved in the process as they can be, and

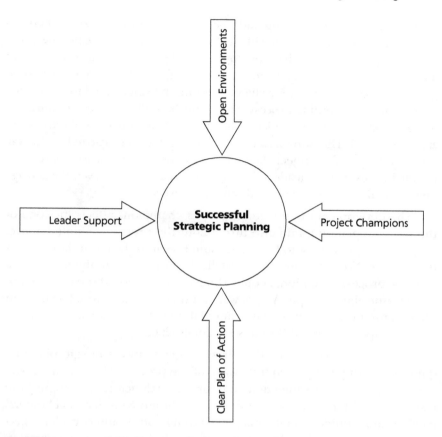

Figure 8.2   Prerequisites for successful strategic planning.

they must be supportive of the efforts of others in the organization as they gather and sort through information. Support also translates into resource availability. As noted earlier, strategic planning efforts often require time and money. They may mean taking on extra duties and responsibilities by certain individuals in the organization, and those extra duties may take those people away from their primary responsibilities. Without the support of leadership, strategic planning initiatives will not be successful (Kaufman et al., 2003).

Key Project Champions

While top-down support for the strategic planning process is critical, the actual mechanics of the process do not happen at the top levels of the organization. Rather, successful strategic planning efforts are championed (or managed) by several key individuals in the organization working together to actually conduct the planning and manage the process. Bryson (1988) defines project champions as individuals "committed to make the process work. The champions [do] not have preconceived ideas about what specific issues and answers would emerge from the process, although they may have some good hunches" (p. 19). These champions must be empowered to make decisions about the planning process. They must have the authority required to move the process forward, which is why support from top levels of the organization is critical. That support and empowerment must be carried all the way through the process. Project champions may conduct the process and come to conclusions that top leadership may not agree with. However, the process only works if it can be done openly and objectively.

The development of a team of project champions affects the tone of the strategic planning initiative throughout the process. As noted above, project champions have to be leaders, and they must be enthusiastic about the process. Not everyone has the skills, knowledge, and abilities to be a strategic process champion. People who have large egos, those who are not enthusiastic about the process, as well as others who are troublemakers in the organization are not the best candidates for the role of strategic planning champion (Harvard Business Essentials, 2005).

Project champions should address bigger-picture strategic planning questions during the prerequisite stage of the process. They should examine the business, environmental, and/or internal factors that might have caused a need for strategic planning. They should consider stakeholders' feelings and attitudes about strategic planning and should consider objections or obstacles that might be encountered during the planning process. They should also be prepared to address the question of why strategic planning is important at that point and what the benefits might be for each individual group of stakeholders. These types of issues will most likely surface when stakeholders start getting involved in the planning process (during future steps); they should be considered up front so project champions have a clear picture of the environment in which they will plan.

Open Environments

Strategic planning should not be done by a small group of individuals working in isolation. All key stakeholders should be involved in one way or another; however, the degree to which each group of stakeholders is involved depends on the type of stakeholder and the relationship to the organization.

> It is possible to be inclusive without falling into the too-many-cooks trap. But a strategic plan should not become the exclusive responsibility of a small

cadre of stakeholders. If the planning process is to succeed, it must incorporate the views of all the constituents who will be affected by the plan or have a role in its implementation. (Mittenthal, 2002, p. 3)

While project champions may lead the initiative, members of a strategic planning committee should be representatives of key stakeholder groups. Others, such as experts in the strategic planning process, may also be involved.

The strategic planning process is an inclusive one. Input from many different stakeholders is considered a part of that process. These stakeholders typically include employees, volunteers, customers (or learners, in the case of planning in adult education venues), and many other people who may be involved with the organization in one way or another. These are the people who have the information that will be most valuable in the process. These stakeholders should be made aware of the process, and they should also understand that they may be called upon to contribute. They must be made to feel part of the process, and they must be recognized for their potential roles within the process. This involves communicating with them from the very beginning and keeping them apprised of planning efforts on an ongoing basis. It also involves creating environments within which stakeholders feel free to share their thoughts and opinions, regardless of whether those thoughts and opinions are controversial. The strategic planning process will not be successful if all stakeholders simply tell project champions what they believe those individuals want to hear. Openness and honesty are important, and stakeholders should not fear retribution from sharing their honest opinions. Stakeholders should also be encouraged to "think outside the box" and present ideas that may be considered outside of the norm(s) of the organization. Strategic planning involves openness and a willingness to change and evolve. Sometimes, the wildest ideas from a stakeholder become the best organizational initiatives in the long run. Those ideas will never be able to surface if the environment is not one in which the stakeholder feels comfortable.

A Clear Plan of Action

A final prerequisite for the strategic planning process is the development of a plan or course of action. Strategic planning may mean different things to different people. It is important that top leadership and project champions clearly define the process and the individual steps that will be taken to carry out the process. Everyone, from top leadership to organizational stakeholders, should be clear on what is happening, who is responsible, and how and when plans will be carried out.

Strategic Planning in Action

Now that prerequisites for successful strategic planning have been identified and addressed, it is time to move into consideration(s) of the actual process. The next sections in this chapter deal with the strategic planning process. A proposed process will be discussed along with individual steps that make up that process.

Doing an Internet search for the term *strategic planning* will result in hundreds of links to definitions, articles, and consulting companies. It will also result in dozens of different diagrams that document steps in the strategic planning process. Some of those diagrams will look extremely complicated and intricate, indicating that the process is very complex. However, that is not necessarily the case. There is no one correct way to go through the strategic planning process, and the process does not have to be complicated in order to be successful. An example of a general process for strategic planning that we developed will be presented later in this chapter. It is a process that can be modified or adjusted based on the administrator's specific situation, or it can be used "as is." It is based on the framework described in the next paragraph and shown in Figure 8.3.

Key elements of this process include examination of the environment in which the organization operates, and a focus on the possibilities open to the organization, along with threats that might affect the organization's viability or success. These four items—strengths, weaknesses, opportunities, and threats—are commonly known as SWOT and an examination of them in the context of the strategic planning is known as a SWOT analysis (Harvard Business Essentials, 2005). The SWOT analysis is one of the most important steps in the strategic planning process. However, it is not the first step. As depicted in Figure 8.3, the first step within the process is the addressing of prerequisites as noted in the previous section. Without that prerequisite work, designed to provide a foundation for planning, the overall process may not ultimately be effective. People must be involved and committed before the formal process starts.

The Strategic Planning Process

Step 1: Address Prerequisites

The first step in the strategic planning process has been discussed earlier in this chapter. It relates to prerequisites that are important to address before the strategic planning process starts. Leader support, key project

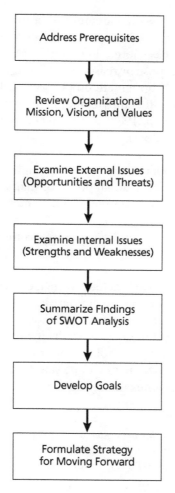

Figure 8.3 A process for strategic planning.

champions, open environments, and a clear plan of action are all prerequisites that should be in place before proceeding any further.

Step 2: Review Organizational Mission, Vision, and Values

After prerequisites are addressed, the organization can move to the next step in the process. This step involves a review of core elements of the organization. Everyone involved in the strategic planning process must be on the same page with regard to the basic purpose and reason for the organization's existence. Those types of things are found in the organizational mission and vision.

An organizational mission statement is "a brief expression of the organization's purpose. It should answer the questions 'Why do we exist?' and 'What, at the most basic level, do we do?'" (Mittenthal, 2002, p. 5). All organizations have a purpose or reason for existing. The mission statement addresses that purpose. "Agreement on purposes defines the arenas within which the organization will compete and, at least in broad outline, charts the future course" (Bryson, 1988, p. 49). According to Cook (1994), mission statements do the following:

- Help promote clarity of purpose through the organization,
- Function as a foundational point for major decisions,
- Are used to gain commitment within the company for proposed goals, and
- Help foster understanding and support for company goals by those outside the company (p. 4).

A mission statement can include verbiage relating to products and services offered, customers served, underlying philosophies, and company goals (Cook, 1994). The purpose of a mission statement is not only to clarify what the organization does (and why it exists), it also can serve as a communication device for stakeholders both internal and external to the organization. A mission statement can be shared with potential customers, investors, learners, and other interested parties. Here are some examples of mission statements:

> *A mission statement for a literacy center:* The mission of the Brown County Literacy Center is to help residents of Brown County achieve the literacy and English skills they need to be successful in life.

> *A mission statement for a HRD department in a large corporation:* Our mission is to contribute to the value of XYZ Corporation through comprehensive training and development programs that help XYZ employees continually develop their job-related skills, abilities, and competencies.

> *A mission statement for an urban university:* Our mission is to provide leadership and inspiration for learning and human development in urban communities.

Likewise, a review of the organizational vision is critical. A vision statement is "a description of the organization's desired future state" (Mittenthal, 2002, p. 5). The vision statement of an organization is often focused on the organization itself. "It projects the future in terms of the program(s), budget(s), or staff size, answering the question "Where do we want to be?" (Mittenthal, 2002, p. 5). It can also be focused on the desired future state of the environment in which the organization operates. In that sense, it is defined as "an aspirational description of what the organization would like to achieve or accomplish in the mid or long-term future" (Business Dictionary, n.d.). Whereas the mission statement looks at the overall purpose of the organization in the context of the external environment, the vision statement is a snapshot of what your organization will look like in the future. However, vision statements do not include details on how the organization will get to the future it describes. This is where the strategic plan comes in. The relationship between the organization's vision and its strategic plan can be summarized as follows: "A strategic plan cannot succeed unless it is derived from a clear vision of what the organization will look like at a specific point in the future" (Mittenthal, 2002, p. 6).

The vision statement for the literacy center noted in the previous example might look like this: Our vision is a completely literate county, with all citizens having the literacy skills necessary to function and thrive in society.

The vision statement for the HRD department noted in the previous example might look like this: We envision an organization of fully trained employees who are prepared for the business tasks of the day and those necessary for tomorrow.

The vision statement of a nature conservancy may be to become a leader at connecting local residents to the environment and to conservation.

The vision statement for an urban university is to become a premiere urban school, recognized for its diversity and known for its excellence in teaching, learning, and research.

Organizational values should also be examined during this stage of the process. Organizational values are guideposts (or standards) for thinking and action all individuals in the organization should use as a framework for making decisions. Because they influence our decisions and actions, they affect how we conduct ourselves within an organization (Finegan, 2000). Values guide actions, so an organization's value statements tend to include concepts like integrity, equality, honesty, and responsibility (among many others). Some examples of organizational values statements follow:

- ▪ Tell the truth,
- ▪ Treat others with respect,
- ▪ Encourage intellectual curiosity,
- ▪ Have fun,
- ▪ Ensure the safety of all employees at all times,
- ▪ Collaborate with others inside and outside the organization, and
- ▪ Maintain a healthy life and work balance.

While a review of the organization's mission, vision, and values is important in the planning process, there may be other documents and pieces of information that are important to review at this point as well. These might include existing strategic planning documents (from previous initiatives) and historical documents related to the organization's planning efforts. Organizational budgets and performance data may be reviewed. In larger organizations, individual department plans might be reviewed as well. Consider interviews or focus groups with stakeholders involved in planning previous efforts, as their perspectives may be helpful. Examine the degree to which the organization has been successful at strategic planning in the past and the degree to which previous strategic plans have been carried out. All of these activities will help set the stage for the strategic planning process. Knowledge gained during these activities will help planners work efficiently and effectively as they move forward. It will help planners become better strategic thinkers. As Lake (2012) notes, "If you don't understand what is happening in your own organization, then you will not be able to achieve your strategic potential" (p. 68).

Why does the strategic planning process include this type of review? Because many stakeholders are involved in the strategic planning process, so there is plenty of room for misinterpretation and misunderstanding. Clarification of key points, discussion of differences in interpretation, and confirmation of understanding by all involved is important during this stage of the process. Therefore a review of the organization's mission, vision, and values ensures that everyone is on the same page moving forward.

Step 3: Examine External Issues (Opportunities and Threats)

After review of the organizational mission, vision, and values (and other pertinent information), it is time to move to the next step in the SWOT analysis. This step involves consideration of the environment outside of the organization. It involves investigating and identifying opportunities that the organization may be able to take advantage of as well as consideration of threats that might affect the existence or overall operation of the organization.

- **Opportunities:** Trends, forces, events and ideas that your (organization) can capitalize on. (Harvard Business Essentials, 2005, p. 2)
- **Threats:** Possible events or forces outside of your control that your company or unit needs to plan for or decide how to mitigate. (Harvard Business Essentials, 2005, p. 3)

"These analyses of the external environment include broad, global (macro) issues like societal changes, new technologies and the economic, political and regulatory environments" (Lake, 2009, p. 5). Analysis of the external environment also includes consideration of environments more immediate to the organization. This type of analysis includes a comprehensive examination of customers, competitors, suppliers, and regulators. "There are both current and potential customers, each with requirements for product/service quality, features, and utility. Are any of these requirements unserved or underserved? There is also a set of current competitors and still others who might enter the arena in which the organization operates (Harvard Business Essentials, 2005, pp. 3–4). Bryson (1988) recommends organizations start by examining the external before moving to the internal. "Organizations spend most of their time talking to themselves about internal happenings, and too little time talking about, and with, the outside environment. The result is a kind of organizational mental illness" (p. 136). Focusing on the external, up front, helps balance a discussion of internal issues.

At this stage of the process, it is important to focus on both opportunities and threats on equal levels. Also, it is beneficial to consider the opportunities that may arise from some current threats. "Unfortunately, organizations all too often focus only on the negative or threatening aspects of [these] changes, and not on the opportunities they present" (Bryson, 1988, p. 54). In analyses of external environments, Bryson (1988) notes that an organization's boards of directors and other governing bodies may be in particularly good positions to assess external opportunities and threats. "This is partly because a governing board is responsible for relating an organization to its external environment and vice versa" (p. 54). This does not mean that internal stakeholders such as employees should be ignored. Single groups of stakeholders typically do not see a complete picture when assessing the external environment. However, when the opinions of

---

Opportunities and Threats

Customers
Vendors/Suppliers
Competitors
Laws, Codes, and Regulations
Work and Lifestyle Trends
Technology
Logistics (Pricing and service availability)
Partnerships
Substitutes

Figure 8.4   Opportunities and threats.

many stakeholders are considered collectively, a clearer understanding of external opportunities and threats may emerge. Consider the items on Figure 8.4 (when investigating external opportunities and threats).

More specifically, the following issues can be examined when conducting an analysis of external opportunities and threats. Keep in mind that not all items apply to all organizations.

Opportunities may include the following:

- Serving new groups of customers,
- Entering new markets,
- Expanding course offerings to meet a broader range of learner needs,
- Diversifying into related offerings,
- Adding complimentary courses or programs,
- Providing more services to learners (vertical integration),
- Complacency among competitors,
- Technology changes/advances,
- Work and lifestyle trend changes, and
- Fast market growth (Cook, 1994; Harvard Business Essentials, 2005).

Threats may include the following:

- New competitors entering the market,
- Increased demand for substitutes,
- Slow market growth,
- Government policies that may hinder the organization,
- Vulnerability to recessions and changes in regional economics,
- Learners' increased bargaining power,
- Changes in learner needs and interests,
- Technology changes/advances,
- Work and lifestyle trend changes, and
- Demographic changes (Cook, 1994; Harvard Business Essentials, 2005)

Notice that some items that appear on the list of threats also appear on the list of opportunities. Items such as technology and issues like work and lifestyle trend changes may translate into opportunities (in some cases). However, these things may exist as threats if they negatively impact an organization's existing operations. For example, online courses and programs have transformed the field of adult education. In certain cases, organizations took advantage of technology and used the opportunity to begin offering online courses to their learners. This type of initiative from a competitor may be a threat for other organizations that did not take the opportunity to offer online learning/online courses other organizations did.

Step 4: Examine Internal Issues (Strengths and Weaknesses)

Having tested the outer world for threats and opportunities, strategists must look inward and evaluate their strengths and weaknesses as an enterprise. As with the outer world, knowledge of the inner world imparts a practical sense about what company goals and strategies are most feasible and promising. (Harvard Business Essentials, 2005, p. 18)

Understanding the company is a key component in this stage of the process, as all aspects of the organization are examined here in depth:

- **Strengths:** Capabilities that enable your organization (or unit) to perform well—capabilities that need to be leveraged. (Harvard Business Essentials, 2005, p. 3)
- **Weaknesses:** Characteristics that prohibit your organization (or unit) from performing well and need to be addressed. (Strategy, 2005, p. 3)

Bryson (1988) recommends that "to identify internal strengths and weaknesses, the organization might monitor resources (inputs), present strategy (process,) and performance (outputs)" (pp. 54–55). The examination of core competencies, or "the company's expertise or skill in key areas that directly produce superior performance" (Harvard Business Essentials, 2005, p. 18) is important during this stage of the process, as is investigation of the organization's financial condition, management, and culture. Consider the items in Figure 8.5 when investigating internal strengths and weaknesses.

Strengths and Weaknesses

Current Performance
Organizational Recognition
Costs and Pricing
Products and Services Offered
Products or Services in Development
Development Capabilities
Employee/Volunteer Knowledge, Skills, Abilities
Organizational Culture

Figure 8.5 Strengths and weaknesses.

Here are some specifics to consider when analyzing organizational strengths and weaknesses:

- Distinct competencies,
- Financial resources,
- Competitive skills,
- Reputation and/or position in the marketplace,
- Business strategies and planning,
- Adaptability and flexibility,
- Proprietary information or products,
- Product/service arrays,
- Cost advantages,
- Competitive advantages,
- Product or service development capabilities,
- Management skill,
- Employee knowledge and ability,
- Volunteer knowledge and ability, and
- Organizational culture (Cook, 1994; Harvard Business Essentials, 2005)

"The bedrock of any successful strategic plan is a warts-and-all consideration of capabilities and strengths, weaknesses and limitations" (Mittenthal, 2002, p. 3). An issue associated with the identification of internal strengths and weaknesses is that many of the stakeholders involved in the strategic planning process may also have vested interests in these areas. This is especially true of employees who may not be as objective as is possible in their analyses of these areas. They also may suffer from limited knowledge and from considering the issue from their perspective(s) alone. As a result, it can be difficult for planners to reach agreement on what the organization's internal strengths and weaknesses are. Another issue is that, while some of these topics can be quantified (such as number of learners, number of courses, etc.), many others cannot. This can result in a variety of differing opinions on the same topic.

> To cut through these different perceptions, [administrators] need a method that involves many perceptive people representing different functions within the organization. Their collective judgment is bound to be more accurate than that of one or two bright individuals who see things from their narrow viewpoints. (Harvard Business Essentials, 2005, p. 25)

Gathering Information for a SWOT Analysis

As you can see by now, the SWOT process involves gathering information from many different sources/areas of an organization. But how is that information best collected? There are several methods that can be used to gather data on strengths, weaknesses, opportunities, and threats. A few of them will be discussed in the following paragraphs.

The method of gathering data depends on several factors. Those factors include planning resources available (namely, relating to time frame and budget) and the type and quantity of information the planner wishes to gather from each stakeholder. The number of stakeholders in a given group is also a factor that should be considered when determining methods for gathering data.

Before any methods of gathering data are organized (specifically those that involve people), planners should examine whether or not the information they want from a particular group could be gathered in an alternative way. In most organizations, there is a considerable amount of hard data available for planners to use and analyze. If data can be gathered by reviewing reports, statistics, or other documents, it's best to use those methods first. This way, planners are not wasting the time of stakeholders with questions that could be addressed by simply reviewing the data. Cast a wide net when considering the types of existing documents to examine overall. Consider previous strategic plans as well as things like learner (or other stakeholder) satisfaction surveys, minutes from board of directors meetings, legislation, laws, and policies, as well as guidelines from accrediting bodies and national-level associations (among other entities).

Interviewing stakeholders is a good way of gathering strategic planning data. Interviewing stakeholders is advantageous to gathering data for strategic planning, because these interviews can be lengthy and expose in-depth perspectives about the organization stakeholders have. An interviewer can probe the interviewee for perspective(s), and questioning them in-depth can provide clarity about those perspectives. If a stakeholder group is hard to reach, interviews may be the only way of gathering data from this group. A downside of interviewing, however, is that it takes a good deal of time and it typically involves only one or two stakeholders at a time. As noted earlier, when interviewing stakeholders, bias may be present and that might affect responses. Additionally, a lack of anonymity might affect responses. Telephone interviews can save time and money, but it can be difficult to establish credibility over the telephone (assuming the interviewer does not know the stakeholder), and the interviewer has less control over the situation and environment (Rea & Parker, 1997; Wallen & Fraenkel, 2001).

Focus groups can be used to gather strategic planning data as well. Focus groups involve the gathering of data from groups of 5–8 stakeholders at a time. Those stakeholders can be from the same group or they can represent a variety of groups. The dynamic nature of a focus group can result in quality data, and the focus group moderator can probe, clarify, and guide the group in a direction appropriate for reaching the goal. Focus group participants can also interact with each other, which may help uncover issues from different perspectives. Sometimes focus groups are dominated by one or two talkative individuals so when this happens all voices and perspectives may not be heard. Also, it may be difficult for focus group participants to discuss sensitive topics in a group setting (Rea & Parker, 1997).

The use of surveys is a good way to reach large numbers of stakeholders, and technology has made surveys very easy to develop and distribute (provided the stakeholder group has access to technology—a key issue in some cases). Using surveys is a good way to contact a lot of stakeholders, and surveys require a fairly conservative amount of time and money to produce and administer. A downside of gathering data via surveys is that they tend to have low response rates and it is difficult to get in-depth information from a survey (Rea & Parker, 1997).

Benchmarking is another way of gathering information that can be helpful in the strategic planning process. Benchmarking involves "learning from the successes, failures and mistakes of others" (Mittenthal, 2002, p. 7). The benchmarking process involves learning about other organizations that may be similar or complementary (in various ways) to the organization conducting the strategic planning. Direct competitors of organizations in the same geographical areas may be reluctant to share specific information about their practices, but benchmarking can be undertaken with complementary organizations and organizations in other geographic areas that may be similar to the organization engaging in the planning. Benchmarking involves contacting other organizations and asking for opportunities to learn from them. Typically, the organization identifies a few practices, policies, or procedures to benchmark (as benchmarking is usually a focused activity, and it is not meant to be undertaken on broad levels). Once a final list of organizations to benchmark with are identified, agendas are established and meetings are scheduled. Benchmarking allows organizations to avoid "reinventing the wheel" when other organizations may have tried similar tactics and strategies and found them problematic and/or ultimately unsuccessful. Reciprocity is important in the benchmarking process. If a planner asks an organization to benchmark, the planner should be prepared to honor that organization's benchmarking requests.

Step 5: Summarize Findings of SWOT Analysis

The fifth step in the strategic planning process involves compiling the findings of the SWOT analysis. This step starts with sorting and categorizing issues uncovered during the SWOT analysis. After this occurs, the process of prioritizing ideas begins. It is from those ideas that action plans will be developed (in the subsequent step).

Sorting and Prioritizing

At this point in the process, strategic planners should have a lot of data to work with. That data will exist in various forms and will have been gathered from many stakeholders. At this point, the next task involves summarizing the data, as well as sorting, prioritizing, and searching for overall themes and consistencies (as well as inconsistencies and differences), and examining how the data can be used to move the process forward. Strategic planners may be overwhelmed with the amount of data they have to work with at this stage in the process and that can affect how planners move forward. The task of taking a mountain of data, sorting it into several major themes, and then prioritizing it can be difficult. In this section, we will discuss a few strategies that can be used to take a great deal of data and end up with several concise ideas to use as the process progresses.

To begin, revisit the SWOT analysis questions:

1. What major external opportunities do we have?
2. What major external threats do we face?
3. What are our major internal strengths?
4. What are our major internal weaknesses? (Bryson, 1988, p. 137).

The result of addressing these questions should become four major lists of items. Items on the lists should then be sorted and prioritized.

Sorting and prioritizing external factors (opportunities and threats) may be easier than prioritizing internal strengths and weaknesses, mainly because of a potential for bias and limited perspective(s) in examining internal elements. This can cause the process to become slow or convoluted at this stage. Using the four lists described above, a process of consolidating ideas, clarifying those ideas, and asking each participant to rank them in order can help ensure the most important strengths and weaknesses become apparent (Harvard Business Essentials, 2005, p. 5). This type of process involves meetings of the strategic planning committee and key stakeholders.

Those stakeholders must represent a variety of different areas. These types of meetings can be productive and can result in consensus going forward.

While the compilation of four lists is an important part of the process at this point, those lists (by themselves) might not tell the whole story. Bryson (1988) notes that supporting types of documents might be prepared at this point as well. He suggests that the following be developed at this step in the process: "various background reports on external forces and trends, clients, customers, and payers, competitors and collaborators, with additional reports on internal resources, present strategy and performance" (p. 119). These background documents provide support or bases for items on the lists. They can be used to provide more detail to justify actions taken in the future.

Discussion among planners and key stakeholders is critical during the sorting and prioritization processes. Discussion by organizational leaders is also important at this step. "Such discussions provide insight into the organization and its environment and also prepare the way for the identification of strategic issues in the next step" (Bryson, 1988, p. 120).

While the sorting and ranking of issues is important, it may still result in several lists of issues that can be overwhelming to address. Prioritization becomes important at this point. Organizations can't address all items on the SWOT analysis at one time. Careful and deliberate steps forward must be taken, and those steps depend on how SWOT analysis items are prioritized. In order to ensure prioritization efforts are appropriate for the organization, planners should refer to the organization's mission, vision, and values during this stage. The result should be a list of prioritized items to address when moving to the next step in the process.

Step 6: Develop Goals

The development of goals is the next step within the process. By this point, issues have been identified, sorted, and prioritized, and it is time to consider where planners and key stakeholders envision the organization going. Now, "the organization should establish goals and objectives for itself and then develop strategies to achieve them" (Bryson, 1988, p. 58). Goals "express desired outcomes and may be focused on discrete parts of the organization's programming or internal operations" (Mitthenthal, 2002, p. 7). Firmly establishing these goals are what the organization wants to accomplish. Goals should be measurable, and subsequently the progress toward goals should be measured often. Mitthenthal (2002) notes that with regard to strategic planning, the terms goals and objectives are sometimes used interchangeably. However, he posits that "goals are generally more comprehensive or far-reaching than objectives (p. 7).

Some goals are focused on results. "A 10% increase in the number of learners in a particular course or program" is an example of a specific goal that focuses on results. "A 15% decrease in student attrition in the cosmetology program" is another example of a goal that focuses on results. Other goals can be focused on processes. These types of goals are typically more related to the internal workings of the organization. "A 5% decrease in volunteer turnover" is an example of a goal related to the internal operations of a volunteer literacy organization. "The development and offering of four new courses this year" is another example. As noted above, goals should be measurable. "Increasing learner satisfaction" is a fairly ambiguous goal, whereas "increasing scores on student satisfaction surveys by four points" is a measurable goal that addresses the same issue. Likewise, "hire more staff" is an ambiguous goal, but hire two more instructors is more specific.

Step 7: Formulate Strategy for Moving Forward

Strategic implementation is "The ongoing implementation of [strategic planning] decisions and actions so that the outcomes are achieved" (Lake, 2012, p. ix). After goals are developed, the next step is to develop strategies and tactics that will be implemented to meet those goals. A strategy is "a pattern of purposes, policies, programs, actions, decisions, or resource allocations that defines what an organization is, what it does, and why it does it. Strategies can vary by level, function, and timeframe" (Bryson, 1988, p. 59). Often you will hear the terms *strategies* and *tactics* used together. Strategies and tactics "consist of approaches or sets of activities needed to achieve the goals and objectives" (Mittenthal, 2002, p. 7). They both involve action that will be taken.

Although they both involve actions that will be taken, there is a difference between the two terms. A strategy is a plan of action designed to meet a goal. It is larger in scope than a tactic, is usually relates to a long-term objective, and it typically involves planning. A tactic, on the other hand, is a specific action. A tactic is short-term in nature and involves a specific action that will contribute to an overall strategy (and ultimately meet the goal) (Owyang, 2013).

As an example, consider the case of a healthcare organization that offers courses in nutrition and fitness for families. As part of the strategic planning process, the organization identified a goal of increasing attendance by 20% over the next year in a course on cooking and nutrition. A strategy to meet that goal may be to connect with potential learners by getting involved in community-related festivals and events, and a useful tactic would be to staff a booth at the local art fair and provide information on courses to attendees. Another tactic might be to sponsor a family fun walk/run event.

An HRD department developed a goal of a 20% increase in employee attendance in online courses related to retirement planning. A strategy used to meet that goal involved using promotional efforts to increase awareness of course availability. A tactic used was to hold a drawing for an iPad for any employee who reviewed the online course descriptions and related course information within a certain time period.

For each goal specified, multiple strategies and many different tactics may be used (Figure 8.6). Strategy development can involve brainstorming, as it is overall a search for practical alternatives that can be implemented to meet goals. The process involves consideration of different options and specific ways to meet goals, evaluating potential barriers that may affect the strategy and then selecting the strategies that are agreed upon. Up to this point in the process, all activities have involved planning. Now the planning becomes primarily action oriented, which can be frightening for people involved in the process. Strategic planning requires a commitment to evolution and change, and sometimes in the planning process organizations get to this point and become hesitant to take action. Or they agree to institute very small changes not in line with the goals set forth within the planning process. All individuals in the organization must be committed to evolving and making changes, whether those changes are large or small ones. "If

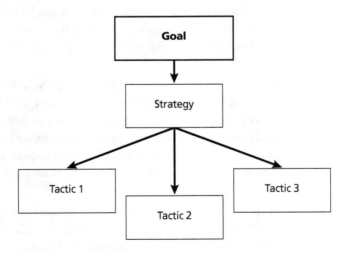

Figure 8.6 The relationship between goals, strategies, and tactics.

they are to remain viable and effective, organizations must be prepared to change as extensively as conditions require (Mittenthal, 2002, p. 9).

After strategies have been agreed upon, tactics can be developed and plans can be put in place. Tactics are often developed for a 6-month or year-long time frame (as compared to strategies, which are typically longer in nature) (Owyang, 2013). An overall plan for implementation can detail the various strategies and tactics for each goal, along with information on time frames, cost, priority, and means of measurement for each goal. This type of document can ensure everyone is on the same page going forward, and it serves as a guidepost for the implementation and monitoring of goals, strategies, and tactics.

A plan for implementation also might include tools for measurement. Once strategies are implemented and actions have begun, it is important to conduct ongoing measurement of goals. This type of measurement serves several purposes. It can allow the organization to connect specific tactics to strategies and goals, which helps determine which tactics were successful and which were not. It also provides an ongoing review of whether or not goals were realistic. It's possible that one or two tactics will help the organization reach a goal much faster than it had anticipated. Or conversely, ongoing measurement may reveal that the organization's tactics are not working and they should be modified going forward.

The End of the Process?

At this point, you might think the strategic planning process is complete. Goals, strategies, and tactics have been developed, and a plan is in place to monitor progress toward goals. While this is the last step in our strategic planning process flowchart, in reality, the strategic planning process within an organization can be ongoing. External and internal factors affecting the organization change. The implementation of strategic plans is not always successful, and even plans that have been implemented successfully may not have the impact that the planners likely imagined (Lake, 2012). So the strategic planning model might include an arrow from the very last box back up to the top to the very first box. In today's environment, markets, learners, economic conditions, laws, regulations, and many other factors are continually changing. A strategic plan is important to develop and implement within an organization, but it should also be examined continually and altered as necessary. In that specific sense, the strategic planning process is never complete.

Concluding Thoughts

Consider the entire strategic planning process as outlined in this chapter. What types of things did you learn about strategic planning? How might you use the strategic planning process to benefit your organization? What might potential benefits and potential barriers be? Several overarching themes run through all of the process, and they will be summarized in this section.

First, the importance of having a plan and carrying it out within a detailed process is important in ensuring the ultimate success of the plan. Sometimes, strategic plans are developed, but they are not implemented. Organizations may shy away from taking action and making recommended changes that may help them reach their goals. Having a specific plan helps ensure all are on the same page moving forward.

The most detailed and appropriate plans will not be successful without the support of high-level leadership, as well as all stakeholders in the organization. Strategic planning cannot be developed and implemented by a small group of people without any supporting influences. It is an organizationwide process that must be supported by high-level leaders in order for it to be successful. While key players in the process (or project champions) may be involved in working on a variety of levels within the organization, support from the high-level leaders is critical.

Ongoing communication throughout the process is also a key factor in successful strategic planning. Communication with leaders, employees, volunteers, and other interested stakeholders helps ensure that everyone is aware of the process (and current updates on process status). "Communication is an effective tool for motivating employees, for overcoming resistance, for preparing people for the pluses and minuses of change, and for giving employees a personal stake in strategy implementation" (Harvard Business Essentials, 2005, p. 117). A communication strategy for strategic planning should be diverse in that it should involve written documents, formal presentations, and question-and-answer sessions. It is important that communication be two-way; it should not come solely from planners or high-level leaders.

Finally, patience is critical during this process. The gathering of information from many different stakeholders; the sorting, interpreting, planning, and implementation processes; the communication with stakeholders; the addressing of issues of resistance and barriers; and a host of unforeseen obstacles that every planner will face during the process means that planners must have significant patience. There is no expedited method for going from the start of the process to the end. Strategic planners with patience and a good understanding of the process are the most effective ones throughout the long term. Those with little patience risk getting burned out and losing focus early in the process.

Summary

Many people and processes have to be in place, and they must work well together if the strategic planning process is to be effective. This chapter outlined a process for strategic planning that can be used by those who are involved in adult education and human resource development. It also included practical tips and hints for successful strategic planning and implementation of plans.

DISCUSSION QUESTIONS

1. Consider your knowledge and perceptions about the strategic planning process at this point. Have you ever undergone such a process, and what was that experience like? What were the results of that process?
2. What are some reasons adult education organizations should engage in strategic planning?
3. Revisit the three scenarios outlined at the start of this chapter. From a strategic planning standpoint, how would you address each of these scenarios?
4. What are the mission, vision, and values statements for your organization (or for an organization with which you are familiar)? How do these elements help shape that organization?
5. If your organizations do not have mission, vision, and values statements, what might those statements look like should they be created? Develop some potential mission, vision, and values statements for organizations with which you are familiar.
6. What types of documents would you review in developing a mission, vision, or values statement for your organization? What stakeholders might provide you with input?
7. What other categories of opportunities and threats (Figure 8.4) can you think of? Which ones might specifically apply to your organization?
8. Consider your organization or an organization with which you are familiar. What external opportunities and threats can you think of?
9. What are some ways your organization might sort and prioritize issues uncovered during a SWOT analysis? Who might be involved in these processes?

10. What barriers or obstacles do you foresee in the sorting and prioritizing processes within your organization?
11. Write some examples of goals for your organization. How will you measure your progress toward those goals?
12. Consider a goal for your organization (or an organization with which you are familiar), and develop a strategy (or strategies) as well as tactics that may help the organization meet that goal.
13. What are the forces in your organization (or an organization with which you are familiar) that may affect how (or if) change is carried out? These forces may be positive in that they are forces for change, or negative, in that they may work against change efforts.
14. Develop a list of possible strengths, weaknesses, opportunities, and threats for the following organizations:
    - A community-based literacy agency located in a major urban area.
    - A community college located in a rural community.
    - A museum in a large city that offers educational programs for local residents.
    - An independent businessperson offering gourmet cooking courses for residents in a midsized city.
15. For each of the above organizations, what might some strategic planning goals look like (assume each organization has gone through the strategic planning process)?
16. After having read this chapter, what are some reasons why organizations with which you are familiar might elect to go through the strategic planning process? What are some reasons why they might not?

References

Bryson, J. M. (1988). *Strategic planning for profit and nonprofit organizations.* San Francisco, CA: Jossey-Bass.

Bryson, J. M. (2011). *Strategic planning for profit and nonprofit organizations* (4th ed.). San Francisco, CA: Jossey-Bass.

Business Dictionary. (n.d.). *Vision statement.* Retrieved November 5, 2015, from http://www.businessdictionary.com/definition/vision-statement.html

Cook, K. J. (1994). *AMA complete guide to strategic planning for small business.* Lincolnwood, IL: NTC.

Finegan, J. E. (2000). The impact of personal and organizational values on organizational commitment. *Journal of Occupational and Organizational Psychology, 73,* 149–169.

Harvard Business Essentials. (2005). *Strategy: Create and implement the best strategy for your business.* Boston, MA: Harvard Business School Press.

Kaufman, R., Oakley-Browne, H., Watkins, R., & Leigh, D. (2003). *Strategic planning for success: Aligning people, performance and payoffs.* New York, NY: Wiley.

Lake, N. (2012). *Strategic planning workbook* (3rd ed.). London, England: Kogan Page.

Latham, A. (2012, March 1). *Clarity quiz—How often should you do strategic planning?* [Blog post]. *Ann Latham Delivers Uncommon Clarity.* Retrieved from http://uncommonclarity.com/index.php/article/how-often-should -you-do-strategic-planning/

Mittenthal, R. A. (2002). Ten keys to successful strategic planning for nonprofit and foundation leaders. *TCC Group.* Retrieved from http://www.tccgrp .com/pdfs/per_brief_tenkeys.pdf

Owyang, J. (2013, January 14). *The difference between strategy and tactics* [Blog post]. Retrieved from http://www.web-strategist.com/blog/2013/01/14/ the-difference-between-strategy-and-tactics/

Porter, M. E. (1980). *Competitive strategy: Techniques for analyzing industries and competitors.* New York, NY: The Free Press.

Rea, L. M., & Parker, R. A. (1997). *Designing and conducting survey research.* San Francisco, CA: Jossey-Bass.

Russell, J., & Russell, L. (2005). *Strategic planning training.* Alexandria, VA: ASTD Press.

US Bureau of Labor Statistics. (n.d.) *Business employment dynamics.* Retrieved from http://www.bls.gov/bdm/entrepreneurship/bdm_chart3.htm

Wallen, N. E., & Fraenkel, J. R. (2001). *Educational research: A guide to the process.* Mahwah, NJ: Erlbaum.

9

Program Evaluation

Everyone Evaluates

Think about the evaluation you have done today. At first thought, you may believe that you haven't evaluated anything. But then, consider what you thought about as you woke up and heard the local weather forecast. You heard the forecast, compared it to some standard you've developed for what you consider an ideal or perfect weather day, and then determined whether today was going to be a nice day, an average day, or a miserable day. Now consider your thoughts about breakfast. You probably went through the same type of process. Did you enjoy it, or was it not very good? Then think about your commute to work—maybe it was very easy, or maybe it was slower than usual. When you got on the subway car, you evaluated the situation and made a decision about where to stand or who to sit next to. All of these are examples of evaluation. Granted, they are examples of very informal, and fairly low-stakes evaluations. Still, they involve the gathering of information, the processing or consideration of that information compared to some predetermined standard we have developed for ourselves, and then the making of judgments or decisions based on that information. The thing to remember

Organization and Administration of Adult Education Programs, pages 201–218
Copyright © 2016 by Information Age Publishing

is that people are continually evaluating as they live their lives—evaluating situations, people, events, conditions, and many other things.

The irony is this: Although people evaluate all the time, they tend to dislike or shy away from the formal process of evaluation when considered in the context of educational programs. This may be because of lack of knowledge on the subject of evaluation. It may be because of fear or unease associated with evaluation. It may be because conducting an effective evaluation can be a lot of work. Often evaluation is looked at in a negative context. Formal education is typically associated with evaluations such as tests, and students are warned of the consequences of failing a test or not performing to their potential. Sometimes evaluation is associated with reprimands, such as during an employee's yearly performance review, when issues of poor performance may be addressed. Evaluation can also be associated with having to "fix" something that is broken or change something that is not working, and change, by itself, can be anxiety provoking. All of these are reasons why evaluation is often avoided. It is not often considered in a positive light. However, evaluation can be positive. It can serve to highlight things that are going well, courses that are successful, instructors who are performing at superior levels, and students who are pleased with their educational experiences. Sometimes those positives are lost in a sea of negatives normally associated with evaluation, but the purpose of evaluation is to examine everything and to find the good as well as the average and the below average (Spalding, 2014, p. 5). Consider these scenarios.

Emily manages a series of educational programs at a community center. She notices that courses taught by one instructor always have waiting lists of students, whereas the same courses taught by a different instructor are not as well attended.

Juan recently became the manager of an HRD department at a midsized manufacturing organization. He is interested in doing an overall review of the department's educational program offerings to determine which programs are most relevant to the company's employees.

Jill's organization is facing some cutbacks, and she feels that she may have to cancel some of the organization's educational program offerings. In order to make decisions, however, she has to learn about which programs are generating the most revenue and which ones are losing money.

Lexi is interested in evaluating the effectiveness of the educational programs her organization offers, but she is not sure where to start or how to begin the process. For this reason, she has found it easier to put it off.

Something that these scenarios all have in common is that they involve the concept of evaluation in one form or another. As explained above, evaluation is a multifaceted concept, and it is one that can be considered from several different levels and from several different perspectives.

Why Is Evaluation Important in Adult Education?

Evaluation can help program administrators determine the value of an educational program (or of various aspects of a program). It is a tool that can be used to help organizations provide the most effective and efficient educational programs for their learners. Nobody wants to continue doing something that is harmful or ineffective, and evaluation can identify those types of things, so strategies, plans, and behaviors can be adjusted and ultimately programs can be more effective. Positive evaluation results can be a source of pride for the administrator and the organization and reason to celebrate good work and accomplishment. Positive practice identified through the evaluation process can be replicated elsewhere in the organization. Even the negative things learned from evaluation can be useful—sometimes they are more useful than the positive things. While reading this chapter, consider evaluation from a more balanced perspective. The bottom line is that evaluation can help programs in many ways, but it has to be done correctly. That means having a good understanding of the concept of evaluation, knowledge of the tools and strategies available for use in the evaluation process, and the ability to interpret evaluation results.

Chapter Overview

This chapter will discuss concepts associated with evaluation that are important for educational program administrators to understand. We'll cover terminology, basic concepts, and principles of evaluation. Reasons and purposes for evaluation will also be presented.

There are many ways to go about conducting an evaluation, and a process for evaluation will be described in this chapter. Factors to consider when deciding whether or not to conduct an evaluation will be discussed, along with content on the use of internal and external evaluators. We'll conclude with a discussion of the role you play as an administrator in the evaluation process.

Evaluation: Definitions and Concepts

There are many definitions of the term *evaluation* as it relates to educational program evaluation. Several of them are presented here. Fitzpatrick, Sanders, and Worthen (2011) define evaluation as "the identification, clarification, and application of defensible criteria to determine and evaluation object's value (worth or merit) in relation to those criteria" (p. 7). Caffarella (2002) defines program evaluation as "a process used to determine whether the design and delivery of a program were effective and whether the proposed outcomes were met" (p. 225). Mertens and Wilson (2012) add to Caffarella's (2002) definition by describing characteristics of evaluation. They note that program evaluation uses formal methodologies, involves the gathering of empirical evidence, often takes place in decision-making contexts that are political and involve multiple stakeholders, and each includes their own sets of interests. While the aforementioned definitions of evaluation focus on formal evaluation, evaluation does not necessarily have to be formal to be useful. In discussing different types of evaluation, Caffarella posits that "although systematic or strategically planned evaluations are important, so are the more informal and unplanned evaluation activities" (p. 225).

Evaluation and Assessment

Although sometimes used interchangeably, the concepts of evaluation and assessment are seen by some as being different. Galbraith and Jones (2010) distinguish between the terms *evaluation* and *assessment* in the context of educational program evaluation. Their definitions are as follows: "Assessment refers to the collection of information, and it measures levels of achievement without comparisons to a set of standards. Evaluation, however, indicates application of the assessment findings to the continued development of student learning or program achievement" (p. 167).

Some believe that the term *assessment* is most appropriate when examining the performance of learners in the classroom, and that *evaluation* is the process of examining and making decisions about educational courses and programs. Those who work in adult education or HRD assess learner performance in a variety of ways—on tests or assignments, on written projects, on participation, and in other similar ways. Sometimes that assessment takes place in a classroom, sometimes it's in the workplace, and sometimes it's in a different venue, depending on the situation and the learning activity. In a formal classroom, that assessment can be associated with letter grades, which relate to a student's final grade in the course. Student performance is important to discuss in conversations about evaluation, and student assessment may be considered when conducting a course or program evaluation, but it is not the primary focus of those who work in educational program administration (Spalding, 2014, p. 11). This chapter will focus on evaluation from a programmatic standpoint (and the term *evaluation* will be used in the context of program evaluation and not in the context of learner assessment) (Figure 9.1).

```
┌─────────────────────────────────────────┐
│          Assessment Versus Evaluation    │
│                                          │
│   We assess the performance of learners  │
│   in our courses.                        │
│                                          │
│   We evaluate our courses and programs   │
│   for effectiveness.                     │
│                                          │
└─────────────────────────────────────────┘
```

Figure 9.1 Definitions used in this chapter.

Among all these definitions, a few commonalities emerge. Evaluation involves the collection of data. It is the examination of an entity (an educational program or course, section of a course, or series of programs) and the comparison of what is being done with what should be done (or against some type of standard or opinion). Based on those comparisons, conclusions about the effectiveness of the program (or the effectiveness or worth of various aspects of the program) can be determined. Actions can also be taken to improve areas of weakness and build upon areas of strength.

The Purpose of Evaluation

In a general sense, purposes of evaluation have already been presented in this chapter. On a more detailed level, Werner and DiSimone (2012) note several reasons or purposes for the evaluation of adult education programs. Although the authors present these reasons in the context of HRD programs, they are equally relevant to all adult education programs. They include the following:

- To examine whether or not an educational program is meeting its objectives,
- To identify strengths and weaknesses of an educational program,
- To examine cost/benefit ratios of the program,
- To make decisions about who should participate in an organization's educational programs, and
- To understand who benefited most and least from a program.

The above purposes are important in themselves, as administrators want to know all of this information about their educational programs. Those charged with administering educational programs must know whether or not the program is meeting its objectives—what the strengths and weaknesses of the program are, what type of cost/benefit ratios are present, who is participating, and who is benefiting from the program. Based on this information, the administrator can make changes to programs in order to continually improve them. Those changes can be in the form of improvements to existing programs or changes in the planning of future programs. If a hospital is running a series of courses for the community on a particular subject and those courses fill up quickly and are very positively evaluated by learners, the hospital might consider adding course sections or developing new courses on related topics. On the other hand, if the courses are not well attended and learners indicate the courses are not meeting their needs, the courses may be revised and planning for related courses in the future may be scrapped (Dunsworth & Billings, 2011).

Cervero (1988) presents seven major categories of questions to examine when conducting an evaluation. While these categories certainly can relate to questions posed during an evaluation, they are also all reasons why we evaluate. They are as follows:

- **Program design and implementation:** These are questions that consider the similarities and differences between what was planned and what was actually implemented.
- **Learner participation:** These are questions that focus on the learner. How many people attended the learning event and what were the backgrounds of those learners? Were (enrolled students) learners similar to those for whom the program or course was targeted?
- **Learner satisfaction:** Were learners satisfied with different aspects of the learning event?
- **Learner knowledge, skills, and attitudes:** What did learners learn as a result of the event?
- **Application of learning after the learning event:** How was learning applied by the learner?
- **Results of learning (or impact):** What were the results of the application of learning?
- **Program characteristics associated with outcomes:** What are the connections between what happened in the learning event and the results or outcomes of the event.

These seven categories can be grouped based on the sequence in which they occur. Administrators can evaluate the development of the program, the implementation of the program (including learner participation), and the outcomes of the program, which include learner satisfaction, application of learned material, and results. We can also evaluate the connections between specifics that happened during the learning event and learning, application, and results.

Evaluation can serve other purposes related to the overall mission of the organization. For example, Werner and DeSimone (2012) posit that evaluation is a good way for HRD departments to demonstrate the value they add to the organization and to build credibility for the educational programs they run. With regard to nonprofit organizations, St. Clair (2015) notes that evaluation can be used by funders and other sponsors to assess effectiveness. This demonstration of value is critical for all involved with educational planning, regardless of venue or situation. HRD departments often have to demonstrate their value to the organization as a whole. A nonprofit organization may have to demonstrate the value of its training programs to its board of directors in order to justify funding for additional training programs. Organizations today have to run as effectively and efficiently as possible, and functions within organizations must add value in order to remain viable in the organization. Evaluation is an excellent way of showing the value that a program planner, instructor, group, department, or organization brings to the table.

Evaluation can involve many people, or stakeholders. When conducting an evaluation, gathering feedback from stakeholders is important. A stakeholder is "a person, group, or organization that has interest or concern in an organization" (Business Dictionary, 2013). The degree of interest depends on the specific type of stakeholder. Some stakeholders, such as the program developers, instructors, and learners in an ESL course are more directly related to the organization. Other stakeholders, such as the employers who hire graduates of the ESL course and the families of students in the ESL course, may be more indirectly connected to the organization. Figure 9.2 is an example of stakeholders for a community-based

---

Stakeholders for a Community Organization

Learners/Students

Instructors

Staff

Managers

Community Members

Other Community Organizations

Local Government and Policymakers

Figure 9.2 Examples of stakeholders.

organization that offers educational programs. Fitzpatrick et al. (2011) have developed categories of stakeholders. They are as follows:

- Policymakers, including local government officials and accrediting bodies,
- Educational program administrators or managers,
- Instructors in the program,
- Learners or participants (primary consumers of the program), and
- The community itself, including family members of the learners and other community groups (secondary consumers of the program).

Stakeholders share an interest in the organization. That interest comes from a variety of perspectives, and the level of interest is not the same for each group of stakeholders. Priorities among different groups of stakeholders may also be different, and these factors can make the evaluation process complex. Some groups, including learners and instructors, may have more direct interest in the organization than general members of the community (who may have an indirect interest). Focus of interest is often different among categories of stakeholders as well. Learners or students may be more focused on learning and growing. Local government and policymakers may be focused more so on rules and regulations that affect the organization.

As an example, consider the various stakeholders that could be involved in the evaluation of a community-based organization focused on literacy. In some cases, educational programs for adults must be certified by state agencies, so those agencies may conduct evaluations of the organization's programs as well. A national accrediting or credentialing agency might require evaluation of the organization's programs by experts in literacy. In both cases, experts would evaluate the organization's programs using a predetermined set of standards for these types of programs, and they would make decisions based on how close the organization's programs came to meeting the national agency's standards. The accrediting or credentialing agency may then accredit the program, and the program could emphasize its state or national accreditation (Fitzpatrick et al., 2011).

Learners are stakeholders, and their opinions can be helpful to program administrators in the evaluation process. Learners are the "customers" of the organization, and their input should be considered when making program decisions. Students are typically asked to evaluate a course and provide the instructor and the organization with feedback on it. Surveys or checklists may ask learners to rate many different aspects of the course, from environmental to instructional factors. Surveys are typically administered at the end of a course, or sometimes they are administered at the end of a particular unit of instruction (if the instructor is looking for specific information on a certain aspect of a program).

Instructors, administrators, and staff members within the agency are also stakeholders. They may be asked to evaluate various aspects of the organization's programs as well. Input from these various groups of stakeholders typically focuses on the aspects of the educational program that are most important to that group. For example, the organization's controller may be interested in learning which courses and programs are more profitable than others. The controller may conduct an evaluation to determine which ones are profitable and which ones are not (Spalding, 2014, p. 12). Or maybe the organization has hired a subject-matter expert in the area of ESL to conduct an evaluation of the organization's ESL-related programs. That subject-matter expert may evaluate the thoroughness or level of completeness of each course in the English program to ensure that relevant and important subjects are covered. Instructors might be asked for their thoughts on curriculum and classroom structure. Evaluation for these groups may be done using surveys or interviews, or it may be informal.

This is just one example of the kinds of evaluation that may occur in an organization. Conducting evaluations could be a full-time job for a program administrator, and in some organizations, educational program evaluation is a full-time job. It can involve many different groups of stakeholders. It can also occur on many different levels within the organization. The next section of this chapter will consider specific levels of evaluation.

Levels of Evaluation

As an administrator of adult education programs, you should consider the concept of evaluation in a number of ways and on multiple levels. Administrators can evaluate an organization's entire offering of courses. They can evaluate specific areas or categories of courses. They can also evaluate individual courses. All levels of evaluation are important, and all must be performed on an ongoing basis if the organization's courses are to be successful.

To illustrate, consider the community learning center and its course structure depicted in Figure 9.3. This community learning center offers several different varieties of educational programs. All educational programs fall under the same division of the organization. Within that division, they are further divided by subject matter (only the basic skills courses are depicted in Figure 9.3). All basic skills courses are grouped together, for

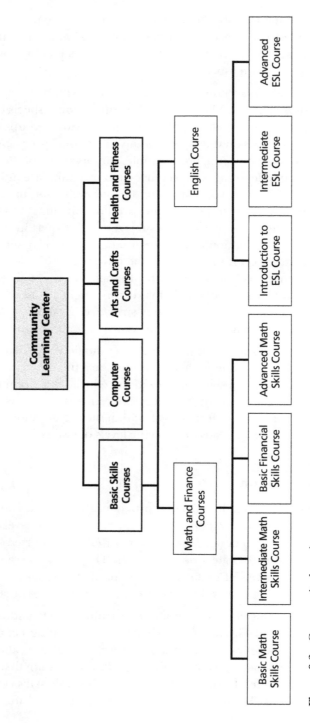

Figure 9.3 Community learning center structure.

example (as depicted in Figure 9.3), as are all computer-related courses, all health and fitness–related courses, and all arts and crafts–related courses. Within the basic skills division, courses are further divided by subject. All math-related courses are grouped together as are all English-related courses. Finally, the individual courses are shown.

Evaluation of the educational programs offered at this center can be done on several different levels. Following is a discussion of those levels:

Program evaluation: All educational programs offered by this center could be evaluated. Evaluation at this level might examine the degree to which the organization's total programs serve the needs of the community. Evaluation could also focus on the degree to which the educational programs align with the overall mission of the organization (Dunsworth & Billings, 2011, p. 3).

Category evaluation: All programs in one category, such as all basic skills programs, could be evaluated. Again, evaluation could focus on the degree to which programs in a category cover information appropriate for learners in that category. Evaluation could also consider the degree to which a category of programs is aligned with the organizational goals and mission.

Subcategory evaluation: In the example above, all English courses could be evaluated to determine their effectiveness and thoroughness (with regard to topics covered).

Course evaluation: Each course within the English category could be evaluated to ensure course goals were being met and learners were satisfied with the instruction they received as well as the course content. Administrators could even evaluate the individual components of a particular course if they wanted to perform evaluations on that level. Typically, instructors do this with sections or units of their courses (or if they do not, they should).

The Process of Evaluation

There are certain processes that should be followed in order to conduct an effective evaluation. Several researchers have developed processes that can be followed when conducting an evaluation (Caffarella, 2002; Fitzpatrick et al., 2011), and the steps outlined below are a combination of various researchers' approaches.

1. Determine purpose and parameters
   - Determine overall timeline and budget

      – Identify evaluators and other key personnel
      – Set parameters and boundaries
      – Examine the evaluation context
2. Make plans for conducting the evaluation
      – Determine data-collection techniques
      – Develop questions and instruments
      – Develop plans for analysis
3. Collect data
      – Analyze results
4. Interpret results
      – Make recommendations
5. Report results

Determine Purpose and Parameters

Evaluations sometimes become exercises in which the proverbial horse is put before the cart. People get so focused on actually "doing" an evaluation that they don't think about the planning that goes into conducting a successful evaluation until they get stuck somewhere or run into some type of difficulty. It is important to plan the evaluation before anything else happens. Planning involves several things, but the major focus of planning is to determine the purpose of the evaluation (and to ensure that everyone involved in the evaluation understands the purpose). If there is no clearly stated purpose for the evaluation, conducting that evaluation becomes a waste of time and money (among other resources) (Dunsworth & Billings, 2011, p. 9). Also important are establishing boundaries within the evaluation. Evaluations cannot address every issue a program may face. Delineation of boundaries and parameters for the evaluation are important during this step of the process.

People involved in the process must be identified and brought in at this point as well. These include people who may conduct the evaluation as well as those who may organize or manage the evaluation. These people may be internal or external to the organization (and there are advantages and disadvantages to each). Also there may be some combination of internal and external evaluators. What knowledge, skills, and abilities does each person involved in the evaluation process bring to the table? What knowledge and skills gaps are there? How will those gaps be compensated for?

In addition to human resources noted above, consider other resources, including technology and financial, required to conduct an effective evaluation. What types of technological systems are in place for evaluation management? A budget for the evaluation process must be considered throughout its early stages. Budgetary constraints may affect things like the scope and parameters of the evaluation as well as the people involved in the process. Budgetary issues may also affect the timeline during which the evaluation takes place. Budgets should be considered throughout the process, and an initial budget should be developed before the evaluation begins.

All of this planning is done within the context of the organization in which the evaluation will take place. Examine the context and the environment during this stage of the process. "Evaluation is inherently a political process. Any activity that involves applying the diverse values of multiple constituents in judging the value of some object has political overtones" (Fitzpatrick et al., 2011, p. 307). What is the political state of the organization, and what types of political issues might affect the evaluation process? What types of organizational issues might affect it?

Once a purpose has been determined, parameters have been set, key players have been identified, and issues relating to resources and environment have been addressed, the process moves to the next step.

Make Plans for Conducting the Evaluation

During the planning process, the methods used for gathering data are determined, and specific questions are developed. A variety of methods exist for collecting data. Surveys, interviews, focus groups, and observations are a few of the formal methods for collecting data. Informal means, such as casual conversations and informal polling can also be employed. Also important to remember at this step is the collection of existing data. Records, transcripts, and other data that may be useful to the evaluation may already be available.

A plan for analyzing data should also be developed at this point. This plan can include methods of data analysis as well as processes and procedures to be used in the analysis of data. Individuals charged with analyzing data can be identified here as well. The overall purpose for the evaluation should be considered throughout the process. During this step it is critical to remember that purpose as it is easy to lose focus of it during the process.

Collect Data

At this point, the evaluator is ready to use the tools developed during the previous step. During this stage, interviews are conducted, surveys are distributed, and focus groups are held. Data is gathered and stored for analysis.

After data has been gathered, it can be analyzed. The data analysis plan developed in the prior step of the process can be implemented at this point (Dunsworth & Billings, 2011).

Interpret Results

Based on data analysis, results can be summarized and recommendations can be made. A major consideration during this part of the process is the importance of consistency from data analysis to interpretation to recommendations. It is important that interpretation makes sense based on data analysis and recommendations are formed from sound interpretation of results.

Report Results

The reporting of results to key stakeholders depends on the purpose of the evaluation and the information each stakeholder may need (or may want to see). There is no single right or wrong way to present results. When reporting results, consider what each stakeholder may want to know. For example, higher-level executives in an organization may want an executive summary of the evaluation of a particular training program employees in their divisions are required to take. Those who work closely with the employees in that division (such as managers and supervisors) may have a need for additional details on the findings.

It is a good idea to compile a list of people who are interested in the results of an evaluation, along with the method used to present those results. Remember that those involved in the process of gathering data, such as people who were surveyed or interviewed, may be interested in results as well. Sometimes those people are not considered at this point. Also remember that students may be interested in the results of the evaluation. Following up with people who participated in the process is an appropriate courtesy, and it helps to ensure those people will work with you on future evaluation projects.

Process Summary

While the steps presented are arranged in a logical sequence for program evaluation, this type of evaluation does not necessarily happen in a logical order. With regard to the evaluation process, Caffarella (2002) notes that sometimes "various elements overlap, need to be revisited, or have already been addressed through other planning activities" (p. 230). Also remember that evaluation can be formal or informal. It may involve working chronologically through a series of predetermined steps similar to those noted above. Or it may be as informal a process as asking a group of learners their thoughts about a particular course. Just like the process of educational program planning, planning for evaluation is not always an orderly activity. However, it can be helpful to have some type of guide or general set of steps to use when possible.

When Not To Evaluate

The process presented above is an effective overall guide for conducting an evaluation. However, the process assumes that answers to the questions within the first step (Determine Purpose and Parameters) are positive and they provide the evaluator with the information they need to successfully progress to the next step. However, suppose that is not the case and the information garnered during this step of the process raises concerns for the evaluator. It is possible at this point that the evaluator may realize the present is not the optimal time to conduct an evaluation. What follows are some potential problematic issues to watch for at this step.

Are there conflicting views on the need for evaluation? Are those views held by people who have power to provide access to resources and other items needed to conduct a successful evaluation? If those who control resources are not willing to cooperate with the evaluator, it is difficult to see how an evaluation can be done. Likewise, if the scope of the proposed evaluation is greater than the resources allocated to it, the evaluation will not be successful. In these cases, the evaluator should consider whether to move forward with the evaluation or not. Is there consensus on how to use evaluation results? Will results be used at all? If evaluation results will not be used, there may be no good reason to conduct an evaluation (Fitzpatrick et al., 2011).

The Administrator's Role in Evaluation

Because the field of adult education is so broad, and those who organize and administer adult education programs work in so many different venues, there is no singular set of rules for administrators with regard to the evaluation of adult education programs. In some cases, the administrator of a program may be in charge of all duties related to every aspect of program evaluation. In other cases, the administrator may receive the results of an evaluation conducted by others within the organization. Sometimes administrators may want to remove themselves from all or part of the evaluation process in order to ensure the evaluation is not biased in any way. Administrators who also supervise employees may have direct authority over those who conduct evaluations, and they should remember that their presence during, or participation in, an evaluation may affect the decisions made by subordinates, or it may affect direct reports in the evaluation process. For example, it may be difficult for an evaluator to provide the results of a negative evaluation to his or her supervisor, especially if the program being evaluated is a favorite or "pet project" of that supervisor. Administrators who are supervisors must be able to examine and consider how their presence and participation might affect the evaluation process and results.

Internal Versus External Evaluators

As stated previously, management of an organization's evaluation processes is often the job of the program administrator. Administrators also make decisions about whether to conduct evaluations using internal or external evaluators. Most evaluations are conducted within the organization itself, and a great deal of that evaluation is informal and ongoing. Formal evaluations can also be conducted internally as well. In some situations, however, external evaluations are required. When an organization is licensed or accredited by an agency, often the agency requires external evaluation of the organization's programs as part of the accreditation or licensing process. Sometimes organizations want to obtain objective perspectives on their programs, and they choose to enlist external evaluators to conduct evaluations. St. Clair (2015) notes that "as the need to demonstrate effectiveness in (educational) programs has grown, a new profession specializing in evaluation has sprung up" (p. 133).

There are benefits and detriments to using both internal evaluators and external evaluators. Internal evaluators have the benefit of understanding the context of the organization and its programs. Because of their knowledge, they can tailor their recommendations more specifically, and this can result in a greater organizational commitment to implement those recommendations. Internal evaluators also are employed by the organization, so they can work to ensure their recommendations are carried out. Typically, it is cheaper and faster to conduct an internal evaluation as well (Conley-Tyler, 2005; Fitzpatrick et al., 2011).

Conversely, internal evaluators may have biases, and they may not be as objective as external evaluators. Also, they may not have the subject-matter expertise or the level of expertise in evaluation that external evaluators might offer (Conley-Tyler, 2005).

There are many advantages to using external evaluators. External evaluators are typically seen as more objective and impartial as well as more credible than internal evaluators. Additionally, external evaluators can bring a variety of perspectives to evaluations, and they typically have more specific expertise in the process of evaluation. People within the organization might reveal more to an external evaluator than to an internal evaluator as well. Because they do not have long-term ties to the organization, external evaluators can present information that may be unpopular or controversial, and they can be blunt in their assessments (Conley-Tyler, 2005; Fitzpatrick et al., 2011).

External evaluators typically are more expensive to employ, and evaluations using external evaluators often take longer than those using internal evaluators. External evaluators do not have the contextual knowledge that is helpful in conducting an evaluation, and because they work with organizations on shorter-term bases, they may not be present to help with the implementation of their recommendations (Conley-Tyler, 2005; Fitzpatrick et al., 2011).

Chapter Summary

Evaluation is a multifaceted concept that should be woven throughout the fabric of educational organizations. Programs cannot continually improve without some type of evaluation to guide their evolutionary process. They cannot show their worth or the value they add to society without evaluation. This chapter covered basic concepts associated with the topic of evaluation. These concepts can be used to develop and implement evaluation plans that can help organizations move forward.

DISCUSSION QUESTIONS

1. Think of an adult education program in your workplace or area of interest. What areas of the program would you most like to evaluate and why? What type of approach (or combination of approaches) for evaluation would be most appropriate?

2. Consider your role as one who organizes and administers programs (either in your workplace or in an organization with which you are familiar). How might your involvement in the evaluation process affect the evaluation? Consider the people involved and your relationships with them as well as potential processes that might be affected.

3. Consider an educational organization with which you are familiar. Compile a list of that organization's stakeholders. Then rank them, if you can, in order of importance to the organization.

4. Think about the last time you conducted a program evaluation. Which steps of the process noted in this chapter did you do and which did you leave out (and why)?
5. Discuss some ways in which evaluation can add value to the training function of an organization. How is this value related to the communication of results from an evaluation?
6. Consider the four scenarios described at the start of this chapter. What would you recommend for each scenario? What additional evaluation-related considerations should each of the people in the four scenarios consider?

References

Business Dictionary. (n.d.). *Stakeholder.* Retrieved from http://www.businessdictionary.com/definition/stakeholder.html

Caffarella, R. S. (2002). *Planning programs for adult learners.* San Francisco, CA: Jossey-Bass.

Cervero, R. M. (1988). *Effective continuing education for professionals.* San Francisco, CA: Jossey-Bass.

Conley-Tyler, M. (2005). A fundamental choice: Internal or external evaluation. *Evaluation Journal of Australiasia, 4*(1/2), 3–11.

Dunsworth, M., & Billings, D. (2011). *Essentials for principals: Effective program evaluation* (2nd ed.). Bloomington, IN: Solution Tree Press.

Fitzpatrick, J. L., Sanders, J. R., & Worthen, B. R. (2011). *Program evaluation. Alternative approaches and practical guidelines.* Upper Saddle River, NJ: Pearson.

Galbraith, M. W., & Jones, M. S. (2010). Assessment and evaluation. In C. Kasworm, A. D. Rose, & J. M. Ross-Gordon (Eds.), *Handbook of adult and continuing education.* Los Angeles, CA: Sage.

Mertens, D. M., & Wilson, A. T. (2012). Program evaluation theory and Practice: A comprehensive guide. New York, NY: Guilford Press.

Spaulding, D. T. (2014). *Research methods for the social sciences: Program evaluation in practice: Core concepts and examples for discussion and analysis* (2nd ed.). Somerset, NJ: Wiley.

St. Clair, R. (2015). *Creating courses for adults.* San Francisco, CA: Jossey-Bass.

Werner, J. M., & DiSimone, R. L. (2012). *Human resource development.* Mason, OH: South-Western.

10

Legal Issues and Ethical Considerations

A Question of Character

The word *ethics* is derived from the Greek word *ethos* which means *character* and from the Latin word *mores*, which means *customs*. "Together, they define the term ethics, which is how individuals choose to interact with one another" (Legal Information Institute, n.d., para 1). Legal issues are those for which there are laws or policies in place that must be followed when addressing them (Woska, 2013). Legal and ethical issues will be examined together in this chapter, although they are not interchangeable in concept or definition. The Cornell University Legal Information Institute notes, "Though law often embodies ethical principles, law and ethics are far from co-extensive" (Legal Information Institute, n.d., para 2). Lying, for example, may be unethical, but it is not illegal. Can you think of other things that may be unethical but not illegal? How about things that may be illegal but ethical? Consider these two concepts, and these questions, in the context of adult education.

Who among us doesn't think they perform their job in a legal and ethical manner? Certainly most (or all) adult educators would say that

Organization and Administration of Adult Education Programs, pages 219–247

219

they hold themselves to high ethical standards and perform their jobs well within the boundaries of the law. However, when pressed for specifics, often peoples' ethical standards differ, as do people's interpretations of both what is within, and outside of, the law. Legal and ethical issues are linked to those responsible for educational program administration in a variety of contexts (Cooper, 2012). Some things may differ: the focus of educational efforts, the operational environment, and the people with whom the administrator interacts. Legal issues and ethical considerations are always present. Topics in this chapter serve as guideposts to help you as an administrator understand the issues that are most relevant to your practice. Also included in this chapter are points of critical reflection, so you can consider legal and ethical responsibilities to yourself, your employees, your organization, and society. In reading through this chapter, make note of the topics and sections you are most interested in for further investigation. Consider additional legal issues not noted in this chapter which may be of importance to program administrators. Subsequent investigation will help develop the knowledge and decision-making processes of the program administrator. Consider the following scenario.

Refreshed after the weekend, you come in to your office on a Monday morning with your list of things to do for the week. You open your email and receive several messages: (a) You just completed a search to fill an open position, and you offered the job to a candidate. The human resources department has written to notify you that one of the candidates who did not receive the position filed a complaint with your state's equal rights division, and the organization's lawyers would like to meet with you to discuss your response to document the search and screening process so that they can respond to the equal rights division. (b) An employee asks to meet with you about a situation and asks if you can promise confidentiality. (c) You receive a phone call from a news reporter about a controversial public program your organization held. The reporter would like to know if you could talk to her about complaints made by community members. (d) You have just been informed that a mandatory training that has long been planned falls on a major religious holiday for one quarter of your staff.

Do these scenarios sound familiar? All of these issues have the potential to take up a lot of time as well as organizational resources. These types of Monday morning messages put a series of personal and organizational decision-making processes into motion that are connected to organizational policy, ethics, and legal obligations.

Why Are Legal and Ethical Issues Important to Adult Educators?

One thing that separates administrators of adult education programs from those who teach in adult education programs is that administrators tend to be required to deal with legal issues more often than instructors are. That is because of the leadership and managerial duties associated with educational program administrator positions. The management of organizations, the supervising of employees, and the administration of educational programs can entail dealing with legal conflicts among employees, learners, and other organizational stakeholders. That is why knowledge of legal issues is important to educational program administrators.

Administrators and educators deal with ethical issues of all kinds as well. The types of ethical issues administrators deal with may be different from those in which adult educators are involved simply because of the different nature of the administrative position. In this chapter, both legal issues and ethics will be discussed from the standpoint of educational program administration.

Chapter Overview

An understanding of legal issues and knowledge of ethical considerations are important in the decision-making processes and in the critically reflective practice of adult education program administrators. Legal issues and ethical considerations compose the main sections of this chapter, and it concludes with potential ethical and legal dilemmas meant for further analysis and discussion.

The first section of this chapter explores legal issues relevant to administrators in adult education and human resource development. Legal issues discussed are categorized by type (hiring, firing, compliance, and contracts, for example).

This chapter will not provide legal advice. It will provide information on common categories of issues that educational program administrators must deal with. It will also provide information on possible resources for administrators.

The second section of the chapter addresses ethical considerations that program administrators may face. "Ethics involves the examination and analysis of the logic, values, beliefs, and principles that are used to justify morality in its various forms . . . Ethics takes what is given or prescribed and asks what is meant and why" (Cooper, 2012, p. 2). The terms *ethics* and *morals* are often used interchangeably. Program administrators should take the time to critically reflect upon their views and how they integrate this critical reflection into practice. It takes a lifetime to build ethical positions, but it may take only a moment to either reinforce or violate those positions.

What Exactly Is a "Legal Issue?"

A legal issue is one for which there are some types of laws or rules that must be followed when addressing or working through it (Woska, 2013). Legal issues can be examined by group or by category. For example, there are many laws that govern the processes that must be used for hiring and terminating employees. Other laws address compliance, contracts, the providing of accommodation(s), and many other topics.

Legal issues can be examined on different levels also. There are different laws at the municipal, state, federal, international, and transnational levels, and an educational organization may have many different laws to follow on each of those levels. For example, consider the legal concept of a protected class. A protected class of people cannot be discriminated against on the job based on a particular protected characteristic. Federal laws prohibit discrimination based on certain parameters such as race, age, and religion (among others). Physical appearance is not a protected class on the federal or state levels, but in some municipalities (such as Madison, Wisconsin), physical appearance is a protected class (MuniCode, 2015).

Because legal issues vary according to specific levels, they become even more complex as they relate to situations such as offering distance education courses across state lines or when working in organizations with locations in more than one municipality, state, or country. For example, when working in another country, laws that govern the number of hours per week employees can work may differ. To further complicate things, legal issues on all of these topics and at various levels are continually changing.

Program administrators must be familiar with laws at all levels as they are apply to their organization's operations (Table 10.1). Decisions made within the organization must be informed by parameters the organization is bound to by law, what they must report by law, or for what they and their organizations can legally be held liable for under the law. Compliance with the law and implementation of policies and procedures within legal guidelines must be considerations for each administrator. Therefore, as administrators face legal issues, they must consider how to most efficiently and effectively operate within the boundaries of the law.

TABLE 10.1	Levels of Legal Considerations
Level	**Consideration**
Municipal and County	Pay attention to legal issues relating not only to where the organization is located, but also to where its programs are held.
State	If the organization works with people in multiple states, be sure to understand the laws within all states in which educational programs are offered. Each state may handle issues of credentialing and licensure in different ways. Distance education programs mean learners may be located in many different states.
Federal	Understand how federal laws affect the operations. Family Education Rights and Privacy Act (FERPA), The Americans with Disabilities Act (ADA), and Title VII of the Civil Rights Act of 1964 are just a few of the federal laws that impact all organizations in the United States.
Tribal Governments	Within the United States and other nation states, program administrators may work as part of a tribal government, or their organizations may offer educational programs held on tribal lands. Be aware of tribal government rules and policies that may govern the organization's work. Tribal governments are recognized as domestic dependent nations within the U.S. and other indigenous peoples within other nation states in which the organization operates may have similar status.
International, Transnational, and Supranational Organizations	International, transnational, and supranational bodies may enforce regulations that can impact the organization's work. For example, the European Union is an example of a supranational organization and an organization may conduct a training session in one of its member states.

Types of Legal Issues

As noted earlier, there are many different kinds of potential legal issues program administrators may face. Some common legal issues program administrators are responsible for are noted in the Figure 10.1. Each of these will be discussed separately in the next section of this chapter.

Hiring

There are laws that govern many aspects of the hiring process, including the advertising of positions, searching and screening (including background checks), interviewing, making job offers, and bringing new employees on board. These types of laws address issues such as discrimination, protected classes, reference and background checks, questions that can and cannot be asked during interviews, preemployment testing, new-hire

---

Examples of Legal Issues

- Hiring
- Conducting performance evaluations
- Remediation, suspension, or termination
- Maintaining privacy
- Accommodation
- Providing education
- Supervising daily organization climate and conditions
- Contracts
- Assuring compliance

Figure 10.1 Legal issues.

paperwork, and many others. Hiring is a time-intensive process for everyone in the organization, therefore, as an administrator, the goal is for every phase of the process to go as smoothly as possible and to be legally compliant. This requires a good understanding of all hiring-related laws.

Organizations often have a specific process in place for each step of the hiring process, and those steps should have been developed with consideration for the legal aspects of the hiring process. In organizations with a human resource department (or a person who manages the human resource function), that department or person should be aware of all hiring-related laws, and they should ensure all laws are followed throughout the hiring process.

Even with a human resource department or an employee designated to manage the human resource function, program administrators in charge of the hiring process should ensure that they are knowledgeable about the most current laws and policies surrounding the hiring process whenever that process is undertaken. They should also review hiring processes, procedures, and legal guidelines with all persons involved so all are on the same page with regard to legal responsibilities and parameters. Everyone involved with the hiring process is responsible for complying with all levels of the law.

Legal issues surrounding the hiring process focus on the fair and equitable treatment of all candidates applying for positions (Buckley, 2016). Establishing processes for developing and publicizing job postings, reviewing and evaluating applications, conducting interviews, and making hiring decisions is important. Scoring rubrics can be used to assess candidates in comparison to the job qualifications. Rubrics can help guide and document interviewers' decisions throughout the application and interview process. A rubric can be developed using the job description as a guideline. Think

Criteria	5 Excellent	4 Very Good	3 Average	2 Below Average	1 Low or None	0 Unable to assess	Score
Requisite experience teaching math							
Experience teaching adults							

Figure 10.2 Example of part of a scoring rubric.

about what the duties of the position are and consider the type of scoring relevant at the application and interview phases. For example, some of the criteria required for a basic math instructor are 2 to 3 years of experience teaching math and experience teaching adults. Part of a rubric for this position might look like that within Figure 10.2.

In the interview, consistency can be maintained using prescribed interview questions (and communication with other interviewers to make sure they do not veer off script). Questions asked should be standard and relevant to the duties indicated in the job posting. Documents used by those involved in all phases of the hiring process should be retained by the organization in the event they are needed in the future. Keeping those documents demonstrates adherence to rules and procedures in the event that questions about the process later arise.

While there are many rules that govern hiring processes, many of them are based around the concept of discrimination (and of giving all applicants equal consideration and opportunity during the hiring process). All of us would say that we do not intend to discriminate, but what would an outsider say about our actions through the hiring process? Do these actions reflect compliance?

Conducting Performance Evaluations

Performance evaluations are a critical part of employee management and serve as documented records of an employee's performance and progress toward goals. Core legal-related elements of the performance review process include consistency of evaluation among different employees or groups of employees, the equity of the process, and timeliness of the process (Mayhew, n.d.). Evaluations should be written or documented with clear summaries, actions, goals, and other specific information such as timelines and dates. Established systems for providing performance evaluations should be in place and clearly documented for all employees. Self-assessments and rubrics may also be used to demonstrate equal treatment and equal access to opportunity.

Remediation, Suspension, or Termination

Many of the same types of legal elements related to the conducting of performance reviews are also applicable to remediation, firing, or termination. Policies, in compliance with legal requirements, should be in place that clearly outline steps to be taken as a result of either positive or negative performance reviews. It is easy to develop policies for positive performance reviews, as these policies often include reward or recognition. Policies for negative reviews must be much more detailed, and legal issues must be carefully considered when negative reviews are necessary. Often, policies for handling negative reviews include providing a process for remediation. These might include job duty clarification, short-term goal setting, or increased training. Whether positive or negative, an administrator must demonstrate due diligence in documenting the "why" (the reasons for the positive or negative performance review) as well as a plan for the future, and they must be certain that disparate treatment issues do not exist. The termination process is not a time for impulsive or "knee-jerk" reactions to complaints. Administrators need to properly investigate situations (and document the findings of those investigations) to show they have gathered sufficient information to support their actions. Gathering this information may involve navigating the political contexts inside and outside their organizations. Termination may be the last step in the process for dealing with negative performance (Falcone, 2010).

The organization may also have specific policies relating to actions that result in immediate suspension (and subsequent termination, if applicable). There should also be a policy for how an employee is informed of suspension and termination, including a procedure relating to what happens after the person is informed. In cases of termination, policies might address whether or not the individual is immediately escorted out of the building and if prearranged security is used in order to help facilitate the process. In these events, plan ahead for both best case and worst case scenarios.

Maintaining Privacy

Program administrators may deal with legally based privacy issues on two levels: that of the employee and that of the adult learner. For both groups, it is critical the administrator and all individuals handling records for both learners and employees understand what type of information they can (and cannot) provide and to whom they can (and cannot) provide it. Most employee records are confidential, and information in them cannot be shared openly. Typically, information pertaining to adult learners, such as grades, attendance records, and personal contact information also cannot be shared (although laws for the sharing of minors' information with parents or legal guardians are different from those pertaining to adults).

Nobody in the organization should assume they know the families or personal circumstances of their learners or fellow employees. Everyone in the organization should know what kind of information can (and cannot) legally be shared with second or third parties. In addition, there may be privacy rules that apply specifically to the kind of education being delivered and the organization in which the administrator works. For example, if an individual is required to attend training as part of a court order or as part of continuing professional education credits to maintain licensure, there may be specific processes for reporting information and specific people to whom that information is reported. Some personnel records that might be confidential in the private sector (such as salary data) are part of public records in the public sector. This affects confidentiality issues for adult educators and program administrators working for the government and in public institutions of higher education.

Accommodation

The Americans with Disabilities Act (ADA) assigns civil rights protections to individuals with disabilities. The Equal Employment Opportunity Commission states a person may be considered disabled if they have a physical or mental condition that substantially limits a major life activity (such as walking, talking, seeing, hearing, or learning), have a history of a disability (a disease that is in remission, for example), or if a person is believed to have a physical or mental impairment. The ADA guarantees equal opportunity for individuals with disabilities in employment, public accommodations, transportation, state and local government services, and telecommunications (U.S. Department of Justice, 2013). This guarantee of accommodation is important to understand for both employees and learners. For example, if an educational organization holds a public program, how will they accommodate individuals who need a sign language interpreter? Do registration and marketing materials indicate how much notice is needed in order to provide accommodations? Can online course materials be accessed and used by those with disabilities? Are the organization's facilities accessible to employees who use wheelchairs? Consider the rules and policies in place to accommodate both employees and learners, and be sure that your organization is prepared to remain compliant with ADA requirements.

Providing Education

The selection of adult learners for competitive educational opportunities is also an area in which administrators should have explicit policies and processes in place. These policies should address learners whom the organization serves as well as employees in the organization. For example, if there are scholarship opportunities to participate in informal programs the organization delivers, or internal training opportunities for which employees are selected, be sure there are systems in place for documenting how and why individuals are chosen. In addition, due diligence, or properly researching sound business decisions and responsibilities, is critical with regard to the administration and planning of employee development programs so that compliance (adherence to the law) is demonstrated and potential negligence (violation of the law—whether intentional or unintentional), is avoided (Buckley, 2016). How administrators determine who has access to educational opportunities may impact learners' opportunities for advancement in their own organizations (Clardy, 2003) or employees' advancement opportunities as well. Adult education administrators often have a central role in the decision-making process and general oversight of training programs. "Points of impact" (Clardy, 2003, p. 133) need to be considered, such as how the administrator determines which individuals qualify for continuing education and how the training program is designed and evaluated.

As stated above, participation in training may qualify employees to advance within the organization. As such, a "domino effect" may occur (starting with training decisions and ending with performance review and promotion decisions), which may have an overall, and perhaps illegal impact on opportunities for certain groups of employees. For example, are training opportunities offered to only those employees we like or not offered to marginally performing employees? Is training always held at a time when those belonging to a specific religious group cannot attend? Are certain training environments accessible to only the employees who are hearing or who can walk? Access-related policies should address these issues.

Supervising Daily Organization Climate and Conditions.

Part of an administrator's role is to both foster and nurture a healthy organizational climate. Organizational climate is defined as "the meanings people attach to interrelated bundles of experiences they have at work" (Schneider, Ehrhart, & Macey, 2013, p. 361). Elements of climate include people's perceptions of organizational policy, procedure, and practice, as well as their perceptions of ways others are treated in the workplace (Schneider et al., 2013). Some workplaces seem to have healthy organizational climates and others may have unhealthy organizational climates that could cause employees to leave the organization or create an atmosphere in which gossip, harassment, and other negative behaviors become the norm, adversely impacting the lives of employees and creating situations in which legal issues, such as lawsuits, may arise.

Administrators need to understand their organization's climate, and they should have an organizational climate "thermostat" so they can continually gauge climate. A healthy climate is one that is conducive to working and learning. Sometimes organizations measure climate conditions with healthy workplace indicators, workplace well-being scales, or life-work satisfaction surveys. For the most meaningful results, these types of instruments can be customized for each workplace.

Although descriptors for a healthy workplace may vary on a continuum within a variety of diverse cultural and work contexts, healthy aspects you may wish to consider are listed in Figure 10.3.

After years of performing administrative work, gauging the organizational climate may seem an intuitive skill to many program administrators, but each administrator continually needs to integrate a deliberately reflective practice for "checking in" with co-workers, subordinates, and leadership. Climates

---

Examples of Healthy Workplace Indicators

- High morale
- Open communication among all levels of the organization
- Respect and appreciation for the work of all members
- Productivity
- Accountability
- Flexibility
- Fair wages and benefits
- Collaboration/independence work balance
- Fairness
- Work–life balance
- Support
- Emotional, mental, and physical safety

Figure 10.3   Healthy workplace indicators.

can change quickly, and administrators need to rely on colleagues and co-workers to help them learn what is working well as it relates to their organizational climate as well as what areas may need to be addressed.

As an administrator, it is important to be aware of certain "red flags" such as high absenteeism, frequent turnover, and inability to retain workers. These red flags may indicate a serious issue relating to the organizational climate of an organization. Climates can be adjusted with changes to policy, procedure, and employee treatment. Also important to consider is that characteristics of a healthy climate can become negative sometimes. For example, teamwork and close camaraderie among employees can contribute to high morale and increased productivity. Yet, when these collaborations and tight-knit alliances become exclusionary to others, teamwork can encourage an "insider/outsider" mentality, and it may be difficult for new employees to join these groups. Excluded employees may even be marginalized or barred from collaborative workgroups. Taken to the extreme, this kind of behavior can result in instances of workplace bullying. When bullying in the workplace occurs, destructive moral, physical, and mental consequences for the targeted employee, as well as legal consequences for employees and the organization, are inherently likely.

Workplace climate is a large issue frequently affected by many small situations. These small situations (or incidents) may not seem important when prioritizing work, but the accumulated and unchecked effects of many small situations can affect larger perceptions of climate. Administrators must be able to detect positive and negative climate issues, interrogate their own belief systems, reward positive behaviors, and address unwanted behaviors before they become destructive patterns that escalate into legal issues for those within the organization. Make time to check the organization's "climate thermostat": Watch for subtleties by staying attuned to dynamics within meetings and those occurring at the water cooler; be sure to periodically conduct formative assessments of workplace climate that allow all personnel in the organization to provide input.

Contracts

A contract is a formal agreement outlining voluntary obligations that are enforceable by law (Blum, 2007). Although contracts can be written or oral, in general it is much easier to document and enforce written contracts. Everyone enters into simple contracts as part of everyday life. For example, when someone goes to the store to purchase a new camera, there is an understanding or agreement that, in an exchange for money, the vendor is selling the purchaser a product that will operate as advertised. In education, tuition

---

Examples of Types of Contracts

- Services and equipment (phone, Internet, printing, copy machine and computer rental, transportation, cleaning, electricity, trash removal)

- Space (operating office space, conference rooms, and outside facility rental)

- People (employees, consultants, adjunct instructors, legal counsel, security, and trainers)

Figure 10.4 Types of contracts.

or fees are exchanged for educational services. Educators promise to deliver, for example, a high quality healthcare training that meets certain goals and objectives in exchange for money paid by learners to attend the training. Or those working in HRD may contract with an information technology specialist to deliver a training session to employees in the organization.

Three general categories for contracts may include contracts for equipment and services, contracts for space, and contracts for people (Blum, 2007) (Figure 10.4).

Administrators might be charged with contracting for services their organization needs such as cleaning and trash removal, equipment like copy machines and computers; and use of spaces such as offices and classrooms. Contracting for services and equipment may be fairly straightforward with all obligations clearly and easily stated. Contracts for use of space(s) may be a little more complex, and it is essential to understand what a contract allows an organization to do (and what it prohibits an organization from doing) within a facility. Contracts may include facility and/or union rules that may govern what can be brought into the building (including food and equipment), as well as what kind of work an organization's staff may do, such as moving equipment and arranging chairs. Some facility contracts specify that furniture, equipment, and services must be obtained from specific vendors. Check the specific rules/regulations for each of these, ask questions when anything is unclear, and also learn exactly what is excluded from the contract as well as what is included in the contract.

Contracts for people include those signed by employees, instructors, or consultants for the organization. These contracts should be developed by legal experts to ensure they address all elements relevant to the situation.

As noted above, it is important to know exactly what is included in any contracts that are signed, as well as what is not included. If something is not listed in the contract, it is not included in the contract, so additional services, features, and considerations will most likely come at an additional price. For example, in contracting with a facility to run courses that require Internet access, do not assume that access is included unless it is stated as included in the contract. In contracting with a company to provide a copier, be certain what kind of copier service and maintenance is provided within the contract. When hiring outside consultants, it is important to know whether expenses are computed as additional costs. Contracts for consultants often include daily rates and fee schedules for the work performed, but many consultants require organizations to pay for a variety of additional expenses separately. These additional expenses may include travel expenses the consultant incurs in getting to and from the organization. Work with legal experts in the organization to be sure any contracts you sign directly meet the needs of the organization. Administrators who work in nonprofit or community-based organizations should consider enlisting the help of a volunteer who has an appropriate legal background to help with contracts.

The same concepts are true when the organization is the provider of services. Every adult education organization wants their learners to have effective and enjoyable learning experiences. Those positive experiences start with clearly stating (within contracts) what type of educational services are to be provided to learners in exchange for tuition and fees.

Assuring Compliance

Compliance refers to adhering to standards, rules, or legislation (Buckley, 2016). An administrator's role is to oversee compliance in multiple ways. Examples of areas in which organizations must be compliant include the following:

- Accommodation,
- Copyright,
- Health care,
- Safety (for both employees and customers or learners),
- Tax,
- Trade, and
- Human resource issues (including hiring, compensation, pay, benefits, and training, among others) (U.S. Department of Labor, 2013).

From an administrative standpoint, compliance involves two separate things. First, administrators want to make sure all they do remains in compliance with the applicable laws. Second, administrators need to be able to demonstrate (through documentation, which includes policies, procedures, and other evidences) that they are complying with all applicable laws. Everyone in the organization needs to understand compliance issues that affect the organization, and they must also be able to demonstrate adherence to compliance if questioned. Be aware of the multiple levels of compliance. Organizations may be subject to compliance-related laws on municipal, county, state, federal, and international levels. They must be compliant with all laws and rules that affect them, and there should be policies and processes in place for documenting that compliance.

Now consider the levels of authority and the structure of the organization within which program administrators work. Program administrators often oversee both personnel and processes in their organizations, and they are responsible for ensuring both personnel and processes are compliant with the law. Although it may not be the administrator's specific job duty to create advertisements for a series of educational programs or to schedule work hours for employees, they may manage these processes in a larger sense, so they must insure that all employees (and volunteers, if the organization relies on volunteer support) who deal with issues involving compliance have knowledge of legal issues affecting their work. This will help to ensure that employee and volunteer performance remains within the boundaries of the law.

The second important aspect of compliance deals with demonstration of how compliance is ensured and that it is recorded within documentation. The methods used to document and communicate information on many of the above topics should be considered from a legal standpoint. All organizations should have policies for documentation related to compliance, as well as policies for how legal information is communicated to people in the organization. Retention policies relating to what documents are kept, how they are kept, and for how long they are kept before being destroyed are important aspects of documentation policies (these should always be developed to meet legal requirements).

Learning About Legal Issues

Laws continually change, and new court decisions continually impact laws. Adult education administrators should continually update their existing knowledge relating to legal issues. They must develop internal processes for handling how changes to laws that affect the organization are incorporated into the organization's procedures. They should also understand how legal issues (and changes to laws) impact their specific profession or industry. For example, adult education administrators working in continuing professional education for nurses and those working for an auto manufacturing company may have some overlapping issues, but there are issues that may be very specific to each of their professions and industries.

The saying "Ignorance is bliss" is not true when dealing with legal issues. Ignorance about legal issues (changes in the law) can be costly. Violations of the law may happen simply because an administrator cannot control all people and all situations; however, they can educate themselves and those in their organizations, and they can create processes to demonstrate and ensure compliance. It is critical to continually ask questions and always seek to learn. Most administrators are not lawyers, nor do most have expertise in legal issues. In these cases, it is important others in the organization have that expertise. As noted earlier, if the organization relies on volunteers, it is advantageous to have volunteer contacts who are in the legal profession who can provide advice. Administrators can pursue multiple avenues to educate themselves about potential legal issues impacting their organizations including those listed in Figure 10.5.

The suggestions shown in Figure 10.5 are just a few examples of potential resources that educational program administrators can use to learn about legal issues affecting them and their organizations. What other resources might be available? Consider legal issues from a general perspective, and consider legal issues that may be discipline-specific as well.

Potential Avenues for Continuing Education About Legal Issues in Adult Education Administration

- Consultation with a lawyer
- Professional association meetings, listservs, newsletters, and journals
- Conferences
- Continuing professional education, and for-credit formal continuing professional education courses
- Non-credit workshops
- Webinars
- Local, State, and Federal Compliance Agencies, such as a State Equal Rights Division or the U.S. Department of Labor

---

Figure 10.5 Potential sources for legal information.

Summary

Legal issues are complicated, but this section gives program administrators several ways to begin analyzing, addressing, and learning about them. Understanding the laws and policies that affect the organization and establishing steps to ensure the organization operates within the boundaries of the law are both critical. How organizations demonstrate commitment to following laws applicable to them is also important. In addition, education about legal issues should be ongoing, and finding appropriate resources to update that knowledge should be a continual aspect of the administrator's professional development.

Ethical Considerations

Ethics can be considered systems of moral principles for individuals, groups, and organizations (Cooper, 2012). Ethical issues can relate to many of the legal issues we have discussed. For example, there are laws addressing reasonable accommodation for those with disabilities, but do administrators have an ethical responsibility to teach their employees about disability or include content in coursework about individuals with disabilities? Some would argue that the inclusion of this content is an ethical responsibility as well as a legal one (McLean, 2008). In many legal situations, ethical considerations come into play. In some cases, minimum legally compliant actions and the ethical actions may not be the same. Addressing legal issues can spur ethical considerations (and vice versa), and combined, the way program administrators deal with each of these contributes to the overall running and reputation of the organization.

Many professions study the application of ethics in specific environments, such as business ethics, medical ethics, or military ethics. Working in adult education, administrators have a unique set of applied ethics because adult learners are typically the focus of the organization's mission. For example, administrators may be involved with an organization that trains physicians, one that provides adult basic education, or one that educates individuals about human rights. Ethical issues faced by program administrators in these diverse environments are situated within a complex set of individual, group, organizational, and discipline-related contexts. Ethical problems may challenge administrators, and ways in which ethical issues are managed and ethical principles are implemented says a lot about the organization and the administrator. This section will address applied ethics as they relate to the duties of adult education administrators.

Applied Ethics for Adult Education Administrators

Applied ethics for adult education administrators involve areas of consideration and practice common in adult education environments. Some professions have a governing body or professional association that issues a discipline-related codes of ethics. The Academy of Human Resource Development (AHRD, 1999), for example, has published standards on ethics and integrity in a document found on their website. These standards serve as guidelines for adult educators working in HRD. There is not universal agreement on whether codes of ethics are helpful, however. There is much debate over whether codes of ethics in professions are necessary, who should reinforce them (if they exist), and whether or not these codes maintain or challenge oppressive systems of the status quo (Sork, 1996).

Types of Ethical Issues

Practitioner groups of adult educators in the United States and Canada identified 12 major types of ethical issues and problems those in the profession typically face (Gordon & Sork, 2001). These issues are shown in Figure 10.6.

Program administrators are not always directly responsible for all of the types of issues shown Figure 10.6, but they may be responsible for the oversight of employees or volunteers who deal with them. Consider what types of ethical issues may arise in each of the 12 major areas. What might ethical

---

Twelve Major Types of Ethical Issues for Adult Educators

- Confidentiality
- learner–adult educator relations
- finance
- professionalism and competence
- conflict of interest
- evaluating student performance
- ownership of instructional materials
- intraorganizational concerns
- credentials
- training design
- employment practices
- enrollment and attendance (p. 213)

Figure 10.6 Ethical issues.

**Main Thematic Areas of Ethical Consideration
for Adult Education Administrators**

- Reconciling aduly learner, employee, and organizational needs
- Human resource management
- Evaluating multiple levels of performance

Figure 10.7 Thematic areas of ethical consideration.

dilemmas of each type look like in the context of your organization? What ethical dilemmas might program administrators, because of their leadership and management roles, face?

The 12 types of adult education ethical issues noted by Gordon and Sork (2001) can be examined by thematic area as well. Thematic areas relevant to adult education program administrators typically fall into three categories: reconciling adult learner, employee, and organizational needs; human resource management; and evaluating multiple levels of performance (Figure 10.7). Each will be discussed in additional detail.

Reconciling Adult Learner, Employee, and Organizational Needs

Adult education administrators must balance the needs of learners, employees, and the organization (not to mention personal needs), and often, the needs of one of these three entities conflicts with the needs of the others. An organization might offer low-cost training to members of its community on a particular topic that is of great importance to the community. However, the organization may lose money running these training sessions, and if the price of attending were increased, fewer community members would be able to attend. Consider the questions administrators might ask themselves when reconciling adult learner, employee, and organizational needs: "How should I send out the email?" "How will others view this action if I change the policy about the cost of admission to our programs?" "How should I respond to a problematic learner when that learner has political power?" "How can I follow through with a mandated budget cut and cause the least personal impact to employees and adult learners?" These kinds of questions are typical of ethical dilemmas that require administrators to reconcile learner, employee, and organizational needs.

Human Resource Management

Managing human resources is a primary job duty of many adult education administrators. Human resource management involves several topics discussed in the legal issues section of this chapter. Those include hiring and termination, performance evaluations, and providing professional development. The adult education administrator, again, may face dilemmas in managing the human resource needs of the larger organization, the unit, department, or program, and the needs of the learner.

For example, a program planner in your organization may have a fundraising goal, and that planner may not have met the goal. The administrator knows that the fundraising environment for the organization's mission is terrible at this point due to current events in the news, but the administrator is being held responsible for the organization's fundraising goals as well. Adult learners' opportunities will decrease due to funding cuts if fundraising goals are not met. What type of performance review does the administrator give the program planner? How does the organization adjust to deal with the consequences of low fundraising? This is just one example of human resource management issues that include an ethical component.

Evaluating Multiple Levels of Performance

Program administrators do a lot of evaluating. They may evaluate overall organizational success, educational programs, employee performance, and learner performance, as wells as many other things. Ethical dilemmas involving evaluation include the criteria by which someone or something is evaluated; the consistency with which that person or program is evaluated, and the methods used to evaluate them. While some methods of evaluation are objective, many are subjective. Even the development of objective evaluation tools can be somewhat subjective. A numeric rubric may be a good evaluation tool, but there is subjectivity involved in creating the categories in the rubric and the ratings associated with each. That subjectivity is not necessarily a negative thing, however, as it simply reflects the values of the administrator and (one hopes) those of the organization.

Ethical Decision Making

Ethical considerations come into play when administrators ask themselves, "To whom am I responsible?" (Brockett & Hiemstra, 2004, p. 17). These responsibilities may be viewed in terms of priority or value. In other words, administrators might weigh certain situations as having higher priority or value than others. A characteristic of ethical dilemmas is the "moral intensity" (Jones, 1991, p. 366), or the closeness, consequences, and perceived social acceptability of the situation to be addressed. The moral intensity of an ethical conflict increases as the proximity of the issue increases. It may be a challenge to consider the ethics of a story or situation that takes place somewhere far away. The moral intensity may be higher and the ethical dilemma may seem greater for the issues that are closer. Moral intensity is greater when administrators can see firsthand the impact of their decisions on individuals affected by the situation. Great moral intensity can manifest itself physically as well as mentally. Those involved may spend a lot of time thinking about ethics, and in doing so, they may develop feelings of anxiety.

Bolman and Deal (2008) discuss four principles of moral judgment, which, in combination with the ethical issues adult educators face, may set cornerstones for an ethical framework of decision making. These are "guidelines about right actions rather than right outcomes" (Bolman & Deal, 2008, p. 226).

- Mutuality. Does everyone involved have the same understanding about the rules or policies in which the situation is occurring?
- Generality. When you think about similar situations, does the action of moral conduct compare?
- Openness. Would you be willing to discuss your decision, decision-making process, and/or the details therein in public? Would you be willing and able to defend your decision making process in a public forum?
- Caring. In what ways do your actions demonstrate your understanding of, and empathy for, the concerns of those involved? (Bolman & Deal, 2008, pp. 226–227).

Recall that ethical issues for administrators were organized within three main thematic areas: reconciling adult learner, employee, and organizational needs; human resource management; and evaluating multiple levels of performance. These thematic areas of focus for an administrator, and the key areas of moral judgment described, can create a framework for ethical considerations for adult education administrators. This framework is shown in Figure 10.8.

These three thematic areas in adult education administration, combined with four points of moral judgment, provide a way of thinking about and framing ethical considerations. Administrators should investigate their specific areas of adult education, associations, and professional groups to find previously established codes of ethics.

There is no single correct way to make ethical decisions. Individuals in the field of adult education have developed frameworks and models that can be used to work through ethical dilemmas. Brockett and Hiemstra

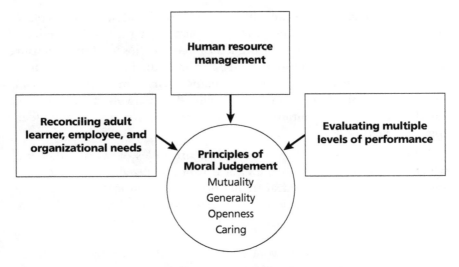

Figure 10.8 Ethical considerations and adult education administrations.

(2004) propose an ethical decision-making (EDM) model for adult education that may help guide ethics-related decision making. The questions they propose include the following:

- What do I believe? About human nature? About the education of adults? About ethics?
- How committed am I to the beliefs I hold?
- Which basic values drive my practice?
- To whom am I responsible?
- To what extent does an ethical dilemma result from conflicting obligations?
- What are my options?
- What are the possible consequences of my actions?
- Which option is most consistent with my values? (Brockett & Hiemstra, 2004, p. 17)

These questions may provide ideas for consideration that help the administrator determine a path of action when faced with ethical dilemmas. Consider them broadly at first and then consider them from the viewpoints of all stakeholders who may be affected by the administrator's actions. From there, narrow your focus and consider priorities, values, and options. While ethical dilemmas may be difficult to address, using these questions can help provide a structure for handling them appropriately.

When Ethical and Legal Considerations Collide

As explained at the start of this chapter, sometimes there are conflicts between what are legally and ethically correct actions. There are times when the legal and ethical issues collide, and program administrators need good counsel in order to work through options and consequences for the administrator, the organization, and the learner (Lipinski, 2002). The most difficult situations are legal issues that conflict with ethical standards. One example is a group of librarians' challenge to a request to give patron records to the Federal Bureau of Investigation— a request supported by the Patriot Act and passed by Congress after the attacks of September 11, 2001, in the United States. In a specific case, four Connecticut librarians felt that it was an "infringement on the intellectual freedom of their patrons" to release such records. The Patriot Act cites national security as the priority. The American Library Association (ALA, 2013) became very involved in the debate as a professional association. The ALA stated the following:

> Protecting patron privacy and the confidentiality of library records are deep and longstanding principles of librarianship that guide the ALA's legislative and policy activities on privacy and surveillance issues. The freedom to read is an inherently important part of our First Amendment rights and civil liberties (para. 9).

This example demonstrates ethical and legal conflict in a nonformal adult education context. It is one of many examples of a legal and ethical conflict that program administrators may face. Keys to addressing these types of issues include sound legal counsel; understanding of organizational goals, priorities, and values; knowledge of the situation; and a plan (such as use of the questions listed above) to work through the dilemma.

Summary

An ongoing theme within this chapter is the importance of being as proactive as possible when handling legal and ethical issues. Proactive action is required in order to comply with legal and ethical issues that confront program administrators. Are potential legal and ethical dilemmas only addressed as a reaction to conflict, or are codes, processes, and policies continually being examined and revised in a proactive manner? The difference in approaches may mean the difference between a healthy and unhealthy organization.

Conclusion

Now that you have read this chapter, you may be better prepared to discuss the ways legal and ethical issues relate to your adult education practice. Do you have a clearer understanding of the ethics and the ethical issues adult educators face? What about the legal issues they face? Both legal and ethical issues are important to program administrators, regardless of the specific areas in which they practice. The questions and scenarios provided below may help you clarify your position(s) and give you cause to consider the areas in which you may need further study.

QUESTIONS FOR DISCUSSION

1. Review the section in this chapter entitled "Levels of Compliance and Considerations." Identify the levels in which you do business or conduct educational programs. Which levels and laws impact your practice?

2. Does your organization have contracts with property managers, equipment owners, or employees? What do those contracts look like? Establish a contract checklist for an educational program you implement and run. What is currently included? Which items should be clarified?

3. Look at a current job description for an employee. How does this help guide the hiring, termination, and feedback processes?

4. What are your current processes and policies for hiring, reviewing, and terminating employees? How are the processes compliant? How do you demonstrate compliance?

5. How are points of impact addressed for a training you administer or one in which you are involved as a participant? How might points of impact affect those of certain protected classes?

6. When you think of the best organizational climate you have worked in, what do you think of? When you think of the worst climate you have worked in, what do you think of? In both situations, were personnel in leadership aware of the organizational climate?

7. Consider your current organizational climate. What specifics do you think about when you consider the climate of your organization? What are some of the healthy and unhealthy aspects of your organizational climate? How can you, as an administrator, affect these aspects of your organizational climate?

8. How has the discussion of legal issues fostered personal reflections of positions of power within society or the organizations you are employed by or volunteer for? How do the positions you hold impact your worldview?

9. Think of a critical incident in your practice involving legal issues. What do you remember most about this incident? How were you involved? How was the issue handled? What did you learn from ways the process was handled? How does that experience connect to what we have discussed so far?

10. What is your action plan for remaining current with changes in the laws that affect your organization?

11. Develop a statement that represents your code of ethics as an administrator of adult education programs. The statement should connect to your context, personal views, and your philosophy of adult education.

12. Identify and review a code of ethics for your profession or another group. What is included in this code of ethics? What is not (but should be) included? With which points do you agree and disagree?

13. How do you think the code you identify impacts the practices of adult education administrators?

14. Think of a time when legal and ethical considerations "collided" in your practice. How did you handle the situation? What went well? What would you do differently? How will this experience inform your own practice as an administrator within adult education environments?

15. Search for a current news story in your field that involves ethical and/or legal controversy or debate. How would you have handled the situation as an administrator? Why would you have handled it that way? How do you think your answer informs your work within your current practice?

Dilemmas for Discussion

As administrators in adult education settings, you know that ethical and legal issues are not often clear and uncomplicated. Often we are presented with vague partial stories—those that involve "she said/he said" sorts of scenarios. Administrators need to have decision-making processes in place for addressing these types of dilemmas. Think about the various contexts in which you work. The decision-making processes for each may vary depending on whether you work in a military context, in higher education, in a corporation, or in a grassroots community development group. The process may be informed by the particular culture or country in which you are working. Consider these scenarios and the legal and ethical considerations that may be important to you. Refer to the questions and themes in the chapter as well as your own national, state, and municipal laws; your organizational policies; and your ethical codes when addressing these scenarios. What aspects are important? What steps might you take, and what questions might you ask? What would your decision-making process be? What would your course of action be?

1. You are the administrator of a large continuing education program for the division of continuing education within a public institution of higher education. The dean, to whom you directly report, tells you to double the registration fees for enrichment programs (Great Books programs, playing guitar, history lectures, etc.) This increase will result in the same amount of revenue, but it will also result in fewer attendees within these programs. The dean feels the image of the programs is important and would like to raise the profile of programs to attract a more affluent clientele.

2. You notice the petty cash box is continually short after public programs your organization holds are over. You discuss this with the outreach programmer and she confesses that she has been taking money. Your organization only pays health benefits for full-time employees. Her family has no health insurance, and her son needs expensive medical treatment that she has no money to pay for.

3. Upper administration has decided to terminate an outreach programmer, Jenny. Your role is within middle administration, and you agree that Jenny's work has been subpar, and even though she has been subject to improvement plans, her work is still not adequate. Jenny is a Native American female. Another outreach programmer, Sandra, has also been subject to program improvement plans, and though she has managed to improve her work, she was subject to subsequent program improvement plans. Sandra is Caucasian, and she is not being terminated.

4. You are the department chair of an adult education program in a higher education setting. A female student files a written complaint with you stating that a professor used an insulting word for women in the classroom to demonstrate a point in the literature. The male professor looked at the female student and said, "How would you feel if you were called a bitch?"

5. You supervise three separate units in a Human Resource Division in private industry. An employee from unit 1 informs you that issues, such as alcohol use of an employee in unit 2, and the sexual orientation of an employee in unit 3, are being discussed within the meetings for unit 1.

6. You lead an ESL program for a community organization within a large urban area. Your students are primarily Latino and Eastern European immigrants. While you do not have any proof, and you

are not required to ask for it, you know that many adult students are undocumented immigrants. You notice that police officers begin patrolling outside the building prior to the beginning of classes.

7. You take on a job as a new administrator within a private Christian university. A student complains that several professors have Christian crosses hanging in the hallway above their doors.

8. Your public higher educational institution has asked you to take on an internationalization mission. You open a new office in "X" country. The human rights record is deplorable. Your unit comes under pressure to increase international student enrollments while working with the current host country's administration, including individuals who are on a travel ban for their alleged involvement in these abuses.

9. You are an HRD administrator asked to conduct a training session in a foreign country at an important factory that supplies essential parts for your industry. You arrive on site and note that the factory conditions are deplorable. You are told they are acceptable within that country, but they would never be acceptable in your own country. The manager pleads with you to stay quiet. Mostly women are employed at the factory, and they are the primary earners within their families. The company has determined that it is fiscally impossible to renovate the facility and still be competitive in the marketplace. You decide to send an email to a colleague describing the conditions of the factory without mentioning your conversation with the manager. The colleague decides to send the email to your supervisor, and you are scheduled to have a conversation with him or her this morning.

10. You are an administrator for a lifelong learning center. You often hold public programs on controversial topics, and you frequently have guest speakers in classes. You are receiving phone calls from members of the community asking you to cancel a program for which you've scheduled a controversial speaker, representing one side of the issue, to speak that day.

11. A very heated presidential election is occurring. Two of your employees are in the minority on an issue, and they are stating other employees have gone "over the line" of free speech by posting a certain candidate's campaign posters in the break room as well as discussing issues about the campaign openly in the workplace. The employees hanging posters and discussing political issues feel they are entitled to their actions via freedom of speech.

12. You are told by an employee that a group of your subordinates, including the employee who is talking with you, went to a bar on

the weekend, and one of the men slapped a woman's bottom. The employees are laughing about it. All of the individuals involved work for you.

13. You are informed that a Caucasian male student is being bullied by a group of Caucasian female students in one of the GED classes in the division of continuing education.

14. You are an administrator at an adult basic-education community program. A father of one of your female adult students calls you. He pleads with you to give him her current contact information; he tells you she has a mental illness, and the family has been increasingly concerned about her well-being.

References

Academy of Human Resource Development. (1999). Retrieved from: http://c. ymcdn.com/sites/www.ahrd.org/resource/resmgr/ethics_standards. pdf?hhSearchTerms=%22ethics%22

American Library Association (ALA). (2013). *The USA Patriot Act.* Retrieved on July 15, 2013, from http://www.ala.org/advocacy/advleg/federallegislation/theusapatriotact

Blum, B. A. (2007). *Contracts* (4th ed.). New York, NY: Aspen.

Bolman, L., & Deal, T. (2008). *Reframing organizations: Artistry, choice, and leadership* (4th ed.). San Francisco, CA: Jossey-Bass.

Brockett, R. G., & Hiemstra, R. (2004). *Toward ethical practice.* Malabar, FL: Krieger.

Buckley, J. (2016). *Equal opportunity 2016 compliance guide.* Philadelphia, PA: Wolters Kluwer.

Clardy, A. (2003). The legal framework of human resources development, part II: Fair employment, negligence, and implications for scholars and practitioners. *Human Resource Development Review, 2*(2), 130–154.

Cooper, T. (2012). *The responsible administrator: An approach to ethics for the administrative role.* San Francisco, CA: Jossey-Bass.

Falcone, P. (2010). *101 sample write-ups for documenting employee performance problems: A guide to progressive discipline & termination* (2nd ed.). New York, NY: AMACOM.

Gordon, W., & Sork, T. (2001). Ethical issues and codes of ethics: Views of adult education practitioners in Canada and the United States. *Adult Education Quarterly, 51*(3), 202–218.

Jones, T. (1991). Ethical decision making by individuals in organizations: An issue-contingent model. *The Academy of Management Review, 16*(2), 366–395.

Legal Information Institute. (n.d.). Ethics: An overview. *Cornell University Law School.* Retrieved from http://www.law.cornell.edu/wex/ethics

Lipinski, T. (2002). *Libraries, museums, and archives: Legal issues and ethical challenges in the new information era.* Lanham, MD: Scarecrow Press.

Mayhew, R. (n.d.). Legal aspects of performance appraisals. *The Houston Chronicle*. Retrieved from: http://work.chron.com/legal-aspects-performance-appraisals-20795.html

McLean, M. A. (2008). Teaching about disability: An ethical responsibility? *International Journal of Inclusive Education, 12*(5), 15.

MuniCode. (2015). *Chapter 39: Department of civil rights: 39.03., Equal opportunities ordinance.* Retrieved from https://www.municode.com/library/wi/madison/codes/code_of_ordinances?nodeId=Chapter%2039%20Department%20of%20Civil%20Rights

Schneider, B., Ehrhart, M. G., & Macey, W. H. (2013). Organizational climate and culture. *Annual Review of Psychology, 63*(1), 361–388.

Sork, T. J. (1996, May). *A few potholes on the road to salvation: Codes of ethics in adult education.* Paper presented at the 37th Annual Adult Education Research Conference, Tampa, FL.

U.S. Department of Education. (2013). *Family Education Rights and Privacy Act (FERPA).* Title 34, Subtitle A, Chapter 1, Part 99 Retrieved from http://www.ecfr.gov/cgi-bin/text-idx?rgn=div5&node=34:1.1.1.1.33

U.S. Department of Justice. (2013). *Information and technical assistance on the Americans with Disabilities Act.* Retrieved from http://www.ada.gov/

U.S. Department of Labor. (2013). *Office of Federal Contract Compliance programs.* Retrieved from http://www.dol.gov/ofccp/

Woska, W. (2013). Legal issues for HR professionals: Workplace investigations. *Public Personnel Management, 42*(1), 90–101.

11

Scenarios, Role Plays, and Activities

Pulling It All Together

Consider all of the concepts that were discussed in this book. Major topics are as follows:

- Methods of organization,
- Leadership and administration,
- Budgeting,
- Funding and supporting programs,
- Marketing,
- Human resources,
- Strategic planning,
- Program evaluation, and
- Ethical considerations and legal issues.

While each of these concepts was presented individually, within separate chapters, program administrators rarely deal with only one of these concepts at a time. That is simply not how the world works. More frequently

Organization and Administration of Adult Education Programs, pages 249–263

than not, an issue faced by program administrators involves a mixture of these concepts. This final chapter includes scenarios, role-play activities, and case studies designed to help you think about how each of these concepts might work together to form real-world scenarios program administrators must address.

As you think about how you might respond to each scenario, react to the artifacts, or role play situations, think about the following questions:

- How might you ground your approach (or analysis) of the concepts and approaches of administration of adult and continuing education programs?
- How do these situations compare to situations you have encountered in your current role as an administrator of adult and continuing education programs (or how might these situations compare to those you might actually deal with)?
- Whose viewpoints are represented?
- What concepts addressed in this book are in play?

Scenarios

Scenario 1 Instructions

Review the following:

1. Scenario: The Continuing Education Division Unit
2. Artifact A: Current Organizational Structure for Continuing Education Unit
3. Artifact B: Email from Linda (in your inbox this morning)
4. Artifact C: Email from the Dean (in your inbox this morning)

Now address the situations discussed in the scenario. How would you handle them?

The Continuing Education Division Unit

Your name is Chris, and you currently serve in the position of an administrator for a unit within a Continuing Education Division of a large, public higher-education institution in an urban area of about two million residents. There are seven units total with 73 staff members within the Continuing Education Division. Your unit is divided into three programmatic areas, with eight staff members, including Ivan, a full-time administrative assistant. The programmatic areas are

- Adult enrichment programs such as learning guitar and exploring areas of the city. These programs are staffed by three program planners. Bob is a full-time employee and he works in a supervisory role supervising two part-time program planners, Linda and Raji.
- Family-life-skill programs including parenting and reading literacy. These programs are staffed by one full-time program planner, Christine.
- Continuing education for business professionals such as marketing, time management, and conflict resolution. These programs are staffed by three full-time program planners, Kyle, Nademe, and Hassim, none of whom is in a supervisory role.

You are under pressure from the newly hired dean of your division to make sure all areas of the programs you supervise make money. Currently, enrichment programs barely break even, and continuing education for business professionals is a big money maker. Family life skill programs depend mostly on "soft" money, or grant money, in order to make ends meet, and when those programs do not support themselves, the continuing education for business professionals' revenue supports them. Although you have been able to rely on some donor support for family-life-skill programs, the current economy has not made it easy to generate community support.

Christine is unable to do all of the programming work necessary and focus on fundraising, so you have tried to take a leadership role in the fundraising area. Christine has worked with the program for about 5 years, and has lived in the community her whole life, so she has many valuable connections with organizations. The family-life-skill programs have existed for the past 30 years, and they are continuously fully attended with excellent anecdotal feedback. Yet the participants are of limited means, and therefore they are unable to pay the kind of fees charged for the other program areas. It has been difficult to evaluate this impact.

The adult enrichment programs break even, and you sense that you have "tapped out" your current list of potential attendees through current marketing methods, which rely on paper mailings and some email blasts based on the information attendees give. Bob has been with the organization for over 20 years and he remains tied to the traditional ways things have been done in the organization. Linda and Raji appear open to trying some new approaches to marketing, however, it is difficult to introduce changes. Program evaluation is currently only executed through "smile sheets" or participant satisfaction surveys, and you think more could be done here.

Kyle, Hassim, and Nademe are constantly busy creating new programs, and they manage their team and work load quite well. For now, their business programs are booming. The team's personal follow-up and customer service with current and potential clients has proven to be an incredible marketing asset.

You are increasingly under pressure to demonstrate viability for each program area, not just the unit as a whole. Each program area is trying to do more with less, and it is difficult to ask any member to take on any more. Each member is adamant that the family-life-skills program is needed.

There have been some strategic planning discussions at your administrative level about potentially consolidating the seven units into three, but nothing concrete has been drawn up. It is unclear what would happen to your position if this consolidation occurred. You need a plan for each program area's viability as well as a plan for how you will communicate that plan to the dean and gain support for it.

Scenario 1/Artifact A is the current organizational structure for the continuing education unit.

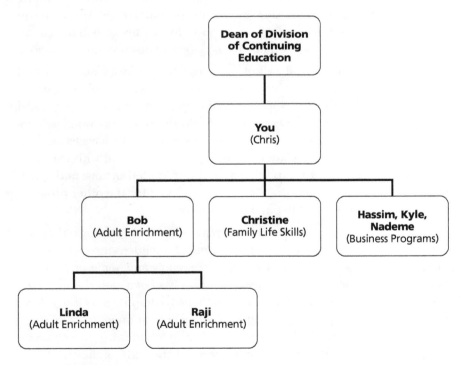

Scenario 1/Artifact A   Current organizational structure for continuing education unit.

There are seven units total and seven Continuing Education Unit Administrators total. Your six colleagues lead units representing engineering, food safety, a water institute, an international education institute, precollege programs, and small business development.

**Scenario 1/Artifact B: Email from Linda
(in your inbox this morning)**

To: Chris
cc: Raji

Hello Chris:

Raji and I were wondering if you might have time for a meeting to discuss potential marketing strategies for our upcoming Tours of the City series. We have some ideas we would like to discuss with you and get your input on them. We could be made available at any morning this week before noon.

Thank you!

Linda

**Scenario 1/Artifact C: Email from Dean
(in your inbox this morning)**

To: All Continuing Education Unit Administrators

Dear Colleagues:

You may have heard rumors, but it is now final that we need to make 2% budget cuts across the board. Each unit can make decisions about how to do this, but I need to see plans for each unit within two weeks. At that point we will meet, consult, and prepare for the future. I appreciate your dedication and devotion to adult education, your learners, and each other, and I know we can generate creative and sustainable solutions to address these new challenges.

Regards,

Dean Sydney Powell

Questions

How will you address the dean's concerns in general? How will you respond to the email you received from the dean this morning? Put together a plan for moving forward.

Scenario 2 Instructions

Review the following:

1. Scenario: The Manufacturing Continuing Education Administrator
2. Artifact A: Employee Demographics
3. Artifact B: Email from CEO
4. Artifact C: Email from plant supervisor
5. Artifact D: Complaint filed
6. Artifact E: A note received under your door

Now address the situations discussed and questions posed in the scenario. How would you handle them?

Scenario 2: The Manufacturing Continuing Education Administrator

Your name is Kelly and you currently serve as an HRD administrator for a locally owned company in a mostly rural county of the United States. The company cans fruit and vegetables. You have approximately 275 full-time and part-time employees total, and your company is one of the main manufacturers in the county. Part of your responsibility is to ensure that all employees continually maintain and update their skills, particularly skills relating to food safety. You have found your colleagues to be very dedicated to their work.

Most of the local employees are friends, as are their families, in this tight-knit community. You are a trusted member of, and leader in, the community. You are faced with several issues at this point. First, the population in the county has been decreasing with the younger generation progressively moving to larger cities. This shrinking demographic has impacted recruitment. Second, you continually struggle to maintain employee skills due to employee turnover. Many individuals are first employed by the company at entry levels; you help coordinate the training, and then they move or leave for other positions. Although there are not many employers in this area, some manufacturers of hard goods are able to offer more competitive wages. You have an influx of Latino and Somali employees in the community, and this has helped fill open positions. These are new populations within the community, and you have the impression, from some training sessions, that some individuals have a very limited command of English.

Although you have a sense, from walking around the plant floor, of the type of current training that may be needed, it is difficult for you to get this information from the supervisors on the floor. Supervisors seem reluctant to fill out detailed performance evaluations for their local colleagues, because they feel it might impact their colleagues' pay or result in reprimands. `You have found, however, that the supervisors are more willing to hold Latino and Somali colleagues responsible for performance issues than they are others. You have noticed that at times the supervisors are not including those who have limited English skills in some training sessions, or there is a lack of information distributed about those training sessions. The supervisors state that it would be a "waste of time," since "they don't understand anything." Although you do not have any specific complaints from employees, you are not sure they are aware training opportunities exist. However, training opportunities provide opportunities for advancement, and advancement will subsequently impact those individuals' rates of pay. You have noticed that Caucasian employees are consistently advancing beyond entry level jobs, and the Latino and Somali employees are remaining in entry level positions.

You have recognized some current challenges and opportunities, and you are trying to be proactive. You have just received news that your company has received a federal grant to provide new food safety training and related workplace literacy training for employees. You started this initiative. The process was very competitive and you are thrilled to have received the funding. A minimum of 12 hours is a mandatory element of the grant, and each employee must demonstrate a basic level of proficiency on written and verbal tests. An outside evaluator will be coming to the department within 6 months to measure progress. You are concerned about how well the company will perform. In addition, you need an internal marketing plan to gain interest in the trainings from all employees as well as "buy in" for the initiative.

You report directly to George, the CEO of this locally owned company; you have a very good working relationship with him, but you are not quite sure he fully understands the current dynamics. George is about ready to retire and turn over company responsibilities to his daughter, Amy, within the next 2 years.

Scenario 2/Artifact A: Employee Demographics

Plant Demographics	5 Years Ago	Current Demographics
Caucasian	95%	75%
Latino	5%	20%
Somali	0%	5%
Male	65%	55%
Female	35%	45%

Scenario 2/Artifact B: Email from CEO

To: Kelly
From: George
cc: Amy

Good morning, Kelly,

As you know, I am going into phased retirement soon and Amy is going to gradually be taking over additional responsibilities. I thought it would be a good idea for us to schedule monthly meetings so that she can understand the importance of your role. Amy will continue to serve as Vice-President. Please contact Amy to set up a schedule and agenda for these meetings.

By the way, I heard you gave an excellent presentation at the high school last week. It really helped the kids understand some important interviewing skills. It was a good public service for our community.

Thank you for your work,

George

Scenario 2/Artifact C: Email from Plant Supervisor

Hi Kelly,

Thanks for bringing in the doughnuts this morning! Great start to a Monday.

Listen, we've got some problems on the floor with the new folks. It seems like they don't really get some of the rules down here, and it's causing some misunderstandings. Can you help?

Also, I got your message about the performance reviews. We'll get them to you as soon as we can. With all the other work we've got going on, it has been hard to get those done too. I don't think that Jay, Steve, or Janet have theirs done either, so we're working on them.

Thanks,

Brian

Scenario 2/Artifact C: Letter Received

Dear Sir or Madam:

The Better Business Bureau has received the above-referenced complaint from one of your customers regarding their dealings with you. The details of the consumer's concerns are included on the reverse. Please review this matter and advise us of your position.

As a neutral third party, the Better Business Bureau can help to resolve the matter. Often, complaints are a result of misunderstandings a company wants to know about and subsequently correct.

In the interest of time and good customer relations, please provide the BBB with written verification of your position in this matter within the next month. Your prompt response will allow BBB to be of service to you and your customer in reaching a mutually agreeable resolution. Please inform us if you have contacted your customer directly and already resolved this matter.

The Better Business Bureau develops and maintains Reliability Reports on companies across the United States and Canada. This information is available to the public and is frequently used by potential customers. Your cooperation in responding to this complaint becomes a permanent part of your file with the Better Business Bureau. Failure to promptly give attention to this matter may be reflected in the report we give to consumers about your company.

We encourage you to print this complaint (attached file), answer the questions, and respond to us.

We look forward to your prompt attention to this matter.

Sincerely,

The Better Business Bureau Complaint Department

Scenario 2/Artifact D: Complaint Filed

Dear Better Business Bureau:

Last week I bought four cans of corn at the local grocery store; I opened each one, and they were peas. I have had very good produce from this company in the past and I was shocked by this. I am concerned that others may be impacted, especially because so many kids have food allergies now. Please let me know how I might be able to address this issue with this company.

Sincerely,

Karen Giles

Scenario 2/Artifact E: A Note Received Under Your Door

Dear Chris -

Names they are calling. One hit.

Please help.

Scenario 2 Alternate Instructions: This scenario can be used in discussion or as a role-play exercise. If using this scenario as a role-play exercise, use the following instructions:

Given what you know about the scenario above via the scene and artifacts, role-play combinations of meetings with the following individuals:

Chris
Brian
Amy
George
Company workers

Scenario 3 Instructions

Review the scenario and address the situations discussed and questions posed in the scenario. How would you handle them?

Health Facility Education Administrator Role Play

Your name is Pat and you are the continuing education administrator for a medium-sized health facility. You are responsible for the oversight of all continuing education, including disaster response training. There are three units, and each unit in the facility has a team leader to organize the response training. The last time you held a disaster response simulation, all units responded very well, and the feedback from outside evaluators was excellent. In fact, the outside evaluators were so impressed that there are possibilities for your team to gain contracts to train others in disaster response training. This would be an excellent opportunity to generate additional revenue and potentially gain a national reputation for training in this particular niche area.

Two toxic personalities and two of the team leaders, Alex and Monica, foster animosity toward you. For example, they recently wrote you a scathing email and cc'd your supervisor about how they disliked the disaster response training simulation and that they were disappointed that we, as a facility, were not paying attention to more important programmatic areas. In your opinion, though, what can be more important than disaster response? The third team leader, Jake, has been fairly quiet, but you have received no complaints from him. You feel this toxic atmosphere is beginning to impact the team readiness for disasters, and Alex and Monica are becoming increasingly aloof and negative in meetings. To respond to this, you provided stricter guidelines for scheduling staff in order to keep the toxic individuals from working on the same shifts; however, this also has impacted the ability of all staff to switch shifts for vacations and other days off.

Normally, nonmandatory brown-bag discussions on current topics related to continuing education were attended to capacity, and now some have been canceled due to lack of interest. You receive an allocation for such programs based on attendance numbers, and things don't look good for next year's budget unless you can increase participation. It is a small thing, but you feel that things are starting to domino and impact your effectiveness as an administrator and a leader. You do not hear anything bad about your work from other employees, so you assume everything is going well.

You have a meeting next week with your supervisor, Tasha. Work climate is on the agenda as well as staffing and marketing for the disaster response training program, both governmental and private. Prioritize agenda items for this meeting, and consider what the discussions on each agenda item would look like. If you were Pat, what would your goals be? What would your goals be if you were Tasha?

Scenario 3 Alternate Instructions: This scenario can be used in discussion or as a role-play exercise. If using this scenario as a role-play exercise, use the following instructions:

Given what you know about the scenario above through the scene and artifacts, role play combinations of meetings with the following individuals:

Pat
Alex
Monica
Jake
Tasha

Additional information for role play exercise—

Alex and Monica Roles: You both feel that Pat has been heavy handed without any input from the front line about what kind of training is necessary. Both of you have worked at the health facility for 10 years. Pat started as your supervisor about one year ago. Monica had applied for the position, but didn't have a master's degree, and others with more formal education made the short list. There is no way that you are going to participate any further in any of this disaster training nonsense. What about the day-to-day training needs of the employees? Those are being completely ignored, and now you're going to be pulled away from the office to do all of these other trainings for outside agencies? Both of you are not happy about this.

Jake Role: You are the newest member of the team and started about 6 months ago. You follow orders from Pat, but you also need to stay in good graces with Alex and Monica. They could really make the work situation bad if they thought you were on Pat's "side." In the midst of all of this, you wonder where the concern is for your learners or the employees who are on the receiving end of training. They seem to have gotten lost in all of this drama.

Tasha Role: You think that Pat has a good deal of experience in the health field, and good ideas, but she needs mentoring as an administrator. Her approach to her team is backfiring. The team also needs to give a bit, but the atmosphere is pretty negative and it is not clear whether Pat will be able to pull everyone together. She has some great initiatives that are going to generate additional revenue, and these are appreciated by your boss as well. You need to get a sense from her about how she might turn things around with regard to management and address the educational needs of staff internally as well as continue to develop important new educational initiatives.

Scenario 4 Instructions

Review the scenario and address the situations discussed and questions posed in the scenario. How would you handle them?

You, Jan, are the associate director of training for a nongovernmental organization working in community development. Your home office is based in Washington, DC, but you have offices all across the United States as well as in other nations. Each year you organize camps in which teachers can gain continuing professional development and at which local children can learn reading, mathematics, and improve their English skills. The camp is one line item of your annual budget, and you are able to be somewhat flexible working with the money to meet the needs of the staff, teachers, and students. Each community has a local program developer responsible for coordinating and training staff as well as for the on-site logistics of the camps. These training directors often conduct trainings, but for some sessions they contract with outside vendors to deliver trainings.

The main office has been communicating with you stating they are beginning to view summer camps as dispensable. In your opinion, this ambivalent attitude is because these sessions are "out of sight, out of mind," and the main office is unable to see the positive impact of training "on the ground." You have evaluation results to demonstrate there is a return on investment, but with budgetary constraints and the fact that this type of training is seen by the main office as "soft-skills" training (and not as valuable as "hard-skills" training), you realize you will have to work hard to justify the continuation of the camp project.

Choose two different countries and communities in which this scenario might take place, and do research about the cultures and the overall social and political environment. How might the contexts impact your approach as an administrator?

Activities

1. Create a concept map, mind map, or another visual organizer conveying your understanding of administration of adult and continuing education concepts individually or in small groups. You can choose your own words or use the titles of each chapter as concepts in order to construct your map.
2. Choose an administrator of adult and continuing education programs who you would like to interview and learn more about. Using a semistructured interview guide, interview this person and

create an analysis of the interview using the concepts described throughout this book. Some questions you may wish to ask include

- What does your typical day look like?
- Could you describe your leadership style?
- How do you go about managing when you have conflicting priorities?
- What is your role in budgeting?
- How do you evaluate the continuing education programs you are responsible for?
- What is a new marketing approach you have recently tried? How did it work?
- How do you conduct performance evaluations?
- Could you describe an ethical dilemma you have had and explain how you resolved it?
- What is the most rewarding part of your job?
- What is the most challenging part of your job?
- Add others as they relate to your interests.

3. Choose a culture or community with which you are not familiar. Interview or ask if you can shadow an administrator of adult and continuing education programs for a day. What did you learn? How might you incorporate what you have learned into your daily practice? If you are not able to meet with the administrator face to face, ask if it might be possible to participate in an online, or virtual, nonconfidential meeting or session.

QUESTIONS FOR DISCUSSION

1. After having explored concepts related to administration of adult and continuing education programs, choose an artifact that best depicts your approach or "you" as an administrator. Explain to the entire class, or a small group, why you chose this artifact.
2. If you had someone else draft a biography of your work as an administrator of adult and continuing education programs 5, 10, or 20 years from now, what would you hope that they would write?
3. Considering the topics discussed in each chapter, what are your strengths as an administrator? What are your challenges or areas you currently need to work on most?
4. What are your learning goals as an administrator and how will you self-assess those goals?
5. What elements of administration (that you learned about in this book) have you decided to integrate into your practice? What have

you decided to eliminate from your practice as a result of what you have read in this book?

6. Throughout this book, we have emphasized the interrelationships of topics that program administrators work with. Consider any two topic areas that were discussed in this book:

   - Methods of organization
   - Leadership and administration
   - Budgeting
   - Funding and support programs
   - Marketing
   - Human resources
   - Strategic planning
   - Program evaluation
   - Ethical considerations and legal issues

7. How does one of the topic areas you chose relate to (and affect) the other area (and vice versa)? Do the same with three of the topics. How do the three topics you have chosen relate to each other?

About the Authors

Steven W. Schmidt

Steven W. Schmidt has had an extensive career in both business and adult education. He is currently a professor of adult education at East Carolina University in Greenville, North Carolina. Before becoming a professor, Schmidt worked in a Fortune 500 company for 18 years, where, among other duties, he organized and managed employee training and development programs. He holds a bachelor's degree in business (University of Wisconsin-Whitewater) and master's and doctoral degrees in urban education with an emphasis in adult and continuing education (University of Wisconsin-Milwaukee).

Schmidt served on the board of directors for the American Association for Adult and Continuing Education (www.aaace.org) for seven years, including a term as president of the organization in 2014. His work has been published in many different educational and business journals, and he has presented his research at regional, national, and international conferences. In addition to co-authoring this book, he is the author of *Case Studies and Activities in Adult Education and Human Resource Development* (Information Age Publishing).

Susan M. Yelich Biniecki

Susan M. Yelich Biniecki has over 20 years as a practitioner in the field of adult education as an administrator, program planner, adult educator, and

Organization and Administration of Adult Education Programs, pages 265–266
Copyright © 2016 by Information Age Publishing
All rights of reproduction in any form reserved.

academic within for-profit, nonprofit, and higher education organizational settings. She served as the assistant director for the Institute of World Affairs at the University of Wisconsin-Milwaukee for over a decade as well as an AmeriCorps Volunteer, a Peace Corps Volunteer, and an administrator of adult education programs for her business abroad. Currently, she serves as assistant professor of adult and continuing education at Kansas State University in Manhattan, Kansas. She holds a PhD in urban education with an emphasis in adult and continuing education (University of Wisconsin-Milwaukee) an MS degree in administrative leadership and supervision in education (University of Wisconsin-Milwaukee) and a bachelor of arts in sociology-anthropology (Ripon College, WI). Yelich Biniecki's research focuses on culture, knowledge construction, and international adult education in nonformal and formal settings. She has presented nationally and internationally and her work has been published in *Adult Education Quarterly, Adult Learning, Journal of Continuing and Higher Education, New Horizons in Adult Education and Human Resource Development,* and other major journals.